CONCENTRATE INTERNATIONAL LAW

Ilias Bantekas
Professor of Transnational Law, Hamad bin Khalifa University (Qatar Foundation) and Adjunct Professor, Georgetown University, Edmund A Walsh School of Foreign Service

Efthymios Papastavridis
Postdoctoral Researcher and Guest Lecturer, University of Oxford, Faculty of Law and Fellow, Athens Public International Law Center and Academy of Athens

FIFTH EDITION

Great Clarendon Street, Oxford, OX2 6DP,
United Kingdom

Oxford University Press is a department of the University of Oxford.
It furthers the University's objective of excellence in research, scholarship,
and education by publishing worldwide. Oxford is a registered trade mark of
Oxford University Press in the UK and in certain other countries

Second Edition 2015
Third Edition 2017
Fourth Edition 2019

Published in the United States of America by Oxford University Press
198 Madison Avenue, New York, NY 10016, United States of America

British Library Cataloguing in Publication Data
Data available

Library of Congress Control Number: 2021935069

ISBN 978–0–19–289568–4

Printed in Great Britain by
Bell and Bain Ltd, Glasgow

Contents

Table of cases

Table of instruments

International Instruments

United Nations General Assembly and Security Council Resolutions

National Legislation

Austria

UK

United Nations Act 1946 (9 and 10 Geo 6, c 45) . . . 57, A4
State Immunity Act 1978 (SIA) (1978 c 33) . . . 94, 102
  s 14(4) . . . 96
Human Rights Act 1998 . . . 58
International Criminal Court Act 2001 (2001 c 17) . . . 60

United States

Constitution of 17 September 1787 . . . 54
Alien Tort Claims Act 1789 (ATCA) . . . 73, 98
'Truman Proclamation' of 12 March 1945 . . . 23
Foreign Sovereign Immunities Act 1976 (FSIA) . . . 96, 101
  s 1611(b)(i) . . . 96

1

The nature of international law and the international legal system

THE EXAMINATION

Exam questions in this field will most likely involve international legal theory and the relationship between the various approaches to international law. In addition, questions concerning the nature of legal obligations, including peremptory norms of international law (*jus cogens*), are frequent. Moreover, there may be questions regarding the conflict of international norms and its fragmentation.

KEY FACTS

- International law sets out the rules that govern the relations between the members of international society, including **sovereign States**, international organizations, and individuals. These rules were mainly created by and for States, but nowadays they encompass more users and address far more issues.
- The structure of the international legal order is fundamentally different from that of national legal systems. Besides the absence of a central legislative organ (ie the equivalent of a national parliament), there is no international police or international judge as conceived in the domestic setting, and both enforcement and adjudication of international rules depend heavily on the consent of the States concerned. However, this does not mean that international law is a 'primitive legal order'; quite to the contrary, it provides a very detailed and multilayered normative structure for a rules-based international society.
- International legal theory has long struggled with contemplating the nature of the international legal system. Theories such as formalism, positivism, or naturalism, which concern every category of law, have been complemented by schools that focus explicitly on international law, such as realism or policy-oriented approaches, as well as by more contemporary theories such as critical legal studies (CLS), feminism, and third-world approaches in international law (TWAIL).
- There are different categories of norms in the international legal system; a common distinction could be between obligations of a contractual nature and obligations towards the international community as a whole (obligations *erga omnes*). In addition, although there is no formal hierarchy among the sources of international law, there is a certain hierarchy of international norms: *jus cogens* (norms from which there can be no **derogation**) and *jus dispositivum* (norms that are susceptible to derogation).

CHAPTER OVERVIEW

The nature of the international legal system

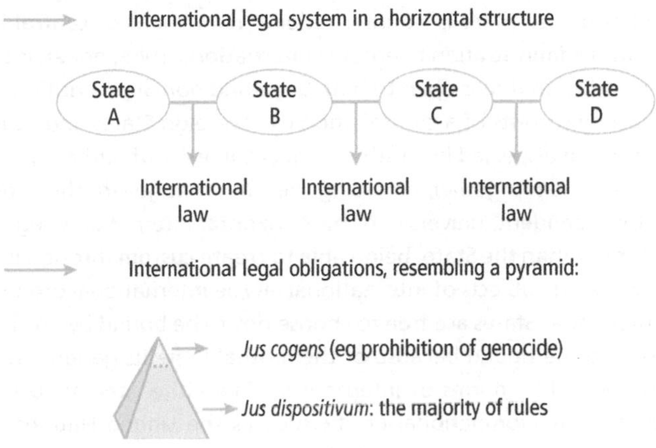

Introduction

International law does exist and it does matter. International law concerns the fight against the Islamic State of Iraq and the Levant (ISIS) and international terrorism or the fight against COVID-19, news that makes the headlines of newspapers worldwide. International law also concerns day-to-day matters, such as the checking of passports at Heathrow airport. International law lays down rules governing the relations of sovereign States, but also grants rights to individuals, from the citizens of a State to asylum-seekers traversing the ocean to find a safe home. International law deals with international crimes, such as genocide, but also regulates the simple **extradition** of a common criminal to his or her State of nationality.

As law in any given era and society is the product of its time, so too international law is the product of international society, evolving as the latter develops. For example, in the nineteenth century, there were enough rules, especially of customary origin, to address the needs of the then State-centred international society. Today, the needs of international society have significantly increased by reason of its transformation and expansion. In the twenty-first century, international law is called to address the needs of the 193 member States of the United Nations, numerous international organizations, an indefinite number of **non-State entities** (eg multinational enterprises or non-governmental organizations), and individuals.

At the same time, the international legal system remains fundamentally different from national legal orders. In the domestic setting, rules spring from a centralized legislative authority on the basis of a well-defined constitutional framework. These rules are enforced by a central authority, the executive branch of government, and when a dispute arises regarding their application, concerned parties have recourse to the judiciary. This vertical system is not reflected on the international plane. There is no international parliament or central legislative body. There exists no central administration to enforce international rules, nor an international court with mandatory jurisdiction that is open to both State and non-State entities.

International society consists of a constellation of sovereign States and other international organizations, which are dispersed in a rather horizontal order of authority. International law is the chain that holds them together, providing the rules that govern their coexistence in this anarchical, yet interdependent, universe. In this horizontal international legal order, the central figure is none other than the State, being able to create **custom** through its practice, adopt treaties, or establish other subjects of international law, ie international organizations.

This does not mean that States are free to choose not to be bound by any rules whatsoever. Rather, they consent to be bound because of the mutual benefits generated as a result. And often they will be bound by norms of international law either stemming from pre-existing customary law or from a supranational entity, such as the United Nations Security Council (UNSC) acting under Chapter VII of the UN Charter. Theorists have long struggled with the question as to why international law is, or should be, binding, as well as with the nature of the international legal system. International legal theory has long been puzzled, apparently drawing analogies with the domestic legal systems, with their hierarchy of norms. Should all international rules possess the same nature, being open to derogation and eternal change? The answer was given fairly recently with the acknowledgement of a set of norms that have, in principle, a superior position in the normative pyramid. These are the so-called peremptory norms of international law that trump every other conflicting rule, and from which there is no derogation. Peremptory norms include the prohibition of aggression, genocide, and torture, among others.

The structure of the international legal system

It is true that the international community seems more 'anarchical' than any other known legal community. This is due to historic reasons, but is also explained by the simple fact that there is no real 'hegemon' (ie leader), as Machiavelli would envisage, or a Hobbesian 'Leviathan' to hold sway. The international legal system is horizontally structured and this has consequences both in relation to its perception and its function. All States are considered equal as sovereign States (the principle of sovereign equality, enshrined in Art 2, para 1 UN Charter) and are not subject to the power of any supranational authority without their consent. Thus, sovereign equality and the need for State consent become extremely important in the international legal order. Indeed, there is no central legislature, but all States may adopt agreements or engage in practice generating customary law on a bilateral, regional, or universal level. No State is subjected to third-party dispute settlement, let alone to the International Court of Justice, if it has not offered its prior consent.

What are the reasons for this? Primarily, international society was never conceived in the same terms as its national counterparts. States could not accept their subjection to a higher authority that could enact and enforce rules or settle disputes without their permission. However, the question as to how States could coexist remained. The answer was to accept the need for some international regulation on the basis of common agreement in order to maintain a minimum public order and stability in international society.

However, this primitive image of the international community has gradually changed. States have increased; new actors have come to the fore, particularly international organizations, transnational corporations, and international civil society. International law nowadays consists of a very complex network of rules regulating a multitude of actors and activities. Even so, State consent remains paramount in the making of and the judicial enforcement of rules.

Illustrative as to the early conception of international law has been one of the first cases before the Permanent Court of International Justice, the celebrated ***Lotus case***:

The Case of the SS 'Lotus', PCIJ, Series A, No 10, Judgment of 7 September 1927

In this case, the Court was looking for the existence of a customary law granting exclusive jurisdiction to **flag States** in respect of high-seas collisions. If such a rule was discovered, Turkey would have been in breach of international law, since it had prosecuted a French national on board a French vessel. Accordingly, the Court examined relevant State practice, but not necessarily to find a rule permitting the exercise of **jurisdiction** by a non-flag State. It would also be content if it was unable to find a rule prohibiting the exercise of such jurisdiction. It is worth quoting the corresponding text:

> International law governs relations between independent States. The rules of law binding upon States therefore emanate from their own free will as expressed in conventions or by usages generally accepted as expressing principles of law and established in order to regulate the relations between these co-existing independent communities or with a view to the achievement of common aims. *Restrictions upon the independence of States cannot therefore be presumed* (p 18).

The last sentence, the so-called *Lotus principle*, namely, 'whatever is not prohibited is permitted in international law', has underpinned the international legal system for a long time. It is also closely associated with the voluntarist approach to international law—in short, 'where there is State will, there is international law: no will, no law'. Recently, the International Court of Justice again used its rationale: in the 2010 *Kosovo* Advisory Opinion, the Court looked at whether international law prohibits the unilateral declaration of independence and, finding in the negative, ruled that Kosovo was entitled to declare its independence.

This case notwithstanding, it is true that, due to the multiplication of States and international organizations, and the immense broadening of the subject matter of international law since the *Lotus* era, international law has gradually evolved from this protean version and become far more advanced and multifaceted. For example, it no longer relies on custom as its predominant source, but rather on treaties. It has also come up with other non-binding agreements, or other declarations or **soft law** instruments that reflect more flexible approaches. More importantly, it has placed the human being at the centre of its attention since the mid-twentieth century, by virtue of the growth of human rights law.

Additionally, international society has established institutions that endeavour to play a rather constitutional role in international relations. Premised upon the domestic 'separation-of-powers' model, the UN General Assembly (UNGA) is a plenary organ, where States can discuss international issues, complemented by the UNSC, an executive organ that may take forcible action in the case of a threat to international peace and security. Finally, the International Court of Justice (ICJ) is an international court where States can settle their disputes. However, these institutions do not establish an order similar to a constitutional one, since the UNGA does not adopt binding rules and recourse to the ICJ is contingent upon the consent of the parties to a dispute. Finally, the police powers granted to the Security Council are subject to the veto of its five permanent members.

Thus, it remains to be seen how the international community will evolve in the twenty-first century. Undoubtedly, new forms of cooperation and new international actors or participants may arise. Also, it is more than certain that the subject matter of international law will continue to increase and areas such as the global commons (space, high seas, deep seabed) or fields such as international economic law will attract more attention.

Fragmentation

Brief mention should be made of the problem of fragmentation of international law. Due to its horizontal structure, it is possible for several legal regimes (ie foreign investment law and human rights law) to exist and develop in isolation from each other, ultimately culminating in the production of divergent rules of international law. This possibility is enhanced by the proliferation of international courts and tribunals that may produce divergent decisions on substantial matters. Moreover, as there is no *lis pendens* rule in the international legal order, there is the danger that one single case may end up in several courts and tribunals, all of which may decide the case differently. For example, different aspects of the same dispute between the UK and Ireland concerning the *Mox Plant case* were submitted to arbitration at the same time under the UN Convention on the Law of the Sea and under the Convention for the Protection of the Marine Environment of the North-East Atlantic (OSPAR Convention), finally ending up before the European Court of Justice (ECJ).

The International Law Commission (ILC) decided to address this issue and established a Study Group under Professor Martti Koskenniemi on 'Fragmentation of International Law: Difficulties Arising from the Diversification and Expansion of International Law'. In 2006, it published its report, which included various methods of obviating such diversification of international rules, including the use of the interpretive tool of Art 31(3)(c) Vienna Convention on the Law of Treaties (VCLT) (1969) or the norms on the resolution of conflict, such as *lex specialis* or *lex posterior*.

Equally important is the knowledge of the case law of all international courts and tribunals, as well as what has been designated as 'inter-judicial dialogue'. When international or national courts decide upon a case concerning a specific and delicate issue of international law, they should be aware of what other courts or tribunals have held on this issue and decide accordingly. This does not mean that they have to adopt the exact same position, but rather to enter into a line of argumentation, which would be conducive to the unity and coherence of the international legal system. For example, when the ICJ ruled upon the degree of control required for certain acts of individuals to be attributed to a State (*Application of the Convention on the Prevention and Punishment of the Crime of Genocide (Bosnia and Herzegovina v Serbia and Montenegro)* (2007)), it disassociated that case from the one decided upon by the International Criminal Tribunal for the former Yugoslavia (ICTY) (*Prosecutor v Duško Tadič* (1999)) and thus justified the adoption of the criterion of 'effective control' rather than of 'overall control'.

REVISION TIP

International law differs significantly from national legal systems, as the relations among its members are not in a structured and vertical order. Relations in international society are looser and horizontal, while notions such as 'sovereign equality' or 'consent' have prominence. International law, however, is necessary in holding together the various parts of this constellation and has significantly progressed in the twentieth century.

The nature of international law: theoretical approaches

The nature of the international legal system has been at the heart of the philosophy of international law. Since the seventeenth century, theory has attempted to comprehend the nature of international law in various ways. Suffice it to refer succinctly to the following main streams.

Naturalism or natural law theory

Naturalism or natural law theory had been the prevailing approach in international law in the primary (prior to the sixteenth century) and classical (seventeenth–nineteenth-century) periods of international law. Premised upon canon (Church) law and the teachings of St Thomas Aquinas, natural law theory addresses the question of the nature of international law by pointing to a set of rules that are of universal and objective scope. This approach was necessitated because these rules emanate from universal and superior values and principles that are eternal to mankind. Such values and principles dictate the limits of the legal system and the free will of the sovereign State. How are these principles of natural law to be found? They could be identified by recourse to canon law or to '*recta ratio*' (right reason) or to universally accepted moral values.

There have been many naturalist schools of thought, all of which share the idea that international legal argument is descending, in the sense that international obligations befall

States, which are called upon to respect them as part of a universal code of truth. Among the proponents of naturalism, one finds prominent international lawyers such as Francisco de Vitoria (1480–1546), Hugo Grotius (1583–1645), Christian Wolff (1679–1754), Emerich de Vattel (1714–67), and Georges Scelle (1878–1961).

It is true that natural law theory, especially in its traditional form, is open to manifold criticism. Most importantly, it blurs the lines between law and morality and thus fails to distinguish international law from political theory or ideology. It is readily apparent how dangerous this can prove, especially as a common conception of morality or political ideology is extremely elusive. However, it must be noted that there are segments of naturalism, even in the contemporary legal order, reflected principally through the notion of human rights or *jus cogens*. The idea that some fundamental rights, such as the prohibition of torture or slavery and the right to life are universal and cannot be derogated from stems from a naturalist perception of international society.

Positivism

If naturalism lies at one end of the jurisprudential spectrum, at the other end we undoubtedly find positivism. The latter is not based on universal and moral principles, but on a structured and coherent legal system that is created by States in light of their interests and desires. In general, positivism rejects any extra-legal considerations, such as morality, politics, etc. It perceives law as a scientific discipline, which is autonomous and self-standing and which can resolve its conflicts without recourse to external sources. According to positivists, law is a coherent system and its rules are derived from a logical and structured process.

Positivism blossomed at the end of the nineteenth century and was the dominant legal theory for many years. It significantly influenced international legal doctrine on account of its eminent proponents, principally Dionisio Anzilotti (1869–1950), Georg Jellinek (1851–1911), Heinrich Triepel (1848–1936), and Hans Kelsen (1881–1973). Jellinek advocated the extreme thesis that international law is based upon the self-restraint of States. Sovereign States enjoy the prerogative of complying with international law according to their own legal system and their own free will. International law is created because States choose to restrain themselves; however, in case of conflict between the law and the interest of the State, the latter prevails.

On the other hand, Kelsen was the most towering figure of legal positivism in the twentieth century, as he tried to conceptualize law as a 'pure' social science. In his seminal work, *Pure Theory of Law* (1934 and later expanded in 1960), he illustrates the legal system as a pyramid: according to him, law is valid only as a positive law. A norm becomes law only because it has been constituted in a particular fashion, born of a definite procedure and a definite rule. The coherence of the legal system is ensured by tracing back its validity to the basic norm, the so-called *Grundnorm*. The validity of this norm is axiomatic, as a prerequisite for the validity of the entire edifice. In his theory, international law has a primary place, since all the constitutional and domestic norms derive their validity from the existence of the States as such; in turn, the existence of the State derives its validity from international law, which sets out the requirements for its creation.

A more refined version of positivist legal theory, prevalent in English jurisprudence, was elaborated by HLA Hart. Drawing on Kelsen, Hart distinguished three categories of rules: (a) primary rules, concerning human action and interaction; (b) secondary rules (rules of adjudication, enforcement, and change), which underpin and operate in relation to the primary rules; and (c) the master 'rule of recognition', which enables the observer to identify the components of the system and to treat them as legal. What mattered was not the acceptance of primary rules but their acceptance of the *system* by which those rules were generated and applied: the combination of primary and secondary rules was perceived as the essence of law. However, Hart approached international law as a marginal form, possessing some, but not all, the characteristics of a developed legal system, and then only imperfectly.

Positivism has equally encountered criticism, especially the strict 'self-restraint theory', for allegiance to the sovereign will of the State. Moreover, it is hard to accept the absence of factors such as morality in a discipline that is called to govern the relations of (international) society.

Realism

Neither naturalism nor positivism averted the calamities of World War II. Thus, many international jurists turned their backs on these theories in the post-Charter era, holding that international law reflects a reality, paradoxical in many respects, but still a reality, and it is futile to try to comprehend it in absolute terms. International law does exist and it is not merely a composition of moral values or sterilized logical structures. Rather, it is the offspring of international society and there is no need to search for the source of legal obligations or why States comply with these. Prominent theorists and lawyers, such as Hans Morgenthau, George Kennan, and Charles de Visscher, espoused realism, while modern scholars, such as Eric Posner and Jack Goldsmith, advocate rather a 'neo-realist' approach.

Formalism

Closely linked with the idea of legal realism is the theory of formalism, which is particularly popular in Europe. It describes the process of discovering international rules. Law is whatever meets the requirements of a broadly accepted definition of law, regardless of whether this definition derives from naturalistic or positivist considerations. It thus resembles realism, albeit infused with positivist features. A good example is the relation of formalism to the sources of international law. For formalism, a certain rule becomes international law only when it takes the form of the three formal sources under Art 38 ICJ Statute; namely, treaty, custom, or general principle of law.

Policy-oriented approach

The policy-oriented school starts from the premise that law operates against a social background. Its purpose is the prescription and application of policy in ways that maintain order in the international community, while simultaneously achieving the community's social goals. This approach has been associated with the New Haven School (University of Yale) of the

1960s and particularly with Professors Myres McDougal, Harold Lasswell, and, more recently, Michael Reisman. It stands on the opposite footing to formalism and represents a very liberal and political perspective of international law. Emphasis is placed on the law-making process and whether this reflects shared community values, such as wealth, enlightenment, skill, well-being, affection, respect, etc. The policy-oriented approach has been criticized by States formerly belonging to the 'Eastern bloc' as a very 'Western and capitalist' approach towards international society and it has not had a great influence on other continents.

The nature of international law: new theories

There have also been various modern theories or so-called new approaches to international law. These approaches are premised particularly on the work of the Critical Legal Studies (CLS) schools that emerged as a legal theory in the USA, namely, schools of thought that are engaged in heavy criticism of the aforementioned theories. Such schools suggest that the nature of international law is limited because it is determined by language, which is biased and trapped in the conventional structures of politics and power. CLS scholars, amongst them David Kennedy and Martti Koskenniemi, attempt to capture the fact that international lawyers try to use arguments both about what States do and what they ought to do and that there is a constant tension between those arguments. CLS pushed forward other approaches to international law, such as cultural relativism and critical race theory. The latter provides a critical analysis of race and racism from a legal point of view.

In addition, reference should also be made to the feminist approach and TWAIL.

The feminist approach

Important feminist theories addressed international law rather belatedly in the 1980s. Feminist scholars oppose male rationalist biases of international rules and the 'objective' or 'neutral' character of the law that ignores women's aspirations. Feminist epistemology seeks to introduce ethics into international relations and adopts empirical, analytical, and normative tools to demonstrate gender biases and reinterpret power relations in international affairs. The movement enters almost all chapters of the discipline and focuses more realistically on the aspects of international law where inequality persists and women still have a marginal or neglected international status.

Third World Approaches to International Law (TWAIL)

Since decolonization, distinguished lawyers from Africa and Asia have been engaged in a debate challenging international law's deficiencies with regard to the developing countries. This gave rise to a critical movement in the 1990s, termed 'Third World Approaches to International Law'. A 'Manifesto' published in 2006 by Bhupinder Chimni summarizes the main theses of the movement, pointing out that neoliberal international law remains hegemonic, bears colonial and post-colonial characteristics, and operates in a 'dualist' fashion of discrimination from the centre against the periphery. Chimni and other Third-World scholars find the record of the UN disappointing, denounce the democratic deficit in most international institutions as lacking transparency and accountability, and consider the world's financial and economic organizations culpable for the current situation of the poverty of billions of people all over the world: people who deserve assistance for their development and need to have differentiated treatment.

Is there any hierarchy in international law?

The international legal system operates on a horizontal structure of authority, in which the subjects of international law are equal and bound by legal rules only if they express their consent. Hence, the adoption of treaties is dependent upon State consent, whereas custom requires consistent practice by some States and the explicit or tacit consent of others. It is not surprising, therefore, that the formal sources of international law (treaties, custom, and general principles) are not set out in hierarchical order. This, however, does not mean that there is no hierarchy of norms in international law.

Jus cogens norms

In 1960, the ILC fuelled the discussion on the distinction of norms. In drafting the VCLT, the members of the ILC put forward the idea that not all rules of international law have the same juridical value, there being certain norms from which no derogation should be allowed. These peremptory norms of international law (*jus cogens*) reflect the most fundamental values of international society and thus stand at the apex of the normative pyramid of the international legal system. This theoretical construction was laid down in Art 53 VCLT, stipulating that:

> a treaty is void if, at the time of its conclusion, it conflicts with a peremptory norm of general international law. For the purposes of the present Convention, a peremptory norm of general international law is a norm accepted and recognized by the international community of States as a whole as a norm from which no derogation is permitted and which can be modified only by a subsequent norm of general international law having the same character.

Nonetheless, the ILC was careful not to lay down an exhaustive list of such *jus cogens* norms, as its purpose was to produce an open-ended list of such norms that would change, depending on the exigencies of international society. *Jus cogens* norms differ from all other international legal rules, conveniently called *jus dispositivum*, in the fact that *jus cogens* can never be altered, even by consent between certain States. Thus, while two States may deviate from a rule of *jus dispositivum*, like the prohibition of fishing within the territorial waters of foreign States, and conclude an agreement allowing it, this cannot occur in respect of the prohibition of genocide. Such agreement would be null and void. What are these *jus cogens* norms? Having in mind their fundamental significance for the international legal order, such norms should include the prohibition of aggression, the prohibition of genocide, and the protection of fundamental provisions of international human rights and humanitarian law, such as the prohibition of torture, slavery, apartheid, etc. Even so, the ICJ has been extremely reticent in enunciating the existence of such norms. First, it insinuated that the prohibition of the **use of force** may be a *jus cogens* norm in *Military and Paramilitary Activities in and against Nicaragua (Nicaragua v USA)* (1986). After many years, the Court did officially acknowledge a norm as *jus cogens*: in *Armed Activities on the Territory of the Congo (New Application: 2002) (Democratic Republic of the Congo v Rwanda)* (2006), the Court accepted that the *prohibition of genocide* was part of *jus cogens*. It made a similar finding in *Questions Relating to the Obligation to Prosecute or Extradite (Belgium v Senegal)* (2012) in respect of the *prohibition of torture*. Notably, in 2015, the ILC decided to revisit the issue of *jus cogens* and included it in the list of the topics currently under consideration.

Erga omnes obligations

Closely related, but not identical, to *jus cogens* is the notion of obligations *erga omnes*, ie international obligations that are not contractual in nature, but are owed to the international community as a whole. For example, the Court in *East Timor (Portugal v Australia)* (1995) recognized the principle of **self-determination** as an obligation *erga omnes*. The latter term, however, finds its provenance in the landmark *dictum* of the ICJ in the Barcelona Traction case in 1970 (see 'Key cases'), in which the Court drew 'an essential distinction' between obligations owed to particular States and those owed 'towards the international community as a whole'. The distinctive feature of such obligations is that its performance does not concern only the State to which the obligation is owed; for example, in the context of a bilateral investment treaty, the only State that does care about the breach of an obligation under the treaty would be the other contracting party. On the contrary, obligations *erga omnes* are of such a nature that all States have a legal interest in their performance. Hence, in the event of a breach of such obligation, all States are entitled to raise the issue before political organs or are considered to have the requisite legal interest and invoke the responsibility of the wrongdoing State before the ICJ.

Specifically, the ILC Articles on State Responsibility (2001) provide for such invocation of responsibility by non-injured States in case of a breach of an obligation *erga omnes* or *erga omnes partes,* which, according to the ILC, pertain to 'collective obligations', ie obligations that apply between a group of States and have been established in some collective interest, such as the environment or security of a region or human rights law. This was also affirmed by the ICJ in the *Questions Relating to the Obligation to Prosecute or Extradite (Belgium v Senegal)* (2012) and *Application of the Convention on the Prevention and Punishment of the Crime of Genocide (Gambia v Myanmar), Provisional Measures Order* (2020).

On the one hand, it is logical that all *jus cogens* norms set out obligations *erga omnes*. For example, all States have a legal interest in the observance of the prohibition of genocide or torture.

On the other hand, obligations *erga omnes* do not spring exclusively from *jus cogens* norms. In other words, a State may assume an obligation, which, even if not of peremptory character, is assumed *erga omnes* or towards a group of states for their collective interest, for example, for the protection of environment ('*oblgations erga omnes partes*'). For example, in *Nuclear Tests (New Zealand v France)* (1974), the statement of the French President that France would not engage in any atmospheric nuclear tests conducted in the South Pacific region was found to bind France vis-à-vis all States.

Article 103 UN Charter

Another facet of hierarchy in the international legal system is Art 103 UN Charter. This provision is, amongst others, the key mechanism for enforcing sanctions adopted by the Security Council under Art 41 UN Charter. It sets forth that 'in the event of a conflict between the obligations of the Members of the United Nations under the present Charter and their obligations under any other international agreement, their obligations under the present Charter shall prevail'. Thus, when, for example, the Council adopts a binding resolution ordering the imposition of sanctions against a State, including the freezing of any assets, UN member States would not be in breach of their international obligations under other bilateral or multilateral agreements in implementing that resolution. This does not mean that conflicting obligations are terminated; rather, they are simply suspended for as long as the sanctions are in force. As a result, States implementing their obligations under the UN Charter are not considered in breach of other conflicting obligations (particularly non-performance) contained in other treaties to which they are parties.

Article 103 has served as the legal basis for the implementation of numerous sanctions regimes imposed by the UN since the 1990s. Nonetheless, it was famously held by the ECJ that Art 103 cannot trump *jus cogens* norms. In *Yassin Abdullah Kadi and Al Barakaat International Foundation v Council and Commission* (2008), the ECJ ruled that the EC Regulation embodying the sanctions against Al-Qaeda imposed by SC Resolution 1267 was in breach of the right to be heard and the right to an effective remedy. According to the ECJ, these rights constitute fundamental principles of international law which not even the UNSC can ignore.

LOOKING FOR EXTRA MARKS?

When there is a conflict between a *jus cogens* and a *jus dispositivum* norm, the former should, in principle, prevail. However, there have been cases before the European Court of Human Rights (*Al-Adsani v UK* (2001)) and the ICJ (*Jurisdictional Immunities of the State, Germany v Italy: Greece Intervening* (2012)) in which this has not been obvious. Both cases concerned the ostensible conflict between *jus cogens* norms (eg war crimes or torture) and the principle of **State immunity**. The latter was considered essentially of a procedural character and hence in no direct conflict with the substantive *jus cogens* rules. In the case now of a conflict between two *jus dispositivum* norms, one may resort to classic Latin maxims that are also applicable in the international system: (a) *lex specialis derogat legi generali*, ie a special legal regime has priority over a general law; and (b) *lex posterior derogat legi priori*, namely, the more recent law overrides an older law.

REVISION TIP

International law sets out obligations that may differ in nature and legal consequences. The most significant difference is between peremptory norms of international law (*jus cogens*) that are not susceptible to derogation and other norms of international law (*jus dispositivum). Jus cogens* norms encompass fundamental principles of the international legal order, such as the prohibition of aggression, torture, and genocide. Such norms impose obligations *erga omnes* upon States or international organizations, namely, obligations owed to the international community as a whole. *Erga omnes* obligations are not of a contractual nature.

KEY CASES

CASE	FACTS	PRINCIPLES
Accordance with International Law of the Unilateral Declaration of Independence in Respect of Kosovo, Advisory Opinion, ICJ Rep (2010), p 403	The Court was asked to assess the legality of the unilateral declaration of independence made by the representatives of the people of Kosovo on 17 February 2008. Absent a treaty, the Court had to assess whether this declaration was legitimate under general international law and whether it was in breach of UNSC Resolution 1244.	The Court construed the question narrowly and sought to address only whether there is a rule prohibiting such a unilateral declaration under customary law and not whether there was a rule permitting it. In analysing relevant State practice, it concluded that 'the practice of States in these latter cases does not point to the emergence in international law of a new rule prohibiting the making of a declaration of independence in such cases' (para 79). This stance was criticized by Judge Simma in his Declaration that is reminiscent of the *Lotus* principle. He held that: 'The Court's reading of the General Assembly's question and its reasoning, leaping as it does straight from the lack of a prohibition to permissibility, is a straightforward application of the so-called *Lotus* principle. By reverting to it, the Court answers the question in a manner redolent of nineteenth-century positivism, with its excessively deferential approach to State consent. Under this approach, everything which is not expressly prohibited carries with it the same color of legality; it ignores the possible degrees of non-prohibition, ranging from "tolerated" to "permissible" to "desirable".'

CASE	FACTS	PRINCIPLES
Barcelona Traction, Light and Power Company Ltd, Judgment, ICJ Rep (1970), p 3	The case related to a claim brought on behalf of natural and legal persons alleged to be shareholders in a foreign limited liability company. It was claimed that unlawful measures were taken against the company. This decision of the Court has principally been cited because of an *obiter dictum* on obligations *erga omnes*. The Court was under severe criticism during that period for failing to uphold the entitlement of Ethiopia and Liberia to invoke the responsibility of South Africa for the apartheid regime in Namibia in 1966. To address this criticism, the Court decided to include a paragraph in the decision postulating the idea of obligations owed to the international community as a whole.	The Court held that: 'an essential distinction should be drawn between the obligations of a State towards the international community as a whole, and those arising vis-à-vis another State in the field of diplomatic protection. By their very nature the former are the concern of all States. In view of the importance of the rights involved, all States can be held to have a legal interest in their protection; they are obligations *erga omnes*. Such obligations derive, for example, in contemporary international law, from the outlawing of acts of aggression, and of genocide, as well as from the principles and rules concerning the basic rights of the human person, including protection from slavery and racial discrimination . . .' (paras 33–4).

KEY DEBATES

Topic	Formalism and the sources of international law
Author/academic	J D'Aspremont
Viewpoint	The theory of ascertainment which the book puts forward attempts to dispel some of the illusions of formalism that accompany the delimitation of customary international law. It also sheds light on the tendency of scholars, theorists, and advocates to deformalize the identification of international legal rules with a view to expanding international law. The book seeks to revitalize and refresh the formal identification of rules by engaging with the postmodern critique of formalism.
Source	*Formalism and the Sources of International Law: A Theory of the Ascertainment of Legal Rules* (Oxford: Oxford University Press, 2011)

Topic	Fragmentation
Author/academic	B Simma
Viewpoint	In his view, irrespective of whether we are in the presence of an emerging system or an uncoordinated mess of diverse mechanisms, the fact is that the present state of affairs, characterized as an 'explosion of international litigation and arbitration', has not led to any significant contradictory jurisprudence of international courts; such cases remain the exception and actually courts have gone to great lengths to avoid contradicting each other.
Source	'Fragmentation in a Positive Light', 25 *Michigan Journal of International Law* (2003–4) 845

EXAM QUESTIONS

Problem question

State A was under the dictatorship of General X, who heavily oppressed its population. This oppression fuelled resistance movements along the whole country, leading to serious disturbances and riots in the major cities of State A. General X responded with military force and very soon there were hundreds of dead and seriously injured people.

State B decided to intervene in State A in order to 'avert a humanitarian catastrophe', as it declared. The intervention was successful and General X was ousted from power.

You are arguing with a friend whether the intervention in State A was lawful; you support that it was lawful because it was justified by a *jus cogens* norm—that is, the prohibition of flagrant violations of human rights. Your friend counter-argues that there is another *jus cogens* norm called the prohibition of the use of force in international law.

How can you resolve this conflict between two *jus cogens* norms? State the arguments of both sides.

See the Outline answers section in the end matter for help with this question.

Essay question

'Fragmentation poses a serious threat to the unity and coherence of international law, which does not possess adequate mechanisms to address it.'

Discuss.

Online Resources

For an outline answer to this essay question, as well as interactive key cases and multiple choice questions, please visit the online resources.

https://www.oup.com/he/bantekas-papastavridis-concentrate5e

Sources of international law

2

THE EXAMINATION

Exam questions in this field will definitely involve the relationship between the sources of international law. In addition, questions concerning the two elements of custom and when the latter is established are frequent. It will be less probable to find questions on general principles of the law or on subsidiary sources. Moreover, there may be questions regarding additional sources of international law, such as United Nations General Assembly (UNGA) resolutions.

KEY FACTS

- A rule (norm) of international law must be derived from one of its recognized sources. Given the absence of a central legislative organ in international law, States have determined in advance those sources from which a binding international norm may emerge.
- The formal sources of international law are enumerated in **Art 38 International Court of Justice (ICJ) Statute**. They include treaties, international custom, and general principles of law. In addition, **Art 38** enumerates two subsidiary sources, namely, judicial decisions and scholarly writings. There is no hierarchy among the formal sources, especially between custom and treaty; it is accepted that they may coexist alongside each other.
- Besides these formal sources, theory also recognizes so-called soft law. This is not binding as such, but is considered as having persuasive value which may, through consistent practice and usage, transform into customary law. Examples of soft law include key resolutions of UNGA or the **1992 Rio Declaration on Environment and Development**.

CHAPTER OVERVIEW

Sources of international law

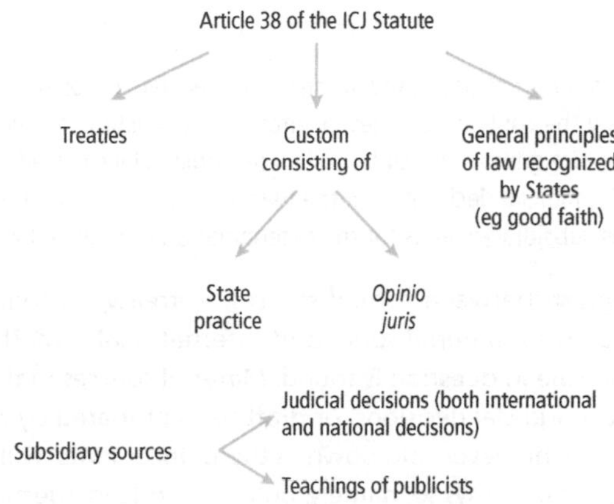

Introduction

Sources of public international law address the question, 'Where do we find the rules of international law?' Municipal rules are derived from legislation enacted by Parliament, other legislative bodies, or the common law as expressed by judicial precedent. The law of the land, thus created, embodies a set of rules the validity of which we accept because they come from these sources.

The sources of international law are different from their municipal counterparts. There is no parliament to enact legislation or a constitution setting out a legislative process; moreover, judicial decisions do not create binding precedent. In this horizontal—as opposed to vertical—structure of the international legal order, the role of sources gains increased importance. At the international level, recourse will be made to what States usually do in their international relations with a legal conviction (custom) and to what States agree in written form between themselves (treaties). In addition, general principles of law common to many nations may prove of assistance in cases where there is no treaty or custom. These are known as the 'formal sources of international law'. As evidence of what custom is, we look to judicial decisions or the writings of renowned publicists (theory). These are called 'subsidiary sources'.

The sources of international law are traditionally found in Art 38 ICJ Statute, which stems from its predecessor, the Permanent Court of International Justice (PCIJ) Statute. Article 38 states that the:

> Court . . . shall apply: a. international conventions, whether general or particular, establishing rules expressly recognized by the contesting states; b. international custom, as evidence of a general practice accepted as law; c. the general principles of law recognized by civilized nations; d. subject to the provisions of Article 59, judicial decisions and the teachings of the most highly qualified publicists of the various nations, as subsidiary means for the determination of rules of law.

It is common to distinguish between *formal sources*, ie treaty, custom, and general principles, and what are known as *material sources* of international law. The latter denotes the documents in which the rule in question is found. Material sources in this sense may be treaties, resolutions of UNGA, judicial decisions, or draft texts prepared by the International Law Commission (ILC). The rule, however, laid down in these documents, will be international law if—and only if—a formal source says so, namely, only if the rule in question has been accepted as custom or part of a treaty that has entered into force. Custom and treaties are in practice the basic sources of international law, with the general principles of law complementing them, especially in procedural matters raised before international courts and tribunals. No hierarchy between the formal sources exists, in particular treaty and custom. They are considered equal. Thus, both treaty law and custom possess equal legal value. More importantly, they can coexist and complement each other; they are not exclusive. In practical terms, however, several differences exist not only between treaty and custom, but also between the treaties themselves; on the one hand, there are treaties that can be quick to draw up, or they can be extremely slow (eg the United Nations Convention on the Law of the Sea: the drafting of the Convention lasted for nine years). On the other hand, custom tends to be slow, but it is flexible because no global or multilateral agreement is required. The more controversial a topic is, the less likely States are to agree a treaty on it (eg use of force or international responsibility).

The traditional reading of sources in the ICJ Statute is subject to criticism, given that international law has evolved significantly since its introduction in the 1922 PCIJ Statute. It is claimed that, instead, emphasis should be placed on the emergence of additional sources, such as the conduct of international organizations. International organizations represent fora for multilateral diplomacy, with the UNGA attracting the participation of all UN member States. Hence, it is reasonable to accept UNGA resolutions as sources of international law. Whatever the merits of these views or criticisms, the fact is that allegiance to the traditional sources of international law has served the international community well. At the present time, it seems unlikely that any other system will be able to replace the traditional approach.

LOOKING FOR EXTRA MARKS?

There does exist a class of agreements that, with exceptions, are not intended to be strictly binding (eg memoranda of understanding), as well as other instruments, such as resolutions and declarations made by international organizations or international conferences (eg 1992 Rio Declaration on the Environment). The latter instruments may comprise what is known as 'soft law'. The term 'soft law' is simply a convenient description for a variety of non-legally binding instruments used in contemporary international relations by States and international organizations, which are mainly *de lege ferenda*, ie they illustrate the law as it should be, rather than as it is (*de lege lata*).

Treaties in force

Article 38 ICJ Statute sets forth that the Court shall apply: 'international conventions, whether general or particular, establishing rules expressly recognized by the contesting States'. Accordingly, the first source of international law is treaties or 'international conventions' under Art 38—that is, international agreements between States in written form and governed by international law. States habitually conclude multilateral or bilateral treaties by which they are bound to particular conduct. Treaties are analogous to contracts in domestic law and the commitments enumerated in treaties constitute international law.

Why should States comply with their treaty obligations? Article 26 Vienna Convention on the Law of Treaties (VCLT) enunciates the fundamental principle of *pacta sunt servanda*, ie 'what has been agreed to must be respected'. It is this principle that renders treaties a formal source of international law.

It is obvious that not all treaties constitute 'law' for all States. In the same manner that a party to a treaty is committed to the obligations therein, a State which is not a party to a treaty is under no such commitment. A 'treaty does not create either obligations or rights for a third State without its consent' (Art 34 VCLT).

Article 38 ICJ Statute refers to 'treaties and conventions in force', thus excluding treaties which have not, or not yet, come into force, or which have ceased to be binding on the parties. The question whether a particular treaty is in force between certain States is to be answered simply by checking whether it has been ratified.

Custom

Introduction

Article 38 ICJ Statute acknowledges as the second source of international law 'international custom, as evidence of a general practice accepted as law'. There is no other category of law in which custom has such a pivotal role as in international law. This is due to the nature of the international legal system and the lack of a central legislative body. Indeed, until the mid-twentieth century, the majority of the rules and principles governing the relations between nations were customary. The inception of the ILC in 1947 brought about the gradual codification of customary law into treaties (eg the VCLT); however, customary law retains its relevance even today: first, it complements treaty law and, secondly, it is the most convenient process for change in international law. Indeed, treaties have a cumbersome system of amendment and modification and this makes custom a very useful tool for addressing new challenges in international life.

What is custom?

The traditional doctrine is that the mere fact of consistent international practice is not enough, in itself, to create a rule of law; an additional element is required. Thus, classical international law sees customary rules as resulting from the combination of two elements: an 'objective' element—that is, established, widespread, and consistent practice on the part of the States (*usus*)—and a 'subjective' element known as the *opinio juris sive necessitatis* (the acceptance of the practice as law or by necessity). The classic case concerning the requirements for the formation of custom is the following:

North Sea Continental Shelf cases (Germany v Denmark/Netherlands), ICJ Rep (1969), p 3

The Court discussed the process by which a treaty provision, and more specifically the 1958 Geneva Convention on the Continental Shelf, could generate a rule of customary law. It held that:

> not only must the acts concerned amount to a settled practice, but they must also be such, or be carried out in such a way, as to be evidence of a belief that this practice is rendered obligatory by the existence of a rule of law requiring it. The need for such belief, ie the existence of a subjective element, is implicit in the very notion of the *opinio juris sive necessitatis* [para 77].

The element of 'practice'

The first or the 'objective' element of custom is State practice. The question then beckons as to which practice is relevant. Since international law regulates the relationships between States, it is only the conduct (action or omission) of States in their relations with one another, or in relation to other subjects of international law, such as international organizations, that is relevant as practice. It follows that the said conduct (which could be either acts or claims) should always be public and possess an international character. The ILC, in its recent Draft Conclusions on the Identification of Customary International Law (2018), has affirmed that 'state practice' consists of conduct of the State, 'whether in the exercise of its executive, legislative, judicial or other functions' (Conclusion No 5), and has recognized as relevant forms of State practice, among others, 'diplomatic acts and correspondence; conduct in connection with resolutions adopted by an international organization or at an intergovernmental conference; conduct in connection with treaties; executive conduct, including operational conduct "on the ground"; legislative and administrative acts; and decisions of national courts' (Conclusion No 6).

Notably, not only acts but also omissions may qualify as State practice; for example, in the *Case of the SS 'Lotus' (France v Turkey)* (1927), the PCIJ examined whether the abstention of non-flag States from exercising jurisdiction in cases of vessel collisions on the high seas gave rise to a customary rule. It found that there was no such practice.

The relevant practice (conduct) must be general, meaning that it must be sufficiently widespread and representative, as well as consistent. The conduct need not be undertaken by every State, so long as it is consistent or nearly consistent. In certain fields of international law, however, the practice of some States possesses more value than that of others. It is the practice of these States, the 'specially affected States', to which we look to see when there is 'practice'. For example, it is mostly the practice of riparian States, ie States bordering a river, that is taken into consideration for the ascertainment of rules on international watercourses. On the other hand, it is equally significant how non-specially affected States respond to certain practice. For example, States without space technology may publicly protest against the space practice of technologically advanced nations, in which case, the practice may not lead to the formation of custom. If they acquiesce, then the practice, if it is consistent enough, will generate custom. As the ILC notes, 'failure to react over time to a practice may serve as evidence of acceptance as law (*opinio juris*), provided that States were in a position to react and the circumstances called for some reaction' (Conclusion No 10(3)).

The practice may even commence from only one State and then be adopted by other States and eventually lead to the emergence of customary law. A textbook example is the emergence of the continental shelf in international law: it all started with the 'Truman Proclamation' in 1945, which was followed by many coastal States, leading to its recognition as customary law by the ICJ in the *North Sea Continental Shelf cases (Germany v Denmark/Netherlands)* (1969).

The time factor

The establishment of custom certainly requires time; provided that the practice is general, no particular duration is required (see ILC Draft Conclusion 8(2)). Nonetheless, there might be cases when the subject matter is new and the formation of custom is instant. For example, when the first satellites were launched into space, it was questioned whether the satellite, in orbiting the earth, infringed the **sovereignty** of the States whose territory it overflew. The matter was resolved by an international convention; however, there have been scholarly opinions claiming the emergence of an 'instant custom' permitting such activity (eg B Cheng, 'United Nations Resolutions on Outer Space: "Instant" International Customary Law', 5 *Indiana Journal of International Law* (1965) 23, p 36).

General versus special or local custom

It is common to consider international custom as general and applicable to all members of the international community, for example, the prohibition of genocide should be respected in all corners of the world. This does not exclude the existence of customary rules that have a local or special scope of application. As regards *local or regional customary law*, the most well-known example is that relating to the practice of diplomatic asylum in Latin America, whereby the States of the region recognize the rights of the embassies in granting asylum to political fugitives. The ICJ considered the application of that rule in the *Asylum case* (1950) (Colombia v Peru), although ultimately it did not find it applicable to the merits of that case.

On the contrary, the ICJ has upheld that a special custom may exist between two States:

Right of Passage over Indian Territory (Portugal v India), Merits, Judgment, ICJ Rep (1960), p 6

In this case, Portugal relied on a special custom between itself and India concerning access to certain Portuguese enclaves on Indian territory. The Court held that:

> it is difficult to see why a number of States between which local custom may be established on the basis of long practice must necessarily be larger than two. The Court sees no reason why long continued practice between two States accepted by them as regulating their relations should not form the basis of mutual rights and obligations between the two States' (p 39).

Habitual character

As was manifested in the *North Sea Continental Shelf cases (Germany v Denmark/Netherlands)* (1969), State practice must be accompanied by a conviction of adherence to an existing rule of law. In the words of the Court:

> [t]he States concerned must therefore feel that they are conforming to what amounts to a legal obligation. The frequency or even habitual character of the acts is not in itself enough. There are many international acts, eg in the field of ceremonial and protocol, which are performed almost invariably, but which are motivated only by considerations of courtesy, convenience or tradition, and not by any sense of legal duty [para 77].

Nevertheless, in stark contrast to the element of practice, which is easy to discern, *opinio juris* seems very vague. It is quite difficult to say with certainty when a State acts or abstains from acting on the basis of some legal conviction. Moreover, it is difficult to tell when both elements are present and when custom is definitely established. Such questions have led many writers to deny the two-element theory and thus emphasize the importance of practice alone. Others have accepted the need for both elements. To mention a selection of these very interesting theoretical approaches: at one end of the spectrum, there are scholars such as Jenks, who accept only the element of practice, or Sir Hersch Lauterpacht, who takes *opinio juris* as granted and looks for *opinio non-juris*—when there is established practice, the presumption is in favour of the existence of customary law and we consider the existence of *opinio juris* as granted; at the other end of the spectrum, Kirgis illustrates the two elements as sliding scales—the more practice exists, the less *opinio juris* we need and vice versa. Finally, D'Amato stresses the significance of the legal articulation of State practice: that is, the manner in which States justify certain behaviour. If it includes a justification in legal terms, then we have the *opinio juris*.

The ILC has affirmed that both elements, namely, practice and *opinio juris*, are required for the formation of customary international law and as forms of evidence of the latter has identified, amongst others, 'public statements made on behalf of States; official publications; government legal opinions; diplomatic correspondence; decisions of national courts; treaty provisions; and conduct in connection with resolutions adopted by an international organization or at an intergovernmental conference' (Draft Conclusion No 10(2)).

LOOKING FOR EXTRA MARKS?

What about a State that persistently objects to the creation of a customary rule? Is it possible to assert that it is not bound by it? The notion of 'persistent objector' has been advanced both in theory and jurisprudence. For example, in the *Fisheries case (UK v Norway)* (1951), the Court stated that the then ten-mile rule of the breadth of the **territorial sea** 'would appear to be inapplicable as against Norway inasmuch as she has always opposed any attempt to apply it to the Norwegian coast'. It is required that the State concerned persistently and publicly objects to the formation of the rule from the outset. However, even though it will be difficult for that State to claim that it is a persistent objector vis-à-vis all the international community as a whole, it can still invoke this in a bilateral context, but note when it comes to peremptory norms of international law (*jus cogens*).

REVISION TIP

International customary law is the practice of States accompanied by the conviction of adherence to what is an obligation or an entitlement under international law. Accordingly, custom consists both of the 'physical' element of 'practice' and the 'subjective' element of *opinio juris*. On the one hand, State practice needs to be general, ie consistent, uniform, and widespread, but not necessarily global or without aberrations. It is true that the practice of States specially affected by the rule concerned will be more important. On the other hand, *opinio juris* will usually be found in legal declarations of States, diplomatic correspondence, and conduct in connection with UNGA Resolutions and will demonstrate that the practice in question was undertaken with a sense of legal right or obligation.

The general principles of law

Article 38 ICJ Statute also includes 'the general principles of law recognized by civilized nations' as a source of international law. When the corresponding provision of the PCIJ Statute was being elaborated, the drafters were concerned that, in some cases, the future Court might find that certain matters are not adequately, if at all, regulated by a treaty or custom. It was thus considered as inappropriate for the Court to be obligated to declare what is known as a *non liquet*, namely, that a particular claim could neither be upheld nor rejected for the lack of any existing applicable rule of law. Thus, the Court could have recourse to the established principles of domestic law that are commonly recognized among the 'civilized nations' in order to find the applicable law in such cases.

This provision remained unchanged in Art 38 ICJ Statute. According to the prevailing interpretation, the principles in question are those which can be derived from a comparison of the various systems of municipal law. The extracted principles must be shared by all, or the majority, of domestic legal systems. Clearly, the word 'civilized' is now outdated, since it echoes another era in which nations were classified as 'civilized'. The idea, however, remains that such principles have to be common to all the major legal systems, for example, both in common law and continental law, as well as Islamic law, where pertinent.

Neither the PCIJ nor the ICJ has based a single decision on such principles, although there have been references to these in various cases, especially before the PCIJ. For example, in the *Legal Status of the Eastern Greenland case* (1933), reference was made to *estoppel*, and, in the *Free Zones of Upper Savoy and the District of Gex* (1932), to the principle of *abuse of right*. Moreover, in the case of the *Right of Passage over Indian Territory (Portugal v India)* (1960), Portugal argued that general principles of law supported its right to passage and submitted a comparative study of provisions in various legal systems for what may be called 'rights of way of necessity'.

Recently, besides estoppel, which often States plead before international courts and tribunals (ICJ, *Obligation to Negotiate Access to the Pacific Ocean (Bolivia v Chile)* (2018); International Tribunal for the Law of the Sea, *Dispute Concerning Delimitation of the Maritime Boundary in Bay of Bengal (Bangladesh v Myanmar)* (2012); Permanent Court of Arbitration (PCA), *Dispute Concerning Coastal State Rights in the Black Sea, Sea of Azov, and Kerch Strait (Ukraine v Russia), Preliminary Objections* (2020); PCA, *Chagos Marine Protected Area Arbitration (Mauritius v UK)* (2015)), reference has also been made, amongst others, to the principle of abuse of process (ICJ, *Immunities and Criminal Proceedings (Equatorial Guinea v France), Preliminary Objections* (2018); *Certain Iranian Assets (Islamic Republic of Iran v United States of America), Preliminary Objections* (2019)). Another reading of this category of sources may be that it refers to general principles of international law, namely, general principles that are directly applicable to international law, such as good faith, equity, proportionality, or due diligence (on the latter principle, see, eg *Corfu Channel case (UK v Albania)* (1949) or *Pulp Mills case (Argentina v Uruguay)* (2010)). However, it is not apparent whether the normative value of such principles finds its source in this category or as customary law.

Subsidiary sources: judicial decisions and teachings

Article 38(1)(d) ICJ Statute makes a clear distinction between the sources mentioned in the preceding sections and judicial decisions and teachings. This is clear from the fact that it refers to the latter as being merely 'subsidiary means for the determination of rules of law'. In other words, while the former sources are considered to be 'formal', the latter are 'material' sources, having, nonetheless, a special degree of authority.

The judicial decisions referred to in Art 38 include judgments by the ICJ as being of the highest authority. However, the Court has made it clear that its judgments do not have the form of binding precedent. In addition, decisions of other international courts and arbitral tribunals serve as subsidiary sources, but they are not alone. The Statute refers to judicial decisions, arguably also encompassing the judgments of municipal courts. Although such judgments may seem of lesser value, in fact decisions of respected national courts carry significant weight in global practice. For example, in the *Arrest Warrant of 11 April 2000 (DR of Congo v Belgium)* (2002), the parties relied heavily on the decision of the UK House of Lords in the *Pinochet case* (*R v Bow Street Metropolitan Stipendiary, ex parte Pinochet Ugarte*) (1999)).

As regards the writings of esteemed publicists, it is true that they had an increased importance in the era of the PCIJ. Today, courts and tribunals rely less on international legal doctrine; nevertheless, the opinions and resolutions of collective bodies of international jurists, such as the ILC or the *Institut de Droit International*, still hold relevance.

The relationship between the sources of international law

There is no hierarchy between the formal sources of international law. Nonetheless, in practice, general principles of national law usually concern procedural matters. As far as custom and treaty are concerned, it has been questioned whether they can coexist or whether a custom ceases following its codification. This was emphatically addressed in *Military and Paramilitary Activities in and against Nicaragua (Nicaragua v USA)* (1986). The Court held that where a customary law is replaced by a multilateral treaty, the customary rule continues to exist, not only in respect of non-parties to the treaty, but also against its parties. In addition, treaty and custom complement each other. For example, the right of **self-defence** is governed by Art 51 UN Charter, as well as by customary law, which provides that its exercise shall be in accordance with the principles of necessity and **proportionality**.

The relationship between treaty and customary law is never static; reference should be made again to the following case:

North Sea Continental Shelf cases (Germany v Denmark/Netherlands), ICJ Rep (1969), p 3

The Court identified three situations in which the existence or creation of customary law might be related to treaty provisions: first, the treaty may embody already established rules of international law; secondly, it is possible that a multilateral treaty sets out rules and principles to which the treaty has a 'crystallizing effect': these would be rules which, even though State practice exists, were not considered to be customary law prior to the adoption of the treaty—the latter thus crystallizes their birth in international law; thirdly, it may be that, after the convention has come into force, States other than the parties adopt its provisions in their mutual relations and this may constitute practice, leading to the development of a customary rule. The Court noted that it is necessary that the provision in question 'should, at all events potentially, be of a fundamentally norm-creating character such as could be regarded as forming the basis of a general rule of law' (para 72).

Are there any new or additional sources of international law?

Besides the formal and subsidiary sources already discussed, it is questioned whether there may be other new sources of international law which correspond to modern times and which reflect an international society that is more democratic and less formal. Such candidates are apparently the resolutions of the UNGA, unilateral acts, and principles such as equity.

The acts of international organizations in general give rise to various legal consequences. On the one hand, decisions of the United Nations Security Council are binding upon all UN member States. This does not mean that they constitute an independent source of international law, as their binding nature is derived from the UN Charter itself (Art 25). On the other hand, there are resolutions of the UNGA that are not binding upon member States per se; nonetheless, they may constitute convenient material sources, in the sense that they may include statements of international law. It is questionable whether resolutions embodying such statements constitute additional sources of international law. Even though it would be consistent with the democratic principle in international law to recognize such law-making authority to the UNGA, these resolutions do not amount to additional sources. Yet, very often they enunciate or crystallize a rule of customary international law, such as the principle of self-determination, as was recently held by the ICJ in the *Legal Consequences of the Separation of the Chagos Archipelago from Mauritius* Advisory Opinion (2019). Also, in the *Military and Paramilitary Activities in and against Nicaragua (Nicaragua v USA)* (1986), the ICJ looked at various resolutions, such as the Friendly Relations Declaration (2625/1970) and Resolution 3314/1974 on aggression, and extrapolated the customary rules on the non-use of force.

Equity has played a significant part in international legal discourse in recent years. The idea of 'equitable principles' or 'equitable result' is instrumental in the law of maritime delimitation. Nevertheless, it is difficult to accept 'equity' as an additional source of general international law.

On the contrary, unilateral acts have a distinct legal value, yet their regulation is far from clear. These acts are unilateral in the sense that, although performed by a single State acting on its own volition, the consequences of the conduct are governed by international law, ie they create unilateral legal obligations on the State. Examples are the acts of recognition, protest, waiver, etc. In the *Nuclear Test case (Australia v France)* (1974), the ICJ held that France had assumed legally binding obligations through unilateral declarations, made to the world at large, to the effect that it would not undertake any further atmospheric nuclear tests in the Pacific. However, this is different from accepting all unilateral acts as independent sources of international law. Rather, States proceed in adopting them in the belief that they are founded on a customary obligation.

It also held that the fact that the previously mentioned principles, recognized as such, have been codified or embodied in multilateral conventions does not mean that they cease to exist and to apply as principles of customary law, even with respect to States that are parties to such conventions. Principles such as the non-use of force, non-intervention, respect for the independence and territorial integrity of States, and the freedom of navigation continue to be binding as part of customary international law, despite the operation of provisions of conventional law in which they have been incorporated.

REVISION TIP

Article 38 enumerates treaty, custom, and general principles of law recognized by the majority of national legal systems as the formal sources of international law. This enumeration has been the subject of serious criticism, particularly as being inappropriate to address the contemporary law-making challenges of international society. Additional sources in the form of resolutions of the UNGA, the principle of equity, or even unilateral acts have been suggested as such. It is true, however, that all these additional sources, but for unilateral acts, may operate more as a material source of international law, rather than as an additional formal one.

KEY CASES

CASE	FACTS	PRINCIPLES
Legality of the Threat or Use of Nuclear Weapons, Advisory Opinion, ICJ Rep (1996), p 226	The Court had to address the question posed by the GA as to the **legality** of the use or threat of use of nuclear weapons under international law, including the law of **armed conflict**, the prohibition of the use of force, and international environmental law. Absent a treaty, the Court had to assess the various declarations of the UNGA to find whether they were creative of customary international law.	The Court interpreted the numerous GA resolutions on the question of nuclear weapons as doing no more than revealing 'the desire of a very large section of the international community to take steps towards nuclear disarmament' (para 73). It did not recognize that the GA has authority to enact international law. More importantly, in assessing the resolutions, it was unable to find a requisite *opinio juris* to that end, due to the inconsistent voting of the member States during their adoption—that is, in one instance State A voted in favour and, in another instance, voted against.

CASE	FACTS	PRINCIPLES
Military and Paramilitary Activities in and against Nicaragua (Nicaragua v USA), Merits, Judgment, ICJ Rep (1986), p 14	The case was initiated by Nicaragua and concerned the various activities of the United States in and against Nicaragua in breach of various rules of international law, including the prohibition of the use of force and non-intervention. Due to the US **reservation** to the optional clause in the ICJ Statute, the Court was forced to apply only customary international law. Although the use of force was regulated under customary law prior to the UN Charter, there was doubt as to whether the existence of conflicts and forcible interventions since 1945 gave rise to any sort of relevant and consistent practice.	The Court held that 'it is not to be expected that in the practice of States the application of the rules in question should have been perfect, in the sense that States should have refrained, with complete consistency, from the use of force or from intervention in each other's internal affairs. The Court does not consider that, for a rule to be established as customary, the corresponding practice must be in absolutely rigorous conformity with the rule . . . If a State acts in a way prima facie inconsistent with a recognized rule, but *defends its conduct by appealing to exceptions or justifications contained within the rule itself, then whether or not the State's conduct is in fact justifiable on that basis, the significance of that attitude is to confirm rather than weaken the rule*' (para 186) (emphasis added). It also held that the fact that the previously mentioned principles, recognized as such, have been codified or embodied in multilateral conventions does not mean that they cease to exist and to apply as principles of customary law, even as regards States that are parties to such conventions. Principles such as the non-use of force, non-intervention, respect for the independence and territorial integrity of States, and freedom of navigation continue to be binding as part of customary international law, despite the operation of provisions of conventional law in which they have been incorporated.

KEY DEBATES

Topic	International custom
Author/academic	M Mendelson
Viewpoint	The author discusses the various theories for the creation of custom in international law. He takes the view that it is time to abandon the concept of *opinio juris*, since it is not so necessary and is, moreover, difficult to identify.
Source	'The Subjective Element in Customary International Law', 66 *British Yearbook of International Law* (1995) 177

Topic	General principles of law
Author/academic	R Kolb
Viewpoint	In the author's view, general principles of law play an important, albeit often invisible, role as catalysts of a law-in-movement. In particular, they offer a legal basis from which new legal doctrines or norms can be derived from case to case in order to fit new social and legal needs. These functions are illustrated more concretely through the example of the powerful principle of good faith.
Source	'Principles as Sources of International Law (with special reference to good faith)', 53 *Netherlands International Law Review* (2006) 1

EXAM QUESTIONS

Problem question

State A had a bilateral agreement with State B, which provided for the reciprocal freedom of movement and financial transactions between their nationals in their respective territories. In application of this agreement, many nationals of State B moved to State A, which was significantly more prosperous in natural and other resources. In addition, State A granted access to the authorities of State B to use its territory for some military exercises. After several years, the relationship between the two States deteriorated and State A decided to denounce the above treaty and expel all the nationals of State B established on its territory. In response, State B initiated proceedings before the ICJ, claiming that State A had violated their bilateral treaty and corresponding customary law, the general principles of good faith and *pacta sunt servanda*, and finally the right to use State A's territory for military exercises. The basis of jurisdiction is the respective declarations under the optional clause of Art 36(2) ICJ Statute. However, State A made a reservation excluding the application of any bilateral treaty binding upon the parties to the dispute.

What will be the applicable law against which the Court will assess the claims of State B?

See the Outline answers section in the end matter for help with this question.

Essay question

The enumeration of sources in Art 38 ICJ Statute is adequate in the twenty-first century. Discuss.

Online Resources

For an outline answer to this essay question, as well as interactive key cases and multiple choice questions, please visit the online resources.

https://www.oup.com/he/bantekas-papastavridis-concentrate5e

The law of treaties

3

THE EXAMINATION

Typically, exam questions in this field concern the validity and application of treaties. They usually avoid technical issues, such as the negotiation of treaties or the role of the entity that acts as the depositary of treaties. Common questions involve the definition of a treaty, the interpretation of treaties, and reservations. Equally, questions about third States or the grounds for termination and suspension of the operation of treaties, such as material breach, are frequent.

KEY FACTS

- The **Vienna Convention on the Law of Treaties (VCLT) (1969)** is the key point of reference. The **VCLT** reflects, to a very large degree, customary international law.
- The **VCLT** regulates treaties concluded between States. It was followed by the 1986 **Vienna Convention on the Law of Treaties between States and International Organizations or between Organizations**, which is not yet in force.
- Treaties are one of the means through which States regulate their international relations. They also constitute one of the formal sources of international law according to **Art 38(1) International Court of Justice (ICJ) Statute**.
- The cornerstone of the law of treaties is the principle *pacta sunt servanda*, namely, what has been agreed to must be respected.

CHAPTER OVERVIEW

The treaty-making process

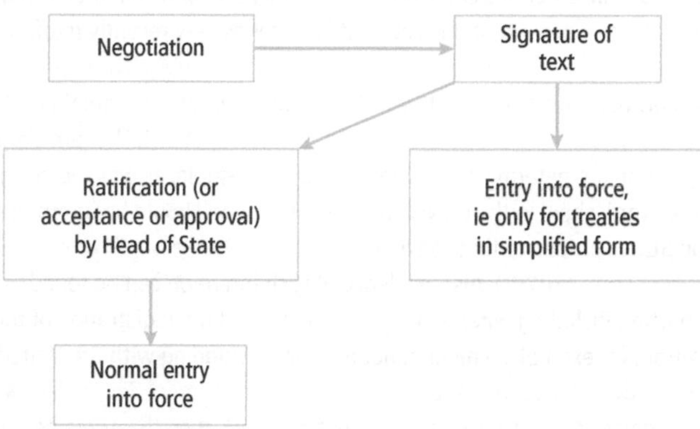

Conceptualizing and defining a treaty

'Treaty' is one of the qualifications used to designate binding international agreements. A treaty is defined by the VCLT as:

Article 2(1)a VCLT

> [a]n international agreement concluded between States in written form and governed by international law, whether embodied in a single instrument or in two or more related instruments and whatever its particular designation.

It is true that a treaty may be described in a multitude of ways. In addition to 'treaty' or 'convention', the same concept is also designated as 'declaration', 'charter', 'covenant', 'pact', 'act', 'agreement', 'exchange of letters', etc.

From the definition given earlier, it is apparent that the VCLT regulates: (a) treaties concluded between States; (b) treaties in written form; and (c) treaties 'governed by international law'. It follows that agreements between States and **international organizations** or agreements between States and non-State entities are excluded from the scope of the VCLT. Agreements between States and organizations are governed exclusively by customary international law until the 1986 Convention enters into force. In addition, oral agreements are excluded from the VCLT. This does not mean that there are no oral agreements which are subject to customary international law. According to Art 3 VCLT, 'agreements not in written form' may also have 'legal force'.

The key requirement for the existence of a treaty is that it must be 'governed by international law'. This means that, since treaties create obligations, there must be an intention therein to establish binding relations. Such intention is evident if, as it was very recently reaffirmed by the ICJ in *Obligation to Negotiate Access to the Pacific Ocean case (Bolivia v Chile)* (2018), an instrument 'enumerate[s] commitments to which the Parties ha[d] consented' (see ICJ, *Maritime Delimitation and Territorial Questions (Qatar v Bahrain)* (1994)). The terms employed by the instrument in question are determinative of its status; for example, as was recently reaffirmed by the ICJ, the use of the word 'shall' in the provisions of a convention should be interpreted as imposing an obligation on States parties to that convention (*Arbitral Award of 3 October 1899 (Guyana v Venezuela), Jurisdiction* (2020)). Also, evidence of such intention can be found in the subsequent practice of the parties, including whether they have requested the registration of the instrument under consideration, for example, a memorandum of understanding with the United Nations in accordance with Art 102 UN Charter (see *Maritime Delimitation in the Indian Ocean (Somalia v Kenya)* (2017) at para 42). If such intention is not manifest, then the agreement in question will not be a treaty. Indeed, several inter-State undertakings may assume the form of international agreements without encompassing an intention to give rise to obligations (eg the 1975 Helsinki Final Act). Finally, sometimes agreements between States will be governed by national law, for example, the local law for the sale of property.

LOOKING FOR EXTRA MARKS?

The VCLT does not require a treaty to assume any particular form or have a particular name. If a dispute arises as to the status of a particular agreement, an objective test determines whether its terms are binding on the parties. This is accomplished by taking into account the agreement's actual terms and the particular circumstances under which it was drafted, as well as their subsequent practice. As a result, the minutes of a meeting may amount to a treaty.

Maritime Delimitation and Territorial Questions (Qatar v Bahrain), Jurisdiction and Admissibility, ICJ Rep (1994), p 112

The two ministers signed a text recording several commitments accepted by their governments, some of which were to be immediately enforced. Having signed such a text, the foreign minister of Bahrain is not subsequently entitled to claim that he intended to subscribe only to a 'statement recording a political understanding' and not to an 'international agreement'.

The 'birth' of treaties in international law

Treaties may be concluded between two (bilateral) or more (multilateral) States, between States and international organizations, and between international organizations themselves. Every treaty is initially negotiated by the competent representatives of States or international organizations, either on a bilateral or multilateral level. The treaty, however, is considered concluded when the parties thereto express their consent to be bound by its terms.

Who has the authority to conclude treaties?

Treaties are negotiated and concluded by the competent representatives of States. The general rule expressed in the VCLT (Art 7, para 1) is that 'a person is considered as representing a State for the purpose of expressing the consent of the State to be bound by it if he or she produces appropriate full powers'. Accordingly, the holder of 'full powers' is authorized to adopt and authenticate the text of the treaty and to express the consent of the State to be bound by it.

There is, however, a group of persons who, by virtue of their functions and without having to produce full powers, are presumed to have such authority. These are the 'Big Three': heads of State, heads of government, and ministers of foreign affairs, as well as heads of diplomatic missions. They may adopt the text of a treaty between the accrediting State and the State to which they are accredited (Art 7, para 2).

Consent to be bound

According to Art 11 VCLT, the 'consent of a state to be bound by a treaty may be expressed by signature, exchange of instruments constituting a treaty, ratification, acceptance, approval or accession, or by any other means if so agreed'. This is a matter for the parties themselves.

Signature

Ordinarily, appending one's signature to a treaty signifies mere agreement as to the finalized version of the text, not that the State in question intends to be bound by the terms of the treaty. It is common nowadays, however, for several treaties, particularly bilateral ones, to be concluded simply by the signature of a State's authorized representative, for example, the minister of finance. These are known as 'treaties in simplified form' or, according to US practice, 'executive agreements'.

If the parties intend a treaty to be subject to subsequent ratification, acceptance, or approval, their signature constitutes only an intermediary stage. It denotes solely that the delegates have agreed upon the text (authentication of the text, Art 10 VCLT) and they are willing to consider ratifying it. In such cases, a signature does not entail an obligation to ratify. It does constitute, however, a juridical act, in the sense that by its signature each State accepts certain legal consequences. Such a legal consequence is the obligation to refrain from acts which would defeat the object and purpose of the treaty in question prior to ratification or an expression of consent not to be bound by it (Art 18 VCLT). It was with this provision in mind that the USA decided to 'unsign' the 1998 Rome Statute of the International Criminal Court in 2002, in view of its policy to sign bilateral agreements with State parties to the International Criminal Court (ICC) prohibiting them from transferring US citizens to the ICC. Such policy would definitely defeat the object and purpose of the Rome Statute, thus the USA preferred to get out of the Art 18 obligation.

Ratification

Ratification means that the ratifying State agrees to be committed by the terms of the treaty at the inter-State level. It therefore emphasizes the State's consent to be bound, as opposed to merely signing the treaty.

Entry into force

Consent to be bound by a treaty, in whatever form (ie approval, acceptance, accession, ratification) will not always entail that the treaty has necessarily entered into force. Bilateral treaties usually enter into force following the exchange of so-called instruments of ratification (essentially an official declaration to be bound that is sent to the depository), while the entry into force of multilateral treaties depends on the intention of the parties. The parties often include a provision stipulating that the treaty shall enter into force only after the deposit of a minimum number of ratifications. For example, the UN Convention on the Law of the Sea, which was signed in 1982, required 60 ratifications for its entry into force; it thus took 12 years to enter into force (16 November 1994).

The 'life' of treaties in international law

The principle *pacta sunt servanda*

The principle *pacta sunt servanda*, enshrined in Art 26 VCLT, stipulates that parties must not only adhere to their treaty obligations, but must do so in *good faith*. Good faith is an autonomous legal principle that permeates the entire law of treaties. Its significance was underscored by the ICJ in the *Gabčíkovo-Nagymaros case*:

Gabčíkovo-Nagymaros Project (Hungary/Slovakia), Judgment, ICJ Rep (1997), p 7

The case concerned the implementation of a 1977 treaty providing for the construction of a hydro-electric dam along stretches of the Danube in Hungary and Slovakia. Hungary claimed that the conduct of both parties demonstrated their repudiation of the treaty, which had thus come to an end. Nonetheless, the Court was of a different opinion, namely, that the reciprocal wrongful conduct of both parties 'did not bring the treaty to an end nor justified its termination'. More importantly, it stressed that 'what is required in the present case by the rule *pacta sunt servanda* … is that the parties find solution within the cooperative context of the treaty' (para 142).

Treaties and third States

The principle of *pacta sunt servanda* applies only to States that have expressed their consent to be bound by a treaty. In other words, only the State parties to a treaty shall abide by its provisions. In respect of non-State parties (otherwise known as third States or parties), a treaty is a *res inter alios acta*, ie it does not create obligations or rights without their consent. The VCLT deals with the issue of treaties and non-State parties in Arts 34–8 and distinguishes between obligations and rights.

Exceptionally, Art 35 VCLT provides that a non-State party may be bound by the terms of a treaty it has not ratified if it expressly accepts to be bound and the parties themselves agree to extend the application of the treaty to third parties. The same rule applies in respect of rights conferred by a treaty upon third parties (Art 36 VCLT).

Interpretation of treaties

Interpretation, it is claimed, is a term of art rather than law. The purpose of interpretation is to establish the meaning of the text intended by the parties. In general, there are three main schools of interpretation: (a) the *subjective*, which looks at the intention of the parties; (b) the *objective* or *grammatical*, which is premised on the text of the treaty; and (c) the *teleological*, which underscores the 'object and purpose' of the treaty.

For the International Law Commission (ILC), however, and the VCLT, the starting point has been the text, rather than the intention of the parties. The idea is that interpretation must start with a careful consideration of the text. This is so because the text is the expression of the will and intention of the parties. This textual interpretation, however, may be qualified in light of the following considerations: (a) the context of the treaty; (b) its object and purpose; (c) the subsequent agreements concluded between the parties; (d) the subsequent practice of the parties; and (e) the relevant rules of international law, namely, international customary law.

Article 31(1) VCLT provides that 'a treaty shall be interpreted in good faith in accordance with the ordinary meaning to be given to the terms of the treaty in their context and in the light of its object and purpose'. The rule in Art 31(1) is that treaty interpretation must be premised upon three elements: the text, the context, and the object and purpose; the underlying principle, however, is that a treaty will be construed in good faith.

The ICJ has consistently upheld the primacy of textual interpretation, while it has downplayed the relevance of the intention of the parties and the preparatory works of the treaty (*travaux préparatoires*). Article 32 provides for recourse to the preparatory works, or to the circumstances of the conclusion of the treaty, in order to confirm the meaning resulting from the application of Art 31 or, more significantly, to determine the meaning when the interpretation according to Art 31 leaves the meaning ambiguous or obscure. Very recently, the ICJ had recourse to the 'circumstances of the conclusion of the treaty' under Art 32 VCLT in the *Arbitral Award case (Guyana v Venezuela) Jurisdiction* (2020).

Territorial Dispute (Libyan Arab Jamahiriya/Chad), Judgment, ICJ Rep (1994), p 6

Interpretation must be based, above all, upon the text of a treaty. As a supplementary means to interpret a treaty, recourse can be made to other methods of interpretation, such as the preparatory work of a treaty (para 41).

Article 31(2) VCLT defines the context of the treaty as encompassing any instrument of relevance to the conclusion of the treaty, as well as the treaty's preamble and annexes. Contextual interpretation also includes reference to the other terms of the treaty, as was recently held by the ICJ in the *Immunities and Criminal Proceedings (Equatorial Guinea v France)* (2020). In that case, the Court examined, amongst others, various provisions of the 1961 Vienna Convention on the Diplomatic Relations in order to find the proper meaning of Art 22 concerning the inviolability of the diplomatic premises. As regards the 'object and purpose' of the treaty, which is, by definition, a vague term, it is often conflated with the *principle of effectiveness*. This principle may operate as an element within the 'object-and-purpose' approach, but it is not limited to this function. In fact, it has two meanings: the first is the presumption that all treaty provisions were intended as possessing legal significance and thus any interpretation that renders a text ineffective is erroneous. The second concerns the object-and-purpose test, emphasizing that the treaty as a whole and each of its provisions were intended to achieve some specific result; an interpretation that inhibits the fulfilment of the text's object and purpose is thus incorrect and another interpretation should be sought (*ut res magis valeat quam pereat*).

Under Art 31 para 3 VCLT:

> there shall be taken into account, together with the context, (a) any subsequent agreement between the parties regarding the interpretation of the treaty or the application of its provisions; (b) any subsequent practice in the application of the treaty which establishes the agreement of the parties regarding its interpretation; (c) any relevant rules of international law applicable in the relations between the parties.

A practical illustration of treaty interpretation taking into account one of the above elements is provided in the following ICJ case, which dealt with the construction of the term '*comercio*' (commerce):

Dispute Regarding Navigational and Related Rights between Costa Rica and Nicaragua, Judgment, ICJ Rep (2009), p 213

The Court held that, even when the meaning of a term is no longer the same as it was at the time of the conclusion of the treaty, the original meaning may have significance. It is true that under Art 31(3)(b) VCLT the subsequent practice of the parties can result in a departure from the original intent on the basis of a tacit agreement between the parties. This, however, can be the result of the parties' intent upon conclusion of the treaty. The intent was, or may be presumed to have been, to give the terms used a meaning or content capable of evolving, like the term '*comercio*' (see para 64).

The significance of Art 31(3)(c) VCLT, namely, the 'relevant rules of international law' as a means of interpretation, was highlighted by the ICJ in the *Oil Platforms case*:

Case Concerning Oil Platforms (Islamic Republic of Iran v United States of America), Merits, Judgment, ICJ Rep (2003), p 803

In this case, the Court had to decide whether the destruction of Iranian oil platforms was a measure essential for the security of the USA, as provided in Art XX para 1(d) of the 1955 Treaty between the USA and Iran. If it had been so, the other provisions of the said treaty would not be applicable and thus no breach on the part of the USA would have occurred. The Court interpreted the above provision taking explicitly into account 'any relevant rules of international law applicable in the relations between the parties' (Art 31, para 3(c)), namely, the rules of international law on the use of force. In interpreting the said provision in light of these rules, the Court came to the conclusion that the destruction of the oil platforms could have been a lawful measure only as a means of self-defence, which was not the case here.

REVISION TIP

The starting point for the interpretation process is always the text of the treaty. This is explicitly stipulated in Art 31(1) VCLT and it has been endorsed by the ICJ. However, the text is not the end point, as many factors such as the context, the object and purpose of the treaty, the subsequent practice of the parties, or relevant customary law may be taken into account.

Reservations

Reservations to treaties are one of the most controversial issues in the law of treaties. A reservation is a unilateral statement made by a State, when signing, ratifying, or acceding to a treaty, the effect of which is to exclude or modify the legal effect of certain provisions of the treaty in their application to that State (Art 2(d) VCLT). The most important case concerning reservations was the 1951 ICJ *Genocide Convention* Advisory Opinion; the Court had to choose between the rigid approach of the League of Nations, which only permitted those reservations accepted by all signatory parties to a treaty, and the more flexible approach of the Pan-American Union, which did not exclude reservations banned by some, but not all, parties. The Court opted for the latter approach and found that even if not all States accept the reservation, the reserving State can still be a party to the treaty.

The Court's approach is now reflected in Art 19 VCLT, which strikes a balance between the integrity of the treaty and the need for flexibility in order to encourage wide participation. The starting point is that parties to a treaty are free to prohibit reservations or to permit only specific reservations. Examples of treaties prohibiting all reservations include the 1982 UN Convention on the Law of the Sea and the 1998 ICC Statute. In all other cases, the default rule is that reservations are permitted, unless the reservation is incompatible with the object and purpose of the treaty.

Article 20(4) VCLT stipulates that, where a party objects to another State's reservation, the reserving State may still be considered bound by the treaty, albeit not in relation to the objecting party, if this is the latter's intention. The alternative is that the objecting party opts for the exclusion not of all the treaty relations inter se, but only with respect to the provision that the reservation concerned.

A rather acute issue concerns the distinction between those reservations that are incompatible with the object and purpose of a treaty from those which are not. Two schools of thought have addressed this issue.

- The permissibility school suggests a two-stage approach whereby the compatibility of the reservation with the treaty's object and purpose is examined objectively. If found to be incompatible, the approval of other parties is irrelevant, whereas, in the event of compatibility, the parties may decide whether to accept or reject it, on whatever grounds they wish.
- The opposability school considers the validity of a reservation as a matter of intention (of other parties) alone and views the compatibility test solely as a guiding principle.

Finally, a distinction is often made between reservations and *interpretative declarations*. The latter are appended to treaties by governments at the time of signature, ratification, or acceptance with the purpose of setting out how the State in question understands particular provisions in the treaty. While these declarations do not constitute reservations, to the degree that the pertinent interpretation serves to modify or alter the legal effects of the treaty against that State, it constitutes a disguised reservation. Thus, such declarations must be subject to careful scrutiny.

Since 1993, the question of the law and practice of reservations to treaties has been included in the agenda of the ILC. The premise was that the VCLT set out the general principles governing reservations but did so in terms that were too general to act as a guide for State practice and left a number of important matters unresolved, including the scope of declarations of interpretation, the validity of reservations (the conditions for the lawfulness of reservations and their applicability to another State), and the regime of objections to reservations, etc. In 2011, after many years of deliberation, the ILC adopted a Guide to Practice on Reservations to Treaties, which tried to give practical answers to the majority of the problems that had arisen in the practice of States and international organizations.

LOOKING FOR EXTRA MARKS?

What happens with reservations to human rights treaties? In the *Belilos v Switzerland case* (1988), the European Court of Human Rights (ECtHR) decided that a declaration made by Switzerland when ratifying the European Convention on Human Rights (ECHR) was in fact a reservation of a general character and therefore impermissible under the terms of Art 64 ECHR. The Court severed the reservation and held that Switzerland was bound by the Convention in its entirety. Moreover, with regard to the International Covenant on Civil and Political Rights (ICCPR), the Human Rights Committee, in its controversial General Comment No 24(52), took the view that the VCLT provisions were inappropriate in the context of human rights treaties. It is the Committee itself and not the State parties which should determine the compatibility of a reservation to the ICCPR. More recently, human rights treaty bodies commenced a 'reservation dialogue' with reserving States in order to withdraw offending reservations. This was also the recommendation of the ILC in its Conclusions on the Reservation Dialogue annexed to the Guide adopted in 2011.

The 'death' of a treaty in international law

Invalidity of treaties

The first set of rules that may lead to the termination of a treaty concerns the invalidity of treaties. These rules may be divided into two groups: relative grounds in Arts 46–50 and absolute grounds in Arts 51–3 VCLT. The main difference is that the former render a treaty voidable at the insistence of an affected State, whereas the latter do not require any legal effects to have taken place. In respect of bilateral treaties, this difference is not insignificant, given that both grounds lead to the invalidation of the treaty. However, in the context of multilateral treaties, the existence of a relative ground vitiates the treaty with regard to the particular State concerned and may not affect the remaining parties (Art 69, para 4 VCLT).

Relative grounds

These are as follows:

1. *provisions of internal law regarding competence to conclude treaties*—under Art 46(1) VCLT, a State may not justifiably claim that its consent to be bound by a treaty was in violation of its domestic law, unless the violation was manifest (ie objectively evident to any State) and concerned a rule of its internal law of fundamental importance (eg constitution);
2. *specific restrictions on authority to express the consent of a State* (Art 47);
3. *error*—according to Art 48 VCLT: 'a State may invoke an error in a treaty as invalidating its consent to be bound by the treaty if the error relates to a fact or situation which was assumed by that State to exist at the time when the treaty was concluded and formed an essential basis of its consent to be bound by the treaty';
4. *fraud* (Art 49);
5. *corruption* (Art 50).

Temple of Preah Vihear (Thailand v Cambodia), Merits, Judgment, ICJ Rep (1962), p 17
Thailand had claimed that the boundary line indicated on a map was in error, since it did not follow the watershed line that was provided in the relevant treaty. The Court rejected this claim by arguing that: 'it is an established rule of law that the plea of error cannot be allowed as vitiating consent if the party advancing it contributed by its conduct or error, or could have avoided it, or the circumstances were such as to put the party in notice of a possible error' (p 26).

Absolute grounds

These are as follows:

1. *coercion of a representative of a State* (Art 51);
2. *coercion of a State by the threat or use of force* (Art 52);
3. *jus cogens*.

Available practice in relation to these grounds is extremely limited.

Termination or suspension of a treaty's operation

Article 54 VCLT sets out the general rule that a treaty may be terminated, or a party may withdraw therefrom, in accordance with the relevant provisions of the treaty itself (eg Art 50 Treaty on European Union, applicable to 'Brexit'), or at any time by consent of all parties. Similarly, the operation of a treaty may be suspended if this is expressly provided for. Also a treaty may be considered to be terminated if the parties conclude a later treaty relating to the same subject matter.

In addition, a party may withdraw from a treaty containing no clause on denunciation or withdrawal, following a period of notice to the other parties, provided that it is established that the parties intended to admit the possibility of withdrawal; or a right of denunciation or withdrawal may be implied by the nature of the treaty (Art 56 VCLT). In this case, the treaty will continue in force for the remaining parties, unless otherwise agreed.

Where a treaty is silent on its termination or suspension and no consent has been provided by other parties, the following grounds may be relied upon:

Material breach

A 'material breach' encompasses the repudiation of a treaty or the violation of any provision therein essential to the accomplishment of its object or purpose (Art 60, para 3). Article 60 VCLT regulates the consequences of a breach of treaty. The ILC has taken a very cautious approach and emphasized that a breach of a treaty obligation, however serious, does not automatically bring the treaty to an end. It merely entitles a party to invoke the breach as a ground for terminating or suspending its operation. This entitlement, however, is subject to certain procedural safeguards set forth in Arts 65–8 VCLT. Obviously, the principle of the sanctity of treaties—namely, *pacta sunt servanda*—is instrumental in this regard.

Supervening impossibility of performance

Article 61 limits the grounds of non-performance to the 'permanent disappearance or destruction of an object indispensable for the execution of the treaty'. If so, a party may invoke the impossibility of performing a treaty as a ground for terminating or withdrawing from it. This ground is unavailable to a party that was itself instrumental in causing those circumstances.

Fundamental change of circumstances

The underpinning idea for justifying this claim of non-performance is that it would be unfair to insist that a party perform an obligation that is no longer feasible on account of the radical change of circumstances since the adoption of the treaty in question. Apparently, this idea runs counter to the principle of *pacta sunt servanda*. Article 62 VCLT very cautiously accepts that a termination on such grounds is possible, but limited.

Article 62 sets out that:

> a fundamental change of circumstances which has occurred with regard to those [circumstances] existing at the time of the conclusion of a treaty, and which was not foreseen by the parties, may not be

> invoked as a ground for terminating or withdrawing from the treaty unless: (a) the existence of those circumstances constituted an essential basis of the consent of the parties to be bound by the treaty; and (b) the effect of the change is radically to transform the extent of obligations still to be performed under the treaty.

Article 62 provides also that claims of fundamental change of circumstances are not applicable in respect of treaties establishing boundaries, especially where the claimant has contributed to the radical change in question.

The landmark case for all these grounds of termination is the ICJ *Gabčíkovo–Nagymaros case*:

Gabčíkovo–Nagymaros Project (Hungary/Slovakia), Judgment, ICJ Rep (1997), p 7
First, with regard to material breach, the Court found that Hungary's notification of terminating the 1977 treaty was premature, as no breach had yet occurred. In any case, Hungary had not acted in good faith and therefore had, by its own conduct, prejudiced its right to terminate the 1977 treaty. In relation to Art 61 VCLT, the Court held that the impossibility of performing the treaty's obligations was attributable to Hungary's failure to perform most of its own projects. Finally, in addressing the claim of Hungary that the political and economic situation had radically transformed the extent of the obligations still to be performed, the Court took a very restrictive view and rejected the claim of fundamental change of circumstances under Art 62 VCLT.

LOOKING FOR EXTRA MARKS?

The rules on the termination or suspension of the operation of treaties are closely linked with, yet distinct from, the law of State responsibility, particularly countermeasures. As the ILC Special Rapporteur on State responsibility explained:

> … the law of treaties is concerned essentially with the content of primary rules and with the validity of attempts to alter them; the law of State responsibility takes as given the existence of primary rules and is concerned with the question whether the conduct inconsistent with those rules can be excused and, if not, what the consequences of such conduct are.

REVISION TIP

The principle *pacta sunt servanda* is so fundamental that every claim for the termination of a treaty should be very restrictively assessed. The rebuttable presumption is that treaties remain in force unless the parties consent to their denunciation or their overall termination.

KEY CASES

CASE	FACTS	PRINCIPLES
Case Concerning the Land and Maritime Boundary between Cameroon and Nigeria (Cameroon v Nigeria, Equatorial Guinea intervening), Judgment, ICJ Rep (2002), p 303	In its judgment on the case concerning the land and maritime boundary between Cameroon and Nigeria, the Court fixed the course of those land and maritime boundaries. According to Cameroon, the maritime delimitation should have been based on valid international agreements, such as the 1975 Maroua Declaration, which Nigeria disputed. The reason was that, at the time, it was signed, but not ratified by the Nigerian head of State.	The Court found that the Maroua Declaration constituted an international agreement concluded between States in written form and tracing a boundary; it was thus governed by international law and constituted a treaty in the sense of the VCLT (see Art 2, para I), which reflects customary international law in this respect. The Court further considered that it could accept the argument that the agreement was invalid. It observed that while, in international practice, a two-step procedure consisting of signature and ratification is frequently provided for in provisions regarding entry into force of a treaty, there are also cases where a treaty enters into force immediately upon signature. In the Court's opinion, the Maroua Declaration entered into force immediately upon signature.
Reservations to the Convention on the Prevention and Punishment of the Crime of Genocide, Advisory Opinion, ICJ Rep (1951), p 15	The Advisory Opinion of the Court was requested by the UNGA in the following terms: 'In so far as concerns the Genocide Convention, in the event of a State ratifying or acceding to the Convention subject to a reservation made … can the reserving State be regarded as being a party to the Convention while still maintaining its reservation if the reservation is objected to by one or more of the parties to the Convention but not by others …?'	The Court determined that if a party to the Convention objects to a reservation which it considers to be incompatible with the object and purpose of the Convention, it can in fact consider that the reserving State is not a party to the Convention; if, however, one party accepts the reservation, then the reserving State is considered a party to the Convention.

KEY DEBATES

Topic	Treaty interpretation
Author/academic	R Gardiner
Viewpoint	Gardiner provides a close analysis of the rules on treaty interpretation as framed by the VCLT and as applied by both international and national courts for 40 years now. It analyses the general history, background, and development of the current rules on treaty interpretation; more importantly, it reads well, is informative, and is rich in useful material.
Source	*Treaty Interpretation* (Oxford: Oxford University Press, 2008)

Topic	The law of treaties and other categories of international law
Author/academic	E Cannizzaro (ed)
Viewpoint	The book first explores the influence exerted by the VCLT on pre-existing customary law. Certain rules of the VCLT which, at the time of its adoption, appeared to fall within the realm of progressive development, can now be regarded as customary international rules. Conversely, a number of its provisions, in particular those which have been the subject of subsequent codification work by the ILC, have become obsolete.
Source	*The Law of Treaties beyond the Vienna Convention* (Oxford: Oxford University Press, 2011)

EXAM QUESTIONS

Problem question

State A ratified a regional agreement on disarmament from conventional weapons and appended an interpretative declaration. This stipulated that it would reconsider the application of the agreement should the political circumstances radically change. In 2020, it again started to acquire such weapons, on the ground that the political tension in the region necessitated it to do so. Following a severe reaction by other parties, it decided to denounce the treaty on the basis of fundamental change of circumstances.

1. Does State A have a right to claim that the acquisition of conventional weapons under such political circumstances was justified pursuant to its interpretative declaration?
2. Does State A have a right to denounce the treaty under Art 62 VCLT?

Discuss.

See the Outline answers section in the end matter for help with this question.

Essay question

'There is no part of the law of treaties which the text writer approaches with more trepidation than the question of interpretation' (McNair, 1961).

Discuss.

Online Resources

For an outline answer to this essay question, as well as interactive key cases and multiple choice questions, please visit the online resources.

https://www.oup.com/he/bantekas-papastavridis-concentrate5e

4 The relationship between international and domestic law

THE EXAMINATION

Questions tend to focus generally on the application of the principles of transformation and incorporation of international law into domestic legal orders. The key is not simply to restate the fundamental bases of these principles, but to back them up with cases that demonstrate how they are applied in practice. Issues other than these principles are unlikely to occupy a single exam question, but readers are advised to have a good understanding of the uses of domestic laws before international courts and tribunals. A basic knowledge of English constitutional law is essential, especially since questions are likely to focus on the reception of international law by English courts. Questions on the laws of jurisdictions other than England with respect to the reception of international law are highly improbable, so it is worth concentrating on the relevant English judicial and constitutional practice.

KEY FACTS

- The international legal system and domestic legal systems are separate entities, despite their frequent interaction. The relationship between the two focuses on: (a) the reception of international law (treaties and custom) into domestic legal orders; and (b) the hierarchy between domestic and international rules.
- It is one thing for States to be bound by treaties at the inter-State level (ie between themselves) and it is another for treaties to produce effects in the States' domestic legal orders. The production of such effects in domestic legal orders depends on the constitutional arrangements of each country. In the UK, this relationship has chiefly been interpreted by the courts.
- English law requires that, generally, in order for treaties adopted by the government to produce effects at the domestic level, they must first be implemented by Parliament through an Act or other legislative action.
- There are two main constitutional theories for importing treaties and custom into domestic legal orders, namely, incorporation and transformation.
- Resolutions of the UN Security Council (UNSC) override all other conflicting legislation in the domestic order of States, save if said resolutions are contrary to human rights. Nonetheless, it is up to each country to decide the method by which such resolutions are to become domestic law.

CHAPTER OVERVIEW

Applying international law in the domestic sphere

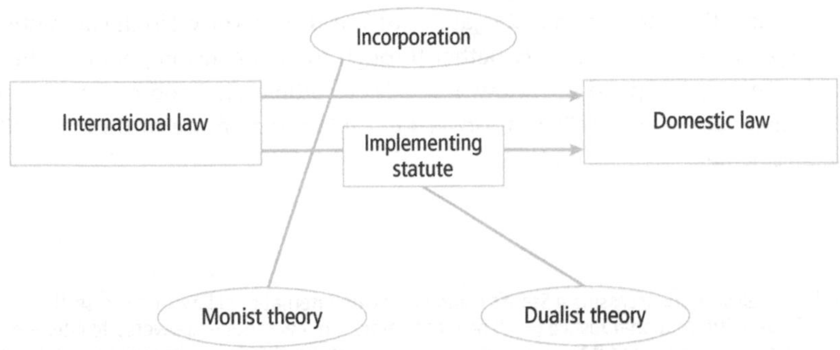

Does international law prevail over domestic law?

Imagine a situation whereby the laws of country X permit the interrogation of terrorist suspects through the use of torture. This would be in conflict with the 1984 Torture Convention, to which X is a party, as well as customary international law, which prohibits all forms of torture (and which is equally binding on country X). What we have here is a clash between a domestic and an international rule and we are asked to determine which should prevail over the other. Most situations will not be as clear-cut. They will involve a conflict between a provision found in a constitution, which is the highest law in the land, and a treaty or custom which came into effect after the constitution was adopted. By way of illustration, the constitutions of civil law countries traditionally prohibited the extradition of nationals to other nations. With the adoption of the European arrest warrant, all signatory countries were obliged to surrender their nationals, thus giving rise to questions of unconstitutionality. In such cases, it is assumed that States are willing to amend the relevant provisions in their constitutions or otherwise treat them as being compatible with their international obligations.

Moreover, it is important to understand how States, in their domestic legal orders, treat that part of international law to which they have not given their express consent, such as customary rules.

Two considerations are relevant. First, States cannot rely on their domestic law as an excuse to violate their international obligations, under Art 27 Vienna Convention on the Law of Treaties (VCLT) (*Treatment of Polish Nationals and Other Persons of Polish Origin or Speech in the Danzig Territory* (1931)). Secondly, the precise relationship between domestic and international law is determined, by and large, by each State's constitution. Constitutional arrangements explain how the international obligations of States are received in the domestic sphere. Once an obligation is found to exist (whether through treaty or custom), it binds the State in its external relations, irrespective of how it decides to ultimately import it into its domestic sphere. Two theories are generally put forward to explain the nature of these constitutional arrangements, namely, monism and dualism.

Certain German Interests in Polish Upper Silesia, PCIJ, Series A, No 7 (1926)
Domestic law is relevant for assessing a State's compliance with international law. In this case, the Permanent Court of International Justice (PCIJ) held that, although it was not empowered to interpret Polish law, there was nothing to prevent it from 'giving judgment on the question whether or not, in applying that law, Poland is acting in conformity with its obligations towards Germany under the Geneva Convention'.

LOOKING FOR EXTRA MARKS?

In *Germany v USA* (*LaGrand case*) (2001), the International Court of Justice (ICJ) accepted that the separation of powers and competencies between federal and state courts and authorities in the USA was a matter of domestic law. However, it emphasized that the effect of said separation on a country's international obligations was a matter of international law alone.

Monism

Monist theory suggests that international and domestic law do not constitute distinct legal orders, but are in fact part of the same order, in the same manner that contract law and criminal law are distinct disciplines, albeit they are both part of the English legal system. However, monism does not deny the likelihood of clashes between international and domestic law. In such situations, just as domestic laws are subject to a hierarchy of sources, with constitutions trumping all other conflicting laws, international law is considered superior to domestic legislation and always prevails.

Dualism

Unlike monism, dualism rejects the notion that international and domestic law are part of the same legal order. For dualists, the two are wholly separate and distinct orders. When a conflict arises between them, the national judge asks whether domestic law (ie regular laws or the constitution) allows the application of a particular international rule. This may happen, for example, because the rule in question is contained in a treaty which the country has ratified. Thus, dualism undertakes a selective process, based on a State's international obligations, in order to determine which international rules are enforceable in a domestic legal system.

REVISION TIP

Countries adhering to the monist theory generally follow the *method of incorporation* for importing international rules into their domestic legal orders. Dualist countries use the *method of transformation*, both of which are explained later. It should be noted that even monist countries follow a mixed system. The UK follows a mixed system whereby it *incorporates* custom, but *transforms* treaties in general.

The reception of international law by municipal law and institutions

This is a very practical matter that concerns how a treaty, custom, or Security Council resolution may be enforced, if at all, before domestic courts and authorities. A treaty or a custom may well establish rights and duties for individuals, as is the case with human rights treaties. The rights-holders will claim the pertinent rights domestically and therefore it is crucial to know how and when these treaties become available to individuals in the domestic legal order (ie when they are *justiciable*). Until a treaty or custom is imported into domestic law, it only binds States in their mutual relations with other States. States follow one of two general methods for the reception of international law into their domestic orders, namely, incorporation and transformation.

Incorporation of treaties

The doctrine of incorporation suggests that, once a country has ratified a treaty, this automatically becomes part of its domestic law without the need for further legislative, administrative, or judicial action. Countries adhering to the doctrine of incorporation render all their treaties part of their domestic law automatically upon ratification of the treaty.

There is one major practical problem with the incorporation of treaties, namely, that they may require further refinement or elaboration at the domestic level. This typically occurs because the obligations in the treaty may necessitate the provision of financial resources by the State, amendment of existing (conflicting) laws, and identification of pertinent rights-holders, among others. Thus, most countries adhering to the doctrine of incorporation distinguish between self-executing and non-self-executing treaties. **Self-executing treaties** are those whose provisions are clear and elaborate enough to be applied automatically in the domestic legal order without the need for further domestic legislation. Alternatively, some self-executing treaties may contain provisions that are considered as non-self-executing, in which case national parliaments may demand the passing of implementing legislation in respect of these non-self-executing provisions.

LOOKING FOR EXTRA MARKS?

The Netherlands is cited as the prime constitutional paradigm that favours the incorporation of treaties, as long as they are deemed self-executing. Under the US Constitution, treaties are considered 'supreme law of the land'. However, the US Senate has ratified very few treaties brought before it by the federal government.

Incorporation of custom

Unlike treaties, the existence of custom is not self-evident, but has to be verified. In practice, this means that when a customary rule is invoked before a court, the judges must first verify its existence. The next step is to determine whether the verified custom, in accordance with the country's constitution, can be incorporated automatically or whether its importation requires an additional Act of Parliament. In common law nations, if a custom is found to exist it will, in principle, be incorporated into the domestic legal system (*Buvot v Barbuit* (1736)), except:

- if the customary rule in question has been consistently repudiated by the authorities of the country (known as the persistent objector rule);
- if it is inconsistent with an existing Act of Parliament (*Chung Chi Cheung v The King* (1939)).

In England, it has traditionally been held that customary international law forms part of its law and therefore once the existence of a custom has been verified it is automatically incorporated into the domestic legal order (*Trendtex Trading Corporation v Central Bank of Nigeria* (1977)). Therefore, the *incorporation* of custom into the UK legal order is in contrast to the *transformation* required in respect of treaties.

Civil law (continental) systems follow a similar process. Article 9(1) Austrian Constitution, for example, stipulates that 'generally recognized rules of international law' are regarded as an integral part of federal law. The term has been construed as encompassing both custom and general principles. In practice, when national courts are confronted with a claim based on an as yet unincorporated customary rule, they rely on scholarly works or the judgments of other foreign courts. This is known as transnational judicial dialogue (*Hoffman v Dralle* (1950)).

Not all customary rules may be incorporated

The courts of countries adhering to the doctrine of incorporation in respect of customary rules tend to limit the application of this doctrine in certain circumstances. This is true especially where the content of the custom in question is unclear or where it is deemed by the courts as being contrary to domestic law and practice. This position is supported particularly by the courts of common law nations. In the UK, for example, a customary rule would not normally be incorporated if it is contrary to precedent (case law) and statute. As a result, some scholars have suggested that the courts of these countries have abandoned incorporation in favour of the doctrine of transformation. This scholarly position is not generally accepted.

Re Keyn [1876] 2 Ex D 63

A German ship collided with and sank a British ship on the high seas. As a result, the passengers of the British ship were killed. The German captain was prosecuted for manslaughter in England and the question was whether British courts could exercise extraterritorial jurisdiction over collisions taking place on the high seas as a matter of customary law. Cockburn CJ held that, even if the majority of nations authorized the use of such jurisdiction, he would still deny it because it would mean changing the relevant English jurisdictional rules altogether. This wholesale change of the law, in his opinion, could only come about by an Act of Parliament and not by the courts' recognition of a new customary rule.

Re Keyn should not be read as requiring an Act of Parliament in order to bring a customary rule in the British domestic legal order. Rather, it is a cautious judgment in respect of a customary rule which, if automatically incorporated, would have changed British jurisdiction on the high seas altogether. The Court was not willing to do this on its own accord.

Incorporation of crimes under customary law

It is undeniable that certain serious international offences, particularly genocide, torture, crimes against humanity, and war crimes, are recognized as such under customary international law. Their automatic importation, therefore, into the domestic legal order of countries adhering to the **incorporation doctrine** should not cause any constitutional problems. However, many countries have not adopted specific criminal legislation in respect of customary crimes, especially where such crimes are not encompassed in an international treaty. As a result, if new customary crimes were to be incorporated in a legal system for the first time, their application against an accused may violate the rule against the prohibition of applying retroactive criminal legislation (*Nulyarimma v Thompson* (2000) (Australia)).

R v Jones (Margaret) [2007] 1 AC 136

A number of people broke into a military base with intent to destroy facilities and equipment. They argued that the base was used by the USA and the UK in order to commit the crime of aggression against other nations. It was for the Court to decide whether the crime of aggression, which did not exist in common law or statute in Britain, could be incorporated by the mere fact that it existed under customary international law. Lord Bingham held that customary crimes were not automatically incorporated. He went on to note, however, that this was not because unincorporated customary crimes lacked definitional certainty.

Incorporation of Security Council resolutions

Under Art 25 UN Charter, all member States are obliged to carry out and implement resolutions adopted by the UNSC. Moreover, States have the same obligation as regards decisions adopted by subsidiary entities established by the UNSC, such as sanctions committees. The binding nature of UNSC resolutions and decisions (by subsidiary bodies) at the inter-State level is distinct from their incorporation into the domestic legal order of States. Constitutions do not generally identify any particular method for incorporating UNSC resolutions. In Japan, for example, they are incorporated by statute, cabinet order, or ministerial ordinance. In the European Union (EU), UNSC sanctions fall within the purview of the EU's common foreign and security policy (CFSP). Thereby, the EU Council adopts a common position that is reflected in a Regulation, which is directly effective in all EU member States. Problems typically arise with the content or application of a UNSC resolution and a State's other treaty obligations, which are usually of a human rights nature. Article 103 UN Charter provides that, in the event of a conflict between the UN Charter and other treaty obligations, the former prevail. In the following cases, the conflict was between the UN Charter and the European Convention on Human Rights (ECHR) or the EU Treaties. The European Court of Human Rights (ECtHR) and the Court of Justice of the EU (CJEU) adopted a cautious approach which, on the one hand, upholds Art 103 UN Charter and, on the other, stresses that Charter obligations must be construed in accordance with States' human rights (treaty) obligations.

Joined Cases C-402 and 415/05 P, *Kadi and Al Barakaat International Foundation v Council of the European Union* EU:C:2008:461

Following the 9/11 attacks of 2001, the UNSC imposed individual sanctions (freezing orders) against the assets of persons suspected of terrorism. Naturally, UN member States ordered their banks to freeze the assets of the targeted suspects, some of whom claimed that the uncritical enforcement of the UNSC's resolutions deprived them of their right to effective judicial protection under Art 6 ECHR. The CJEU agreed that the lack of judicial review against the UNSC's resolution did indeed deprive the applicants of their right to judicial remedies. Therefore, UNSC resolutions need to be interpreted in accordance with fundamental rights.

***Nada v Switzerland*, App No 10593/08 (2012)**

As in the *Kadi case*, the relationship between a UNSC resolution and the domestic legal order may be determined also by reference to the country's other international obligations, such as human rights treaties. In *Nada v Switzerland*, the Swiss authorities had implemented a UNSC freezing order against the applicant without scrutinizing the human rights implications of that action, relying instead solely on the country's obligations under Chapter VII UN Charter. The ECtHR did not limit its assessment to the hierarchical relationship between the ECHR and the UN Charter, but rather pointed to the fact that Switzerland had failed to take 'all possible measures to adapt the sanctions' regime to the applicant's individual situation'.

Al-Dulimi and Montana Management Inc v Switzerland, App No 5809/08 (2016)

In this case, the ECtHR did not find a conflict between Art 6 ECHR and Art 103 UN Charter in respect of sanctions adopted by the UNSC. It stressed that sanctions regimes constituted a 'legitimate purpose', but their implementation at the domestic level should be proportionate to their intended aim and within the context of the obligations imposed by the ECHR.

LOOKING FOR EXTRA MARKS?

In *HMT v Mohammed Jabar Ahmed and ors* (2010), the UK Supreme Court was called to assess an order adopted by the Treasury pursuant to the United Nations Act 1946, which gave it power to freeze the assets of suspected terrorists listed by subsidiary bodies of the UNSC. The UK Supreme Court held that, because orders implementing the 1946 Act did not require parliamentary approval, the courts needed to be extra careful to guarantee that orders did not breach fundamental human rights. The fact that freezing of assets under the order failed to provide judicial recourse meant that the order itself was ***ultra vires*** (in excess of powers). It was stressed that all international obligations assumed by the UK, including UNSC resolutions, must be interpreted in accordance with fundamental rights.

The doctrine of transformation

Unlike the doctrine of incorporation, whereby all treaties and customary rules adopted by a State are considered automatically part of its domestic legal order, the doctrine of transformation is based on a wholly different rationale. Countries adhering to transformation require that, in order for a treaty ratified by the constituent organs of the State to become the law of the land, it must be implemented into domestic law by an Act of Parliament, as is the case with the UK. In practice, implementing legislation need not necessarily be extensive or cover in detail all the provisions contained in the treaty. It may simply be a verbatim reproduction of the treaty itself. Alternatively, Parliament may deem that most, if not all, of the provisions of the treaty may be found in existing legislation and hence refrain from adopting new legislation. The significance of implementing legislation is not so much in its elaboration of the treaty in the internal domestic order. Rather, it serves to confer rights and duties on persons and legal entities at the domestic level. If it were not for this implementing legislation, the effects of the treaty would be valid and enforceable only at the inter-State level.

This observation is important when considering Britain's treaty-making powers. There, treaties are ratified by the Queen on the advice of the prime minister, albeit after the treaty is laid before Parliament for consideration for a period of 21 days (the **Ponsonby rule**). Parliament has no other direct involvement. Nonetheless, without implementing legislation adopted by

Parliament, treaties ratified by the Queen remain effective only at the inter-State level (ie between States themselves) and produce no effects whatsoever on the British domestic legal order. In the UK legal order, treaties possess an interpretative dimension, whereby the courts may infer, in their construction of a particular treaty, that Parliament did, or did not, intend for it to conflict with existing legislation.

REVISION TIP

Although a minor point, one may distinguish *transformation* (ie the use of a domestic statute to turn an international obligation into a domestic one) from *implementation*, which generally refers to the taking of practical measures to give effect to an international obligation. An example of implementation is the establishment and policing of a quarantine adopted under the terms of a treaty, as opposed to the statute that sets up the quarantine. Sometimes, however, the use of the term '*implementation*' is used in scholarly work to denote the legislative act adopted in the process of *transformation*.

The Parlement Belge (1880) 5 PD 197

Two ships, one British and one Belgian, collided near Dover. When legal action was brought against the Belgian ship, the *Parlement Belge*, before the British courts, its owners argued that it was covered by **immunity** on account of a treaty between the two countries to that effect. The problem was that said treaty had not been transformed into British law by an Act of Parliament. The Court of Appeal held that, absent an Act of Parliament, the treaty had not become part of English law. The rationale was that because treaties can deprive British subjects of their private rights, only Parliament is competent to alter the status of private rights. See also the *International Tin Council cases* (see 'Key cases').

Medellín v Texas, 552 US 491 (2008)

The case concerned the application of the Vienna Convention on Consular Relations to death-row inmates. The Convention had been ratified by the USA, but Congress had not enacted implementing legislation. In the same case, the ICJ had issued an injunction on the USA to halt the executions. The US Supreme Court held that the Convention was binding on the USA at the inter-State level but, absent domestic legislation, it produced no effects in the US legal order. The result would have been different had the Convention been self-executing. Moreover, judgments and decisions of the ICJ were found by the Supreme Court not to be binding domestically in the absence of an act of Congress or other constitutional authority.

REVISION TIP

The UK was one of the first signatories to the ECHR and British nationals have long brought cases against the UK before the ECtHR. Nonetheless, the rights in the ECHR became part of English law only in 1998, when the Human Rights Act was adopted by Parliament as a means of implementing the ECHR.

Recognition of foreign judgments

States usually adopt bilateral and multilateral treaties when agreeing to enforce foreign judgments in their domestic legal spheres. The 1970 Council of Europe Convention on the International Validity of Criminal Judgments, for example, obliges member States to enforce foreign penal judgments, whereas Council Regulation (EC) 44/2001 of 22 December 2000 on jurisdiction and the recognition and enforcement of judgments in civil and commercial matters applies equally to civil judgments. Contractual freedom also dictates that foreign arbitral awards are enforceable worldwide in accordance with the 1958 New York Convention on the Recognition and Enforcement of Foreign Arbitral Awards.

KEY CASES

CASE	FACTS	PRINCIPLES
JH Rayner (Mincing Lane) Ltd v Department of Trade and Industry (*Tin Council cases*) [1990] 2 AC 418	The International Tin Council (ITC) was an international organization established by treaty between various countries, including the UK. The treaty in question was never implemented by Parliament, but this did not prevent the ITC from having its headquarters in London and enjoying international legal **personality**, as well as privileges and immunities in the UK, as a result of a statutory order. When the ITC went bankrupt, its creditors brought legal proceedings in the UK. The problem was that the ITC's founding treaty had not been transformed into English law and there was uncertainty as to whether a claim based on an untransformed treaty was possible.	It was held that: 'the Crown's power to conclude treaties with other sovereign states was an exercise of the royal prerogative . . . [but this] did not extend to altering domestic law or rights of individuals without the intervention of Parliament and a treaty was not part of English law unless and until it had been incorporated into it by legislation'. Lord Oliver went on to emphasize that individuals do not derive any rights under, nor are they deprived of obligations by, untransformed treaties. As a result, the claims against the ITC were non-justiciable and were therefore rejected.
R (on the Application of Al-Jedda) v Secretary of State for Defence (2008) 47 ILM 611	An individual had been detained by British forces operating in Iraq on grounds of security. His detention remained indefinite and he was not charged with an offence. Although the conditions of the detention violated Art 5(1) ECHR, the British government claimed that it was nonetheless justified in detaining him in this manner because SC Resolution 1546 granted to all nations a broad authorization to detain suspected terrorists. The question was whether obligations stemming from the SC (on the basis of the UN Charter) superseded the UK's human rights legislation.	Lord Bingham noted that actions taken pursuant to SC resolutions override the UK's human rights obligations, irrespective of whether these are derived from domestic legislation or other international treaties (ie the ECHR). This conclusion was the result of Art 103 UN Charter. Nonetheless, the UK was under an obligation to reconcile as best as possible its two competing obligations. In the case at hand, this entailed ensuring that the detainee's rights under Art 5 ECHR were not infringed 'to any greater extent than is inherent in such detention'.

CASE	FACTS	PRINCIPLES
Wena Hotels v Egypt, ICSID Decision on Annulment (5 February 2002)	This concerned an investment dispute. The parties had entered into a contract to regulate private leases but, at the same time, a bilateral investment treaty (BIT) existed between Egypt and the investor's country of nationality which extended several investment guarantees to all investors holding the nationality of both countries. The governing law of the contract was clearly Egyptian law, whereas the applicable law under the BIT was international law. At some point, the investor claimed that Egypt had breached the private leases contract and had additionally failed to afford an investment guarantee. Which law applied to these disputes—Egyptian or international law?	The tribunal held that the applicable law of each dispute was to be determined according to the source of the obligation claimed. The dispute as to the private leases arose from the parties' contract and therefore the parties' choice of law (ie Egyptian law) was applicable. The dispute as to the investment guarantee arose from the BIT, an international treaty, where the applicable law was designated as being international law.

KEY DEBATES

Topic	The incorporation of customary crimes in English law
Author/academic	R O'Keefe
Viewpoint	Traces the debate in ***R v Jones***, where Lord Bingham held that a customary crime 'may, but need not, become part of the domestic law of England without the need for any domestic statute or judicial decision'. This incorporation of customary crimes was subject to two limitations: (a) the Knuller rule, whereby the courts cannot introduce new crimes; and (b) that Parliament typically enacts statutes in respect of treaty and customary crimes, and that if it refuses to do so with regard to a particular offence, this is the end of the matter. In the present instance, the International Criminal Court Act 2001 intentionally excluded aggression from its ambit, thus leading to the conclusion that it should not be treated as a domestic crime in England.
Source	'Customary International Crimes in English Courts', 72 *British Yearbook of International Law* (2002) 293

Topic	The contractualisation of international law
Author/academic	I Bantekas
Viewpoint	Many of the spheres of international law traditionally regulated by treaty or custom are gradually subject to private contract and, at the same time, State actors choose to interact with other State and non-State actors outside the framework of domestic and international law, in what is known as the sphere of transnational law. A good illustration may be drawing sovereign financing agreements with intergovernmental and private banks, as well as the outsourcing of human rights obligations to the private sector.
Source	The 'Contractualisation of Public International Law', in (2020) 17 *International Journal of Law in Context* 1–7

EXAM QUESTIONS

Problem question

Antonio is a national of country X who was accused of having committed the crime of nuclear terrorism. He was captured by a British warship in international waters and sent to the UK to stand trial. The UK ratified the Convention against Nuclear Terrorism, but has not passed implementing legislation. In any event, the crime itself is considered a serious offence under customary international law and most States in the world have adopted relevant provisions in their criminal statutes. To further compound the situation, the UNSC issued a list of names suspected of terrorism and demanded that all UN member States arrest those persons (if found on their territory) and freeze their personal assets and those of close family members. Antonio was on this list. His wife received housing and childcare benefit in the UK because she was disabled. The UK government suspended these payments to his wife and children and offerred them no judicial recourse to challenge the measures against them. Critically discuss whether:

1. Antonio may be tried in the UK on the basis of the nuclear terrorism Convention and whether the terms of the Convention are enforceable in the UK's domestic legal order;
2. Antonio may alternatively be tried in the UK on the basis of the customary nature of the crime of nuclear terrorism (your response should take into consideration the legal complexities of incorporating customary law into the UK legal order);
3. an SC resolution overrides any domestic legislation to the contrary and whether, under such circumstances, a UN member State is nonetheless obliged to carry out the terms of the resolution; and
4. the absence of judicial remedies and the freezing of assets that constitute the basis of a family's survival are legitimate under the case law of the CJEU. Are human rights considerations relevant to the reception of SC resolutions in the domestic order of UN member States?

See the Outline answers section in the end matter for help with this question.

Essay question

Critically discuss the various limitations imposed on the doctrine of incorporation in respect of customary rules. Why have English courts taken a cautious approach to the incorporation of custom?

Online Resources

For an outline answer to this essay question, as well as interactive key cases and multiple choice questions, please visit the online resources.

https://www.oup.com/he/bantekas-papastavridis-concentrate5e

5

Personality, statehood, and recognition

THE EXAMINATION

General questions on the nature of legal personality are rare and so they are mostly focused on the particular subjects of international law. Among these, one should certainly pay particular attention to the classical and contemporary elements of **statehood**, as well as the legal personality of international organizations. Students should also be aware of the way that **recognition** of States and governments works because this is also a topic that students can critically develop in an exam.

KEY FACTS

- 'Subjects of international law' refers to the same concept as the term 'international legal personality'. The classical distinction between subjects and objects of international law is now pretty much obsolete.
- International legal personality means possessing rights and duties directly under international law, alongside a capacity to enforce these rights or the obligations in favour or against the person or entity. Therefore, where a treaty or custom confers enforceable rights and duties upon any entity, the latter possesses international legal personality in respect of those rights and/or duties.
- Although numerous entities (ie States, individuals, international organizations, etc) may possess international legal personality, they do not all enjoy rights and duties to the same degree. For example, States can conclude treaties and use armed force to defend themselves, whereas individuals cannot. Therefore, international legal personality should be viewed from the point of view of capacity in each and every case.
- The primary subjects of international law are States because they make the law and it is they that confer rights and duties on other actors. Some degree of international legal personality is enjoyed by international organizations, individuals, and non-governmental organizations, such as multinational corporations, national liberation movements, and others. It all depends on the conferral of rights and duties by States in each particular case.
- Recognition of States (by other States) rests on two competing theories. The first contends that recognition is irrelevant to statehood (**declaratory recognition**), whereas the second argues that it is a foundational criterion of statehood (**constitutive recognition**).

CHAPTER OVERVIEW

Subjects of international law

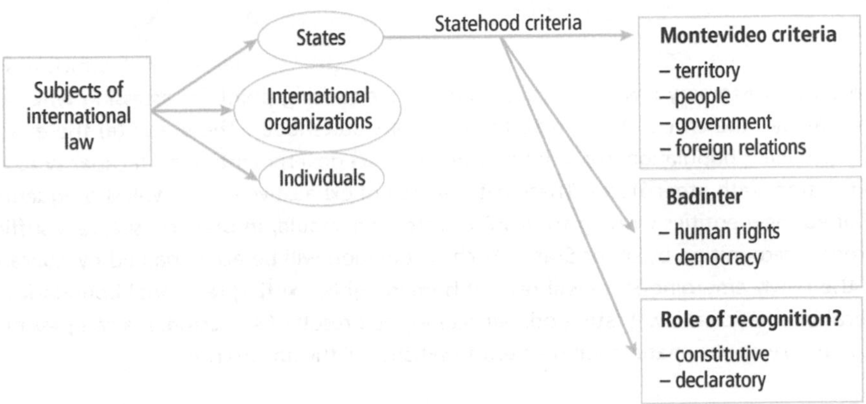

Subjects of international law

International legal personality entails having rights and duties under international law and a capacity to enforce these. States possess unlimited legal personality. Through treaties and custom, they are also able to confer international legal personality to other actors, such as individuals and international organizations. The rights and duties of the latter are not unlimited and are instead dependent on the wishes of States. An example of a 'right' is the entitlement of States to defend themselves against external aggression. The criminalization of war crimes, on the other hand, is an example of an obligation placed upon individuals. Rights and obligations would be meaningless if they were not enforceable. Rights and duties under international law can be enforced before international courts with limited jurisdiction, such as the International Court of Justice (ICJ) and the International Criminal Court (ICC); investment tribunals, such as those established under the 1967 International Convention on the Settlement of Investment Disputes (ICSID); ad hoc criminal tribunals, such as those for Yugoslavia and Rwanda; and quasi-tribunals, such as human rights treaty bodies (eg the Committee against Torture), as well as before national courts. Indeed, national courts entertain most legal actions concerning rights and obligations under international law. Moreover, enforcement need not necessarily be judicial in nature. An obligation may well be enforceable by the resolution of an organ of an international organization (eg UN Security Council (UNSC)) or through inter-State negotiations, which could lead to an agreement for damages or reparation.

States and the criteria for statehood

Article 1 Montevideo Convention on the Rights and Duties of States (1933), which has crystallized into customary law, is typically taken as the starting point for assessing whether an entity satisfies the criteria to be a State (ie to have statehood). These are: (a) the existence of a permanent population; (b) a defined territory; (c) government; and (d) capacity to enter into relations with other States. These criteria are not exhaustive and, as will subsequently be explained, new entities wishing to acquire statehood should, in practice, secure a sufficient degree of recognition by other States. Such recognition will be accompanied by guarantees that the newly emerging State will respect human rights, existing territorial boundaries, and general international law. Statehood, particularly as a result of **secession**, is a complex matter that is in no way automatic, even if an entity satisfies all the above criteria.

Permanent population

Population size is not a criterion for statehood, given that certain small-island States, such as Nauru, had a population of less than 10,000 upon independence. What is required is a core stable population that has a firm allegiance to the State on the basis of a shared nationality. This does not mean that said population must share the same ethnic, religious, or other composition, given that the conferral of nationality is generally independent of such common characteristics. It is immaterial if a foreign migrant population working there has surpassed the local population in number. It is also irrelevant if a large number of nationals of the State are nomads and move around the territory of their country or across neighbouring countries in order to graze their cattle, as long as their transit to the neighbouring nations is temporary (*Case Concerning Western Sahara*, ICJ Advisory Opinion (1975)).

A defined territory

It would be absurd for an entity to claim statehood without the possession of defined territory. What this criterion excludes, therefore, are situations where a rebel group merely occupies certain territory, but is still battling to hold on to it against other States. As a result, it excludes all self-proclaimed States that have acquired territory by unlawful armed force and annexation, as is the case with the so-called Turkish Republic of Northern Cyprus (TRNC). Statehood, on the other hand, is not denied simply because a particular border is disputed or not fully recognized by the international community. The territory of Israel is still contested by most of its neighbours, but it is no less a State than its detractors. The ICJ has made it clear that there is no rule of international law whereby the land frontiers of a State must be fully delimited (*Germany v Denmark and the Netherlands* (*North Sea Continental Shelf cases*) (1969)).

LOOKING FOR EXTRA MARKS?

Provinces/States within federal entities (as is the case with the USA) do not possess the same degree of international legal personality as that enjoyed by regular States and they do not possess statehood. Nonetheless, federal constitutions, such as that of Germany, allow provinces to enter into treaties or other relations with foreign States and international organizations.

Government

All that is required is that the entity in question possesses a sovereign government that is free from external domination. Given that many countries in the world are governed by dictatorial and undemocratic regimes, there is no requirement that governments are democratic. The TRNC has not been recognized by any State other than Turkey because its government is universally considered an emanation of Turkey.

An existing State does not forego its statehood simply by reason of being descried as 'failed', which generally refers to its inability to provide physical security, legitimate political institutions, economic management, and social welfare to its people, as is the case with Somalia. Failed States, even those subject to significant foreign intervention, continue to be sovereign and retain their statehood in full. This is further reinforced by the fact that the practice of recognizing governments (as opposed to States) has lost significant traction since the end of the Cold War.

Capacity to enter into foreign relations

It is not obvious in what way this requirement is different from the criterion of government. In practice, this means that an entity is able to enter into treaties, conduct business, exchange diplomats, and undertake other activities with other countries. In large part, although most scholars and judgments are silent on this matter, an entity's capacity to enter into foreign relations is dependent on its recognition and legitimization by other countries. An entity whose statehood is not accepted by other countries will be unable to enter into foreign relations with them, even if it is fully capable of doing so (see 'Recognition of States and governments' below).

REVISION TIP

The four criteria of statehood in the Montevideo Convention have long been recognized as being part of customary law. The criteria of government and foreign relations capacity should be distinguished, even though the latter seems like a natural extension of the former.

The relevance of human rights in the determination of statehood

It should be remembered that the discussion on statehood concerns new entrants in the community of States because the statehood of existing countries cannot be denied, unless, of course, they disappear or disintegrate.

Following the disintegration of the former Yugoslavia in the early 1990s, the federal provinces that comprised it sought their independence. A committee appointed by the European Union (EU), known as the Badinter Committee, stipulated that in order for the EU to recognize the statehood of these new entities, they would have to satisfy respect for the UN Charter, fundamental human rights, and democracy, as well as guarantee the rights of all minority groups within their territories. Moreover, they were obliged to respect the inviolability of existing borders and settle all disputes amicably.

The principle of **self-determination** is significant in the creation of *new* States, but it is also subject to severe limitations, in that it is only very exceptionally available to seceding entities. The external dimension of the principle dictates that, although majorities can decide to secede, State practice strongly discourages secession (Badinter Committee, *Opinion No 2* and principle 5 of the UN General Assembly Resolution 2625 (1970), known as the Friendly Relations Declaration) unless this is achieved through a process (ie referendum) that is in conformity with the country's constitution. The annexation of Crimea by Russia is considered unlawful because it was achieved outside the Ukrainian constitutional framework, irrespective of Russia's contentions that it was inhabited by a predominantly Russian majority. State practice and ICJ case law confirms that self-determination may lawfully lead to secession (outside a constitutional framework) where: (a) this is connected to non-self governing territories (colonies); and (b) a group (peoples) are subject to gross abuse by the majority or the mother State. This suggests that minorities, while enjoying a great number of rights under international law (eg in respect of language, culture, religion, self-government), do not possess the right to external self-determination (ie to secede). This was why a number of countries opposed Kosovo's unilateral declaration of independence from Serbia, particularly countries with politically active minority populations. The ICJ's Advisory Opinion on this unilateral declaration simply noted that unilateral declarations are not unlawful under international law (*Accordance with International Law of the Unilateral Declaration of Independence in Respect of Kosovo* (*Kosovo Declaration case*) (2010)).

Reference re Secession of Quebec [1998] 2 SCR 217

The Canadian government asked its Supreme Court to rule on whether a unilateral secession brought about by a referendum—which the French-speaking Quebecois had recently lost—would have been lawful under Canadian and international law. The Court held that international law did not favour disintegration as long as the State in question 'represents the whole of the people or peoples resident within its territory, on a basis of equality and without discrimination and respects the principles of self-determination in its own internal arrangements'. As a result, even if the plebiscite had been in favour of secession, this could not have been achieved unilaterally, but rather on the basis of an agreement among all of Canada's provinces and in accordance with the rights of other Canadians and minorities.

The legal personality of international organizations

Article 2(a) ILC Articles on the Responsibility of International Organizations (ARIO) (2011) defines an international organization as: 'an organisation established by a treaty or other instrument governed by international law and possessing its own international legal personality. International organisations may include as members, in addition to states, other entities.' International organizations are established by States and it is the founding States of each organization that determine their *powers* and *functions*. Powers and functions are written into the organization's founding (or constitutive) instrument. An example of this is the United Nations (UN) Charter. Some organizations are set up for a variety of purposes, such as the UN, whereas others are set up for a very specific purpose, as is the case with the International Sugar Organization. There is considerable debate as to the legal personality of international organizations and two theories are usually put forward, namely, the *inductive* and the *objective* approach. According to the inductive approach, the rights and duties of organizations under international law are derived from their constitutive instrument. This includes not only those rights and duties that are expressly stated therein, but also those that may be implied on the basis of the object and purpose of the organization. The objective approach suggests that the international legal personality of organizations is not dependent on their constitutive treaty, but on whether or not they fulfil certain conditions under general international law. This theory is particularly important because the constitutive instruments of many organizations, including the UN Charter, do not specifically state whether the organization enjoys international legal personality. The conditions required under the objective approach are the establishment of the organization by treaty and independence from the member States that established it. In practice, a combination of the two approaches is where the truth lies. It is generally accepted that international organizations are bound by customary international law.

Implied powers

The charter of an organization may only spell out certain powers. Yet, during the lifetime of the organization it may be required to exercise further powers if it is to fulfil the functions and tasks assigned to it. These are known as **implied powers**. The UN General Assembly (UNGA) possesses authority to protect and promote human rights, but the UN Charter does not mention whether it can establish peacekeeping or observer missions in order to fulfil this power. The ICJ in the *Certain Expenses of the UN case* (1962) stipulated that this task could only be fulfilled by establishing such missions, in respect of which UN member States had a responsibility to make financial contributions.

Reparation for Injuries Suffered in the Service of the United Nations (Reparations case), ICJ Rep (1949), p 174

The ICJ held that the UN could not possibly carry out the intentions of its founders if it was not endowed with some degree of international legal personality. Moreover, the UN was found to possess implied powers (ie powers not expressly included in the UN Charter) if these were essential for carrying out tasks specifically assigned to it. The same view was later iterated by the ICJ in its *Certain Expenses of the UN* Advisory Opinion (1962), where it held that irregular peacekeeping expenses authorized by the UNGA were expenses of the UN because the action contemplated fell within the UNGA's mandate under the UN Charter.

LOOKING FOR EXTRA MARKS?

International organizations may delegate powers and functions to other entities, particularly new organs founded by them for a specific purpose (known as subsidiary bodies or organs). However, they cannot delegate to those organs the original powers conferred upon them in the organization's constitutive instrument.

Consequences of the international legal personality of international organizations

International organizations possess a legal personality that is wholly distinct from the personality of each and every State that established them, despite the fact that their member States act as their executive organs and adopt decisions that bind the legal personality of the organization. This means that any claim which the organization might have against any State or other entity belongs to the organization itself and is brought in its own name. Equally, any liabilities attributable to the organization are incurred by it alone and not by its member States (*AOI and ors v Westland Helicopters Ltd* (1988)). Equally, organizations and their staff enjoy privileges (such as tax exemptions) and immunities in the countries where they operate. These are usually derived from: (a) domestic laws conferring immunities and privileges; (b) headquarters agreements, between the organization and the host state; (c) a multilateral agreement, such as the Convention on the Privileges and Immunities of the United Nations (1947); and (d) the organization's constitutive treaty.

Dual liability of organizations and member States

It is clear that if States are able to attribute otherwise personal action to international organizations to escape their own obligations, then, in equal manner, the States affected by the measures adopted by such organizations can claim that they were required by treaty to adhere to them. In both cases, there is an artificial absence of obligations and a corresponding absence of liability. Such a result is untenable, lacks legal foundation, and has rightly been condemned by international and domestic courts, despite claims to the contrary by collaborating States. This type of liability is recognized in Art 61 ILC AIRO, which reads:

> A State member of an international organization incurs international responsibility if, by taking advantage of the fact that the organization has competence in relation to the subject-matter of one of the State's international obligations, it circumvents that obligation by causing the organization to commit an act that, if committed by the state, would have constituted a breach of the obligation.

The European Court of Human Rights (ECtHR) has made it clear that member States to the European Convention on Human Rights (ECHR) cannot evade their human rights obligations 'under the guise of complying with the recommendations of an international organisation' (*Capital Bank AD v Bulgaria* (2005)).

MacLaine Watson & Co Ltd v International Tin Council (Tin Council cases), 81 ILR 670

The International Tin Council, an international organization, became insolvent and its creditors pursued legal action in London, not only against the Tin Council itself, but also against its member States. The House of Lords held that, since international organizations possess a distinct personality from that of their member States, the latter are considered third parties to the debts and liabilities of organizations and are therefore not liable for said debts.

REVISION TIP

International organizations possess rights and duties from their founding treaty, as well as under general international law. The *Reparations case* made sure that organizations enjoy implied powers in order to fulfil functions and tasks assigned to them. Organizations have a personality that is distinct from that of their member States.

Natural persons

Individuals (or natural persons) enjoy international legal personality in three principal fields; namely, human rights, international criminal law, and economic integration/foreign investment. Article 34 ECHR allows individuals to bring claims against States before the ECtHR. The same is true in respect of other treaty-based human rights courts, commissions, and quasi-tribunals. Individuals are also liable for crimes under international law and can be prosecuted before international tribunals or domestic criminal courts (Art 25 ICC Statute). Finally, individuals may be granted enforceable rights and duties under economic integration agreements, such as the right of movement and establishment, as is the case with the EU (*Van Gend en Loos v Netherlands Inland Revenue Administration* (1963)) (see chapter 13 on individual criminal responsibility under international law).

Multinational corporations and non-State actors other than individuals

A company incorporated in country A may set up a new company in country B, under the laws of country B, and become its majority shareholder. An additional company is then incorporated in country C under the laws of the latter, the majority of whose shares are owned by the two companies in countries A and B. This form of inter-country multi-shareholding is the essence of multinational corporations (MNCs). Although each company is subject to the laws of the country of incorporation, the degree of shareholding dictates whether 'control' of each branch is foreign or international, rather than purely local. MNCs are chiefly regulated by domestic law and only rarely by extraterritorial legislation. It is only the ethical/human rights and tax practices of MNCs that have become the subject of inter-State 'regulation'. As regards the former, this has come about through non-binding instruments, such as the UN Guiding Principles on Business and Human Rights. Many instruments, some set up by international organizations, are based on voluntary compliance, such as the UN Global Compact. Some treaties call upon States to control corporate conduct in the criminal sphere, such as Art 26 UN Convention against Corruption 2003.

Non-State actors, such as private corporations and individuals, routinely enter into contracts with States and State entities. These contracts are binding upon States under the terms of the parties' chosen governing law and it is now well established that States do not possess immunity from jurisdiction where the agreement foresees international commercial arbitration.

The State is obliged to submit to, and respect, the award of the arbitral tribunal (*Texaco v Libya and BP v Libya* (1974)). Where the activity in question is classified as an investment, any dispute between the investor and the host State may be resolved through investment arbitration. This may be envisaged in a bilateral or multilateral investment treaty, the parties' contract, or a domestic law to that effect. Foreign investors enjoy an independent right of action (ie without the need for diplomatic protection) against host States in cases of expropriation and other forms of mistreatment. Even the shareholders of a foreign company enjoy an independent right of action against the host State (ie other than the legal person) (*CMS v Argentina*, ICSID Decision on Jurisdiction (2003)).

Other non-State actors include rebel movements, terror groups, and charitable or humanitarian non-governmental organizations (NGOs). Their limited international legal personality is diffuse. Humanitarian NGOs such as Amnesty International, for example, may petition human rights mechanisms on behalf of victims and possess consultative status with intergovernmental organizations. Rebel groups may receive limited recognition as de facto governments and participate in inter-State summits, whereas the conduct of terror groups may amount to an **'armed attack'** for the purposes of self-defence, but they are not otherwise afforded any rights under international law.

LOOKING FOR EXTRA MARKS?

In *Re South Africa Apartheid Litigation* (2014), an action in tort was brought against US corporations, alleging that they were complicit in violations during the apartheid era by manufacturing vehicles and computers for the then racist regime of South Africa. The US District Court distinguished between whether particular conduct violates a universal international norm, which is regulated by international law, and the question of who bears liability for the conduct, which is a matter for domestic law. The Court had no problem finding that corporations can indeed incur liability in tort, rejecting the idea that a group of individuals could escape liability simply because they had incorporated into a legal person. This judgment is in sharp contrast with *Kiobel v Royal Dutch Petroleum* (2013), where the US Supreme Court held that, in order for the Aliens Tort Act to grant jurisdiction to US courts for extraterritorial conduct, they must raise sufficient concern for the USA and because 'corporations are often present in many countries, it would reach too far to say that mere corporate presence suffices'.

Recognition of States and governments

Even if an entity fulfils the Montevideo Convention criteria for statehood, it will still seek recognition by other States. This is because external recognition provides **legitimacy** and allows the exercise of beneficial and meaningful foreign relations. Recognition is sought for statehood itself, and increasingly less so in respect of newly installed governments. Besides the reasons already mentioned, recognition of statehood is important because it leads to admission in international organizations and access to capital markets.

It should be pointed out that issues of recognition usually arise as a result of State succession (ie when a constituent nation breaks up into two or more new State entities, as was the case with the break-up of the USSR). In the break-up of the USSR, the transition to statehood was without contention as a result of the Alma Ata Declaration (1991), whereby all States agreed to respect and recognize each other's sovereignty.

The declaratory and constitutive theories of State recognition

According to the declaratory theory, recognition of a State is merely a political gesture, without any legal significance. Therefore, if an entity fulfils the criteria for statehood, it automatically achieves statehood even if other nations fail to recognize it as such (*Deutsche Continental Gas Gesellschaft v Poland* (1929)). *Opinion No 1* of the Badinter Committee emphasized that 'the effects of recognition by other States are purely declaratory'.

The constitutive theory, on the other hand, suggests that, without sufficient recognition, a new entity claiming to be a State cannot attain statehood. According to this theory, recognition is yet another criterion for statehood.

The declaratory theory is the one with the greatest degree of approval, at least in theory and in scholarly writings. Nonetheless, new States are keen to be recognized by other nations, particularly powerful ones, because this ensures their political survival. In the *Kosovo Declaration case*, a number of nations that were home to ethnic and other minorities refused to recognize the statehood of Kosovo and made strong appeals in this regard to the ICJ. As a result, Kosovo's progression to statehood has stalled, if not wholly terminated, thus demonstrating that universal recognition is a crucial element in the achievement of statehood.

Courts asked to determine the legality of acts adopted by non-recognized States (eg divorces) are generally inclined to distinguish between the non-recognition of a State as such and the day-to-day administrative acts performed by the authorities of such entities. As a result, they generally tend to recognize administrative acts emanating from such entities, but not their statehood (*Hesperides Hotels v Aegean Holidays* (1978)). This distinction is very important.

Emin v Yeldag [2002] 1 FLR 956

The case concerned a divorce granted by the authorities of the TRNC, which the applicant brought for enforcement in the UK. The UK does not recognize the TRNC as a State, but only accepts that, with the aid of Turkey, it is in effective **occupation** of northern Cyprus. The British Court distinguished between the official acts of the TRNC and other personal transactions of people living therein, giving full recognition only to the latter.

The struggle for recognition by de facto States

Entities seeking statehood typically apply for membership of intergovernmental organizations with the aspiration of global legitimacy and implicit recognition by the organization's member States. This was the case with Palestinian membership of the United Nations Educational, Scientific and Cultural Organization (UNESCO) in 2011 and the International Criminal Court in 2015. In 2012, UNGA Resolution 67/19 accorded Palestine 'non-member observer State' status in the UN, with 138 votes in favour, 9 against, and 41 abstentions. Despite the matter being frozen at the level of the Security Council, the UN now refers to the State of Palestine and, as such, it may accede or ratify treaties under the aegis of the UN. It is telling that in its Order of 2018, in *Palestine v USA (Relocation of the US Embassy in Jerusalem)* (2018), neither the USA nor the ICJ called into question the right of Palestine to identify itself as a State and address the ICJ in a manner that is only available to States.

Other entities include the Kurdistan Regional Government in Iraq (Iraqi Kurdistan), which, although an autonomous region at present: (a) has declared a referendum for the near future; (b) retains its own standing army, which answers only to the Iraqi Kurdistan government; (c) dictates its own external relations; and (d) enters into contracts on its own behalf with foreign investors as regards its natural resources. While Iraqi Kurdistan possesses all the criteria for statehood and behaves like a State, it has not yet sought formal independence from Iraq, nor recognition from the international community.

REVISION TIP

The declaratory theory is the one mostly accepted. Nonetheless, recognition is important in fulfilling the Montevideo criterion that States should have the capacity to enter into relations with each other. This was dictated by the frequent dictatorial coups that occurred in the developing world and the embarrassment of recognizing governments that were eventually unpopular and short-lived. We have already shown (see 'Multinational coporations and non-State actors other than individuals') that de facto or aspiring States such as Kosovo or Palestine view membership of intergovernmental organizations as recognition and legitimacy of their statehood.

KEY CASES

The facts of the most significant key cases have already been explained in various sections of this chapter.

CASE	FACTS	PRINCIPLES
Legal Consequences of the Separation of the Chagos Archipelago from Mauritius in 1965, ICJ Advisory Opinion [2019] ICJ Rep 2	When Mauritius became independent from the UK in 1965, its new government agreed with the UK that the Chagos Archipelago would remain under British rule for a period of 50 years, which was subsequently renewed. As a result, Chagossians were not allowed to reside there. UNGA requested the ICJ to determine whether the process of decolonisation had been completed lawfully.	The Court connected the right to self-determination to non-self-governing territories and decolonization. While admitting that self-determination is a fundamental human right, there is little support for its application to situations of secession (eg Catalunya, Kosovo), albeit a safety valve is possible where people are grossly oppressed. All other situations concerning external self-determination should be resolved through constitutional processes. The Court found that the UK had failed to complete the decolonisation of the Mauritius.
Reparation for Injuries Suffered in the Service of the United Nations (*Reparations case*), ICJ Rep (1949), p 174	A Swedish diplomat under the service of the UN was sent by the UN to Jerusalem, where he was assassinated. Although Israel had not yet become a State, the UNGA asked the ICJ whether it had the legal capacity to bring a claim against Israel for reparation. The practice at the time would have been for Sweden to bring the claim on behalf of its national (principle of diplomatic protection).	The ICJ effectively held that the international legal personality of international organizations was dependent on the functions assigned to them by their member States. This personality is independent from that of the member States and international organizations are able to bring claims for harm they have sustained. Moreover, the ICJ stipulated that the powers of organizations are more extensive than those prescribed in their founding treaties. It referred to *implied powers* which exist so that they can fulfil all the functions mandated in their founding treaties.

KEY DEBATES

Topic	Was the Catalonian independence referendum lawful?
Author/academic	A Peters
Viewpoint	Does the autonomous province of Catalonia in Spain have a unilateral right to secede from Spain, in violation of the Spanish Constitution and without its people having been oppressed by the central government? Scholars and politicians are divided on this issue, but the majority (as well as prevailing State practice) seems to suggest constitutional processes in a democratic country are central to internal self-determination questions.
Source	'Populist International Law? The Suspended Independence and the Normative Value of the Referendum on Catalonia' EJILTalk! (2017), www.ejiltalk.org/populist-international-law-the-suspended-independence-and-the-normative-value-of-the-referendum-on-catalonia/.

EXAM QUESTIONS

Problem question

Country X is largely homogenous, but is home to an ethnic minority, the Batas. They comprise roughly 10 per cent of the entire population. For years, they have tried to secede, but have been prevented by X from doing so. They have suffered abuse and human rights violations as a result and, having had enough, the Batas decided to declare their independence and begin an internal armed conflict with X. Although the war is far from over, the Batas have effective control over the territory they live in. Critically discuss whether:

1. the Batas satisfy the Montevideo Convention criteria for statehood, as well as the Badinter criteria;
2. the achievement of statehood can come about by non-peaceful means, as is the case with an armed revolution;
3. minorities within an existing State do not, as a rule, possess the right to statehood and external self-determination under international law—if not, consider what rights they do have;
4. although the Batas are not recognized by many nations as a State, it is still possible for the day-to-day administrative acts of this new entity to be recognized by the courts and authorities of other countries.

See the Outline answers section in the end matter for help with this question.

Essay question

Critically discuss whether Kosovo satisfies the criteria for statehood required under contemporary international law. Your answer should take into consideration the practice of States with regard to the recognition of Kosovo and you should critically discuss whether recognition has a declaratory or constitutive character.

Online Resources

For an outline answer to this essay question, as well as interactive key cases and multiple-choice questions, please visit the online resources.

https://www.oup.com/he/bantekas-papastavridis-concentrate5e

6 Sovereignty and jurisdiction

THE EXAMINATION

The principal reason that States enjoy jurisdiction is because they are sovereign. Sovereignty is a very fluid subject that is not susceptible to practical assessment and therefore it is unlikely to be demanded in an exam in the form of a stand-alone topic. On the other hand, there are many possible questions concerning the jurisdictional competences of States and students will be well advised to possess a good understanding of all five jurisdictional principles. In addition, it is not uncommon for questions dealing with jurisdiction to cover exceptions to jurisdiction, particularly immunities or other defences to jurisdiction. Therefore, students are advised to consult chapter 7 'Immunities' and familiarize themselves with the links between the two notions.

KEY FACTS

- Jurisdiction refers to the power of States to enforce their laws and authority (judicial and police actions) over persons and property.
- The various bases of jurisdiction (eg territorial, passive personality, etc) are exercisable by States in accordance with their national laws, unless otherwise mandated by a treaty. In practice, this means that States are generally not obliged to exercise extraterritorial jurisdiction, this being exceptional and subject to sovereignty-based limitations.
- Although a State may possess legitimate jurisdiction over a person or property, such jurisdiction may be suspended by the operation of a particular immunity. In this case, the jurisdiction is simply suspended, not extinguished. This means that when the immunity ceases to exist, the court may validly assert jurisdiction once again.
- Jurisdiction may be civil or criminal in nature. In the latter case, it refers only to powers over persons. International law textbooks and university courses do not, as a general rule, deal with civil jurisdiction, save for legal actions brought against State entities and international organizations on commercial grounds (eg debts incurred by embassies or public corporations). Other law suits concerning private transnational disputes (eg family, property, or tort) are resolved by reference to the jurisdictional rules of the forum country (ie the country where the suit is lodged), as well as by specific international treaties that resolve jurisdictional conflicts in these fields. This area of law is known as private international law or otherwise as conflict of laws.
- The jurisdiction exercised by a domestic court may be in conflict with the jurisdiction available to the courts of several other countries, especially where all of these possess a link with the crime, the offender, or the victims. Jurisdictional conflicts of this nature are best dealt with through inter-State cooperation, as is the case with extradition, through existing treaties, or by ad hoc agreements. The jurisdiction of national courts may, moreover, be complementary (ie parallel) with that of international courts or tribunals. The statutes of the respective tribunals will determine which of the two has primary jurisdiction. There is nothing awkward about more than one State having legitimate claims of jurisdiction over a case. In fact, sometimes international law aims to give jurisdiction to as many States as possible (eg in respect of transnational crimes) as a means of ensuring the administration of justice.

CHAPTER OVERVIEW

Jurisdiction

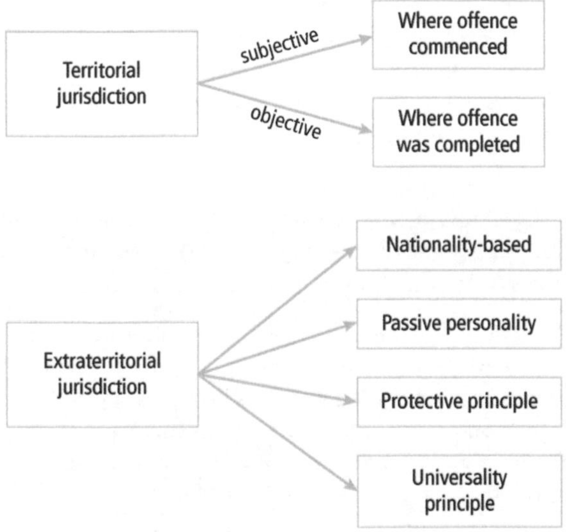

Sovereignty

This concept belies the entirety of inter-State relations and is a fundamental building block of international law. It refers to the authority or power of all States to determine their own affairs without external interference. An obvious corollary of sovereignty is the power to enforce one's laws in one's own territory, as well as to object to any form of external intervention. Sovereignty is very much an extension of self-determination, although theoretically the latter belongs to the peoples of a nation, whereas sovereignty is vested in the executive apparatus of the State. The traditional notion of sovereignty is diminishing in an era where States are willing to confer extensive powers to international organizations, such as the European Union. This is equally true in situations involving indebted nations dependent on loan conditions imposed by international financial institutions such as the International Monetary Fund.

Sovereignty is subject to several limitations. Although States are free to refuse to cooperate or converse with other nations, they are not allowed to violate international law, as would be the case with the unlawful use of armed force, contrary to the UN Charter. Equally, all States must adhere to the principle of self-determination and respect human rights, and may not unilaterally redraw their borders. This is true even of those nations whose borders were drawn on their behalf by their former colonial rulers (the principle of ***uti possidetis juris***).

Netherlands v USA (Palmas Islands Arbitration) (1928) 2 RIAA 829

The case concerned contested sovereignty claims over the Palmas islands. The sole arbitrator pointed out that: 'sovereignty in the relations between States signifies independence. Independence in regard to a portion of the globe is the right to exercise therein, to the exclusion of any other State, the functions of the State.' He noted that this exclusive competence over one's own territory 'is the point of departure in settling most questions that concern international relations'.

Jurisdiction: the basic idea

Jurisdiction is the power of States to make law and enforce it against persons and objects, especially in their territory. This power can take three particular forms: namely, to make laws, which is known as prescriptive jurisdiction; to apply laws through the courts, known as judicial jurisdiction; and to enforce laws, known as enforcement jurisdiction.

These three powers encompassed within the notion of jurisdiction are territorial in nature—that is, they can be exercised without limitation against all persons, entities, actions, and property on the territory of the State (save against persons and property benefiting from immunity). This means that, as a general rule, States do not enjoy jurisdiction in respect of persons or property situated outside their territory (so-called extraterritorial jurisdiction). The rationale for the preference in favour of territoriality, besides sovereignty, is the proximity between the local authorities and the object or purpose of the suit, which in practice makes investigation and prosecution much simpler. Although international law favours **territorial jurisdiction** with a view to preventing conflicts of sovereignty between nations, it does not exclude other forms of extraterritorial jurisdiction, if that is expressly provided in treaties or is otherwise permitted under customary international law. An obvious example would be serious international crimes, such as genocide, which the territorial State is unwilling to prosecute. Clearly, the international community cannot afford to let genocide go unpunished and will allow non-territorial countries to investigate and prosecute the offenders.

There are four types of extraterritorial jurisdiction; namely, nationality-based, passive personality, protective, and universal.

Moreover, there may well arise situations involving conduct taking place on the territory of more than one nation (transnational), as is the case with computer crimes, which may cause harm to multiple victims around the world. Clearly, in such circumstances more than one State has jurisdiction over the same offence or offender. International law does not prescribe a general hierarchical rule in order to resolve jurisdictional conflicts. In principle, and in relation to criminal conduct, a State may assume jurisdiction if this is not precluded by another rule of international law (*France v Turkey (Lotus case)* (1927)) and, equally, the State that has apprehended the accused enjoys primacy of jurisdiction. The system is based on inter-State collaboration and countries may validly surrender their jurisdiction in any particular case by means of extradition or by simply not exercising their entitlement.

REVISION TIP

A State does not have the authority to exercise judicial or enforcement jurisdiction except over persons who are lawfully present within its jurisdictional remit (ie its own territory or territory over which it exercises effective control, such as occupied territory). An exception to this fundamental rule is the principle of **universal jurisdiction**, which is explained later.

Territorial jurisdiction

A State's territory consists of its land and maritime masses, as well as its airspace. States exercise absolute and unimpeded jurisdiction on their land territory, as well as the airspace above that territory.

Maritime jurisdiction: the general rule

In respect of maritime belts, States possess absolute jurisdiction in their **internal waters**, but less so in their territorial sea. As a general rule, jurisdiction over offences committed on board a vessel lies with the flag State (ie the country with which the ship is registered), save for piracy on the high seas or such conduct in territorial waters that is injurious to the coastal State (Arts 27, 30, 97, and 105 UN Convention on the Law of the Sea 1982 (LOSC)).

LOOKING FOR EXTRA MARKS?

There are three exceptions to flag State jurisdiction for offences committed on the high seas. The first relates to piracy *jure gentium*, which is subject to universal jurisdiction under both customary international law and Art 105 LOSC. Any ship can seize a pirate vessel on the high seas, irrespective of its flag. The second exception relates to stateless vessels on the high seas, which are deemed devoid of any national protection (*United States v Marino-Garcia* (1982)). The third concerns situations in which the flag State waives its jurisdictional entitlement and confers it upon another country by mutual agreement.

Objective and subjective territoriality

Where conduct occurs on the territory of two or more States, both may claim jurisdiction on the basis of the territoriality principle. The country where the offence commenced (subjective territoriality) seems to have an equally valid claim as the country where the effects of the conduct were completed or consummated (objective territoriality). Of course, one may also view both of these forms of territorial jurisdiction as an encroachment on the other's sovereignty.

The effects doctrine

Certain States adhering to the objective territoriality principle have chosen to exercise jurisdiction not only because the unlawful conduct was completed on their territory, but alternatively because its effects may have materialized there. In principle, it is possible for the harmful conduct never to have been completed on the territory of country A, yet for its completion elsewhere to produce harmful effects upon persons and property in country A. This is known as the **effects doctrine** and the USA has employed it extensively for criminal conduct, as well as for anti-competitive practices occurring wholly abroad (*USA v Aluminium Co of America* (1945)). The extensive use of the effects doctrine has been criticized for causing political tension, with countries enjoying much closer links to the contested conduct. As a result, in more recent times the US Supreme Court has constrained the use of the effects doctrine by claiming that an anti-competitive practice committed abroad and which harmed consumers in the USA could not be used as a basis for asserting the jurisdiction of US courts in that case (*F Hoffmann-La Roche Ltd v Empagran SA* (2004)).

Exceptional territorial jurisdiction

Frequently, States try to avoid assuming jurisdiction over cases that would risk overburdening their justice systems or raise the likelihood of State responsibility and compensation. This has arisen in situations of military occupation abroad where the occupying powers have argued that their domestic laws—and by extension their obligations under treaty law—were not applicable to the occupied territory. The European Court of Human Rights (ECtHR) has consistently held that an occupying power owes similar human rights obligations to an occupied population as it does to its own people, and its local laws and international human rights obligations apply in full in the territory of the occupied nation. The only limitation to this rule is that the occupier must be in 'effective control' of the territory in question (*Loizidou v Turkey* (1997)). This extension of the occupier's existing human rights obligations to the occupied territory has been endorsed by the ECtHR in respect of the British military presence in Iraq (*Al-Saadoon and Mufdhi v UK* (2010), as well as in *Al-Skeini and ors v UK and Al Jeddah and ors v UK* (2011)). This is despite the fact that the House of Lords had initially entertained a contrary view as to the extraterritorial reach of British laws (*R v the Secretary of State for Defence, ex parte Al-Skeini and ors* (2008)). The matter is now well settled in European jurisprudence.

REVISION TIP

The jurisdiction of States and their attendant entitlements (legislative, judicial, and enforcement) should be distinguished from the jurisdiction of international courts and tribunals. The latter's powers are prescribed by treaty and are generally not vested with legislative powers. Among all international criminal tribunals, only the ad hoc criminal tribunals for Yugoslavia (International Criminal Tribunal for the former Yugoslavia (ICTY)) and Rwanda (International Criminal Tribunal for Rwanda (ICTR)) possess overriding enforcement powers against UN member States. On the other hand, the jurisdiction of the International Criminal Court (ICC) is generally complementary to that of its member States. This means that member States of the ICC possess a primary entitlement over the ICC in enforcing and exercising their own jurisdiction in a particular case. The ICC's jurisdictional entitlement is therefore secondary (or complementary) to that of its member States.

Extraterritorial jurisdiction

Nationality-based jurisdiction

This type of jurisdiction allows States to prosecute their own nationals for criminal conduct committed abroad. The application of this principle assumes that the conduct in question is punishable in the offender's home State, even if it does not constitute an offence in the country where the offence took place. For example, country A may prosecute its national X for having sex with children in country B, despite the fact that country B does not prosecute X. The rationale for the nationality principle has traditionally been the avoidance of impunity for crimes committed abroad in cases where the territorial State was unable, or unwilling, to prosecute.

Joyce v Director of Public Prosecutions [1946] AC 347

Joyce had fraudulently acquired British nationality and, during World War II, broadcast pro-Nazi propaganda in Germany. The House of Lords held that, despite the fraudulent acquisition of nationality, he had a duty of loyalty to the Crown and was therefore liable for the crime of treason, which is enforceable against a State's own nationals.

LOOKING FOR EXTRA MARKS?

Countries traditionally applying the nationality principle (typically, civil law nations) have refused to extradite their own nationals. This attitude has now changed with the advent of the European arrest warrant, which obliges member States to extradite their nationals in respect of a mandatory list of offences (Council Framework Decision 2002/584/JHA [2002] OJ L190/1).

Passive personality jurisdiction

This type of jurisdiction is based on the nationality of the victims of extraterritorial criminal conduct and is exercisable by the victims' country of nationality. It has historically been considered the weakest of all jurisdictional principles because the claim of the territorial State is much stronger in comparison. Nonetheless, in the wake of terrorist attacks against US nationals abroad in the mid-1980s, the USA has increasingly exercised passive personality jurisdiction. Its justification has been that most countries are either unable or unwilling to apprehend terrorists in respect of crimes committed on their territory. Passive personality jurisdiction is affirmed in multilateral treaties, as is the case with Art 5(1)(c) UN Torture Convention (1984). It was also among the chief legal bases (the other being universal jurisdiction) for the Spanish extradition request to the UK for ex-President Pinochet of Chile (*Pinochet Ugarte* (1998)).

United States v Yunis (No 3), 681 F Supp 896 (DC, 1988)
Yunis had hijacked an airliner with American passengers and was involved in other terrorist incidents. He was lured by US secret agents onto the high seas for a supposed drugs deal, but was arrested and flown to the USA to face terrorism charges. The Court upheld the validity of the arrest and the jurisdiction of US courts for terrorist crimes committed abroad and directed against US nationals.

The protective principle of jurisdiction

This principle is employed to confer judicial and police powers on a State in respect of extraterritorial conduct that threatens its national security interests. The scope of this type of jurisdiction is broad and may be abused by powerful nations. There is no general consensus as to the meaning of 'national security', but it is not confined solely to violent acts, such as the bombing of embassies or the murder of government agents. US courts have naturally accepted that attacks abroad against the country's armed forces and its equipment give rise to jurisdiction on the basis of the protective principle (*USA v Yousef* (2003)). It may also encompass non-violent activity, such as the computer hacking of government agencies and espionage (*USA v Zehe* (1985)). Evidently, the protective principle may be in conflict with the interests and ordinary jurisdiction of the territorial State. Its employment is not usually confined to judicial and legislative types of jurisdiction, but also to enforcement action entailing the use of armed force. This was the case, for example, with the toppling of the Taliban regime in Afghanistan in response to its assistance of Al-Qaeda operations outside the USA.

Attorney-General of Israel v Eichmann (1962) 36 ILR 5
The accused was responsible for the planning of the Jewish Holocaust by the Nazis. He was abducted by Israeli agents in Argentina and stood trial in Israel. The Israeli Supreme Court held that, even though Israel was not in existence when the Holocaust took place, it was in its national interests (as an extension of the interests of Jewish people) for all offenders to be prosecuted. Other jurisdictional principles were also claimed in this case.

REVISION TIP

Remember that jurisdiction refers to the power of the State, which takes three forms; namely, legislative, judicial, and enforcement. Jurisdiction may thereafter be civil or criminal. Criminal jurisdiction is further distinguished between territorial and extraterritorial. Territorial jurisdiction can be objective or subjective, whereas its extraterritorial counterpart is based on four types; namely, nationality-based, passive personality, the protective principle, and universal jurisdiction.

Universal jurisdiction

Unlike the other three types of extraterritorial jurisdiction, the universality principle does not require any kind of link between the offence, the offender, the victims, and the State exercising criminal jurisdiction. Universal jurisdiction is justified on two bases:

1. the universally repugnant nature of certain international crimes;
2. their location in areas beyond the territorial authority of any State, namely, the high seas and outer space.

Piracy on the high seas (or *jure gentium* piracy) is subject to universal jurisdiction, irrespective of the nationality of the pirate ship. However, not all universally repugnant crimes give rise to universal jurisdiction. This type of jurisdiction is conferred either by treaty or by the operation of customary law. The Geneva Conventions 1949 on the laws of war subject grave breaches (ie very serious war crimes) to universal jurisdiction, as does Art 105 LOSC with respect to piracy. Beyond these treaties, there is fierce debate as to which other international crimes attract universal jurisdiction under customary law. A conservative school of thought restricts the range of offences subject to customary universal jurisdiction, whereas a more **expansive school** takes the opposite view by relying on the aforementioned *Lotus case*. This school claims that, as long as the exercise of universal jurisdiction over a particular offence is not prohibited by treaty or resisted by a large number of States, then it is legitimate. Customary universal jurisdiction is thought to encompass, at the very least, genocide, crimes against humanity, and torture. National courts keep on adding others, as is the case with aggression by the House of Lords (*R v Jones (Margaret)* (2007), although in this particular case, aggression was held not to have been criminalized under English law).

It is disputed whether universal jurisdiction is an obligation or simply an entitlement which a State may choose not to exercise. While there is no definitive answer to this question, it is irrational to expect nations with limited finances to pursue crimes in far-away places, with all the logistic and financial implications this entails (*Jones v Ministry of Interior Al-Mamlaka Al-Arabiya AS Saudiya [the Kingdom of Saudi Arabia]* (2006) per Lord Bingham, para 27).

LOOKING FOR EXTRA MARKS?

The Princeton Principles of Universal Jurisdiction is an informal document adopted by leading international scholars, which contains the principles and crimes subject to universal jurisdiction. This is very much in the tradition of the expansionist school. In addition, most contemporary transnational crime treaties allow States to effectively exercise all types of jurisdiction. This is the case, for example, with the Council of Europe Convention on the Counterfeiting of Medical Products (2011).

Instances where national courts refuse to exercise their ordinary jurisdiction

A national court may well enjoy jurisdiction over a particular offence, yet refuse to exercise jurisdiction either because the accused is covered by the privilege of immunity (covered in chapter 7 'Immunities') or, increasingly, because his or her arrest was illegal. There are two schools of thought on this issue:

1. The rule in England and Wales is that the prosecution of an accused in violation of international extradition treaties and fair trial guarantees, particularly by means of transnational abduction, constitutes an abuse of process. As a result, courts adhering to this rationale have refused to exercise jurisdiction until proper procedures are followed (*R v Horseferry Road Magistrate's Court, ex parte Bennett* (1993)).
2. The US Supreme Court has taken a much different view. In a case where a Mexican national was abducted by US secret agents on charges of kidnapping and murdering a US federal agent, with a view to being prosecuted in the USA, the US Supreme Court upheld the jurisdiction of the US courts. The Court noted that while the abduction itself may have been a violation of general international law, it was not explicitly a violation of the US–Mexico extradition treaty (*USA v Alvarez-Machain* (1992)). This approach demonstrates an unconvincing attempt to justify the jurisdiction of US courts in cases of extraterritorial abduction.

Jurisdiction of international courts

For an analysis of the jurisdiction of the ICJ, see chapter 10 'Peaceful settlement of disputes' and for international criminal tribunals and particularly the ICC, see chapter 13 'International criminal law'.

REVISION TIP

There are no hard rules for settling jurisdictional conflicts. The system is largely based on comity and priority is generally granted to the country where the accused is detained. Moreover, countries with otherwise weak jurisdictional links enhance their claim where the courts of the territorial country are unable, or unwilling, to prosecute.

KEY CASES

CASE	FACTS	PRINCIPLES
Boumediene v Bush (2008) 47 ILM 650	Following the 9/11 terrorist attacks in 2001, the US government detained a large number of individuals at its naval base in Guantánamo Bay, which is situated in Cuba. The territory of the base was leased to the USA under a treaty with Cuba signed in 1903. The USA had argued that detainees at Guantánamo Bay possessed no habeas corpus claims before US courts, on the ground that the naval base was not part of US territory and the USA did not exercise sovereignty there. The petitioner challenged this argument and the case reached the US Supreme Court.	The Supreme Court held that although Cuba possessed *de jure* sovereignty over Guantánamo Bay, the USA exercised effective sovereignty and this alone sufficed to trigger the jurisdiction of US courts. The jurisdiction of US courts was, moreover, strengthened by the fact that Cuban courts do not themselves possess jurisdiction.
Case Concerning the Arrest Warrant of 11 April 2000 (Democratic Republic of the Congo v Belgium), ICJ Rep (2002), p 3 (Separate Opinion of Judges Higgins, Kooijmans, and Buergenthal)	Belgium issued a law in 1993 which vested its courts with jurisdiction to entertain criminal suits on the basis of the universality principle. Consequently, a Belgian prosecutor indicted the then incumbent Congolese foreign minister for a series of international crimes, including crimes against humanity. In response, his country lodged a suit before the ICJ, arguing that the indictment violated the privilege of immunity enjoyed by foreign ministers. The validity of this argument was accepted by the Court. Universal jurisdiction was ultimately not the main issue in the case, but was discussed at length in a separate opinion to the judgment.	There is no rule of international law that prohibits the exercise of universality by national courts. There is, however, inconsistent State practice as to whether it is required that the accused is actually in the hands of the prosecuting State at the exact moment of prosecution. It is accepted that the accused need not be in the hands of the prosecuting State and his or her presence may just as well be sought by means of extradition. What is absolutely prohibited is the exercise of criminal jurisdiction on the territory of another State without its consent.

CASE	FACTS	PRINCIPLES
France v Turkey (Lotus case), PCIJ, Series A, No 10 (1927)	A French and a Turkish ship collided on the high seas, resulting in the death of the Turkish ship's crew. The Turkish authorities proceeded to arrest the captain of the French ship and prosecuted him for manslaughter. The French authorities intervened and brought legal action against Turkey before the Permanent Court of International Justice, arguing that collisions on the high seas attract flag State jurisdiction only.	The Court assimilated the Turkish ship with Turkish territory and from there it was not a great leap to claim that the offence occurred on Turkish territory. This part of the judgment is bad law, given that the LOSC makes it clear that high-seas collisions attract only flag State jurisdiction. The case is best known for the claim that States may exercise any form of jurisdiction, as long as it is not prohibited by any rule of treaty or customary international law.
USA v Yunis, 681 F Supp 896 (1988)	Yunis, a Lebanese national, was involved in the hijacking of a Jordanian airliner, which carried, among others, two American nationals. Under the guise of a drugs deal, US secret agents lured Yunis to international waters off Cyprus and arrested him. The accused argued that the USA had for a long time resisted the application of the passive personality principle and thus claimed that its courts did not enjoy jurisdiction.	Although passive personality jurisdiction is controversial, it is wholly legitimate and, in any event, the Hostages Convention includes it among its acceptable forms of jurisdiction. This type of jurisdiction is increasingly accepted when applied to terrorist and other organized attacks on a State's nationals by reason of their nationality.

KEY DEBATES

Topic	Africa's opposition to universal jurisdiction by European countries
Author/academic	H van der Wilt
Viewpoint	The African Union has accused European States of 'legal colonialism' by making extensive use of universal jurisdiction against African nationals. They claimed that this was abusive and in violation of African sovereignty. The counter-argument is that such jurisdiction has been assumed because African countries have failed to prosecute those responsible for heinous crimes on the continent.
Source	'Universal Jurisdiction under Attack: An Assessment of African Misgivings towards International Criminal Justice as Administered by Western States', 9 *Journal of International Criminal Justice* (2011) 1043

Topic	Jurisdiction to enforce criminal laws abroad
Author/academic	AJ Colangelo
Viewpoint	The USA has gone beyond its own constitutional constraints, which have long favoured the exclusive territorial competence of all States. The extension of its laws and arrest practices abroad in the absence of consent violates both domestic and international law.
Source	'Constitutional Limits on Extraterritorial Jurisdiction: Terrorism and the Intersection of National and International Law', 48 *Harvard Journal of International Law* (2007) 12

EXAM QUESTIONS

Problem question

A UK national living in London fraudulently sold shares over the internet to persons in Guatemala and Aruba and subsequently fled to Aruba to escape prosecution. The UK does not have extradition arrangements with Guatemala, where the offender's conduct constitutes a criminal offence, much in the same way as in the UK. The laws in Aruba, on the other hand, only criminalize internet crime if the conduct commenced there and the UK has already entered into a bilateral extradition treaty with Aruba.

1. Critically discuss the available bases of jurisdiction open to the UK and Guatemala and advise the government of the UK how, if at all possible, it can prosecute the offender.
2. If Aruba ultimately decided to prosecute the offender itself, would he have a valid claim against the exercise of this jurisdiction?

See the Outline answers section in the end matter for help with this question.

Essay question

Critically analyse the consistency of existing State practice in relation to jurisdiction based on the passive personality principle.

Online Resources

For an outline answer to this essay question, as well as interactive key cases and multiple-choice questions, please visit the online resources.

https://www.oup.com/he/bantekas-papastavridis-concentrate5e

7

Immunities

THE EXAMINATION

Questions concerning immunity may touch upon topics falling within the subject of jurisdiction, given that immunity is an exception to the ordinary jurisdiction of national courts. Questions on immunity often relate to the distinction between personal (ratione personae) and functional (ratione materiae) immunities. Another important topic is the distinction between acts described as either sovereign or public (***jure imperii***) and commercial transactions (***jure gestionis***). You may also be asked to offer a critique of immunity afforded to conduct that is of a criminal nature. The immunities afforded to international organizations may either fall under the general law of immunity or form part of questions dealing solely with international organizations.

KEY FACTS

- Immunity serves to stay (stop or freeze) the jurisdiction of national courts. It is a procedural bar to their ordinary jurisdiction, not a substantive bar. This means that it stops the courts from actually hearing the case, not that the substance of the claim is no longer valid. As a result, if and when the immunity is subsequently lifted in the future, the claim may be brought before a court once again.
- A distinction is made between State (or sovereign) immunity and diplomatic and consular immunities. The first concerns States as such (covering both acts and persons), whereas the latter concerns the personal immunities of a State's representatives and State assets abroad.
- The international law of immunity is primarily found in customary international law in the form of domestic legislation and decisions of national courts. The International Court of Justice (ICJ) has also issued judgments that have fundamentally shaped the law in this area. There is also a small body of treaties that are largely devoted to diplomatic and consular immunities, as well as general jurisdictional immunities of States.
- Immunity from the jurisdiction of national courts should be distinguished from the ordinary jurisdiction of international courts and tribunals. The jurisdiction of international courts is derived from their statutes, not from customary international law or from treaties dealing with immunities. Therefore, immunity before international tribunals may be completely different to immunity under treaty and customary international law.
- Immunities should not be confused with amnesties. The former are afforded by the laws and courts of foreign nations, whereas amnesties are granted by the home country of the accused. Unlike immunities, an amnesty constitutes a substantive bar to the prosecution of an accused person because amnesty laws forgive the perpetrator for the actual crime he or she committed.

CHAPTER OVERVIEW

Immunities

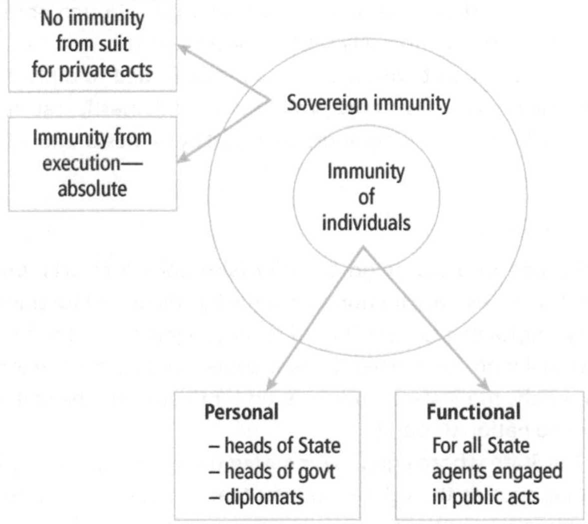

The meaning and purpose of immunity

Immunity is a privilege afforded to States and their agents, whereby national courts of other nations are denied jurisdiction in respect of certain categories of law suits pending before them. On the basis of immunity, national courts and executive authorities are also precluded from enforcing foreign judgments against the property of States on their territory. The purpose of immunities is to shield States and their dignitaries from legal action abroad in order to allow them to conduct their international relations unhindered. Moreover, immunity is a natural extension of the principle of sovereign equality of nations under which one sovereign cannot be tried in the courts of another (*Schooner Exchange v McFaddon* (1812)).

Immunity is a principle derived from international law and therefore any unwillingness or failure to enforce it domestically gives rise to State responsibility. *Absolute* immunity grants the relevant privilege to all government actions and agents (including commercial and private acts), whereas its **restrictive** counterpart restricts it solely to sovereign acts.

The sources of immunity

Although immunity has traditionally been regulated under customary international law, it has recently been the subject matter of two specific treaties, namely, the 1972 European Convention on State Immunity and the 2004 UN Convention on Jurisdictional Immunities of States and their Property. It should be noted, however, that although both reflect customary international law, they have been sparsely ratified. Moreover, the 1961 Vienna Convention on Diplomatic Relations deals in part with the immunities afforded to diplomatic personnel. An important aspect of the relevant law is the proliferation of domestic statutes, such as the UK's State Immunity Act 1978 (SIA) and judgments delivered by domestic and international courts.

Sovereign or public acts

Acts of States performed in a sovereign capacity (also known as acts *jure imperii*)—as opposed to commercial activities—are immune from the jurisdiction of foreign courts. This is true even in respect of wrongful conduct attributed to State agents, as is the case with war crimes. Although the individual who committed the war crime would incur criminal liability without the privilege of immunity, the State cannot be sued for the tort (ie the damage resulting from the war crime) before a national court (*Germany v Italy (Jurisdictional Immunities of the State)* (2012)). Of course, the State whose agents committed the wrongful act may be sued before an international tribunal, such as the ICJ, on an inter-State basis (ie one State seeking damages from another), assuming that both have previously consented to the jurisdiction of the ICJ. The judgment of the ICJ in *Germany v Italy* has put an end to the practice of certain courts, particularly those of Italy, to entertain law suits in tort against foreign States (*Ferrini v Germany* (2006)). The rule is therefore that all acts performed by a State in a public capacity—including violations of the laws of war—are immune from civil suit before the courts of other nations.

Private or commercial conduct of States

It is not always easy to discern when a State is acting in a private (also known as *jure gestionis*), as opposed to a public, capacity. By way of illustration, waging war or making political decisions in the United Nations (UN) are clearly public acts. Equally, when a State oil corporation sells oil in international markets, it is acting in a commercial capacity. However, when a State sells government bonds to finance its health-care or education system, there is a mix of both public and private acts, making it difficult to assess which of the two is more prevalent. It is crucial to answer this question through a solid test because conduct undertaken in a private/commercial capacity is not immune from the jurisdiction of foreign courts.

There is no single test under international law for ascertaining the commercial character of an act of a State. However, it is generally accepted that the best determinants are the *nature* and *purpose* of the act. This is consistent with Art 2(2) UN Jurisdictional Immunities Convention (2004), Art 10 of which stipulates that commercial transactions of States are not immune from the jurisdiction of foreign courts. The Convention mentions other activities that are equally not immune; namely, employment contracts (Art 11), acts causing personal injury or damage to property (Art 12), immovable property-related activities (Art 13), and certain others (Arts 14–17). Moreover, a State may waive its privilege to immunity by entering into a contract with a foreign private entity stipulating that, in respect of all future disputes, it waives its immunity from the jurisdiction of national courts and arbitral tribunals.

The mere fact that an entity exercises a public function, such as a public airline or a public factory, is not sufficient, per se, for it to be granted immunity under international law. It is a precondition that it must be an organ of the State and not a *separate* entity (*Pocket Kings Ltd v Safenames Ltd* (2009)).

I Congreso del Partido [1981] 3 WLR 328

The Cuban government was involved in the sale and transportation of sugar through its own merchant fleet or by chartering foreign vessels. On one occasion, it withheld the sugar belonging to private merchants and they, in turn, brought an action before the English courts which demanded the seizure of a vessel belonging to the Cuban government. The House of Lords (per Lord Wilberforce) held that Cuba had acted as owner and not as a sovereign, especially since the relevant contract was premised on Cuban law, and therefore found that it did not enjoy immunity.

Kuwait Airways Corporation v Iraqi Airways Co [1995] 1 WLR 1147

Following the invasion of Kuwait, Iraq ordered its government-run airline, Iraqi Airways, to transport aircraft belonging to Kuwait Airways to Iraq. The House of Lords held that, although the taking of the aircraft was done in time of war, which would otherwise render it a public act, in the present case it was not. This was because:

> an act done by a separate entity of the State on the directions of the State does not possess the character of a government act . . . The mere fact that the purpose or motive of the act was to serve the purposes of the State will not be sufficient to enable the separate entity to claim immunity . . .

REVISION TIP

The privilege of immunity from the jurisdiction of foreign courts covers all public/governmental acts of the State (based on their nature and purpose). It does not cover entities that are merely under the direction or employment of the State. Immunity does not cover those acts of the State that possess a commercial character although, in many cases, it is difficult to distinguish with clarity a public from a private act.

Immunity against enforcement

In accordance with Art 19 UN Jurisdictional Immunities Convention, post-judgment measures of constraint (eg attachment, seizure, etc) against State property are generally impermissible, unless the State in question has consented by treaty or contract. This principle was further reiterated by the ICJ in *Germany v Italy (Jurisdictional Immunities of States)* (2012), examined later. Limited exceptions have, nonetheless, been accepted by national courts. In *Republic of Argentina v NML Capital Ltd* (2014), the US Supreme Court affirmed a worldwide post-judgment discovery order directed to several banks in the USA, thereby rejecting Argentina's argument that the order was barred by the US Foreign Sovereign Immunities Act (FSIA). It held that the FSIA focuses only on two types of immunity, namely, from jurisdiction and execution, and hence it is silent on discovery in aid of execution of a foreign-sovereign judgment debtor's assets.

In addition, the French Supreme Cassation Court has held that, if a State enters into an arbitration clause which contains an express undertaking to honour a subsequent arbitral award, French courts will consider that State to have waived its immunity from execution of the award in France (*Société Creighton Ltd v Ministère des Finances et le Ministère des Affaires Municipales et de l'Agriculture du Gouvernement de l'Etat de Qatar* (2003)).

LOOKING FOR EXTRA MARKS?

The property of central banks is always immune from suits and attachment, irrespective of the purpose for which it was intended to be used (*AIG Capital Partners Inc v Kazakhstan* (2005)). This result is confirmed by s 14(4) SIA and s 1611(b)(1) FSIA. It was more recently reiterated in *La Générale des Carriéres v FG Hemisphere Associates* (2012), decided by the Privy Council on appeal from the courts of Jersey.

Act of State doctrine

The **act of State** doctrine has been developed in common law jurisdictions and, unlike immunity, which is a procedural bar to law suits against States, it serves as a substantive bar. This means that the existence of an alleged tort committed by a State or its agents cannot be assessed by the courts of foreign nations if it was part of a government act. This would be the case if the tort in question was incorporated in a law or a ministerial decree. The rationale for this defence is that the courts of one nation cannot sit in judgment of the public acts of other nations. This defence applies in civil suits and when the courts uphold it, it means that any further action is dependent on the wishes of the executive branch of government. In *Underhill v Hernandez* (1897), the US Supreme Court refused to assess the legality of the detention incurred by the plaintiff in the hands of an insurrectionist movement which was later recognized as the successor government of Venezuela. The doctrine requires the defendant to establish that the performed activities were undertaken on behalf of the State and not in a private capacity. In another US case, the accused had used his position as former president and dictator of Venezuela to commit financial crimes. The Fifth Circuit Court rejected that these acts were attributable to Venezuela (*Jimenez v Aristeguieta* (1962)).

The act of State doctrine does not necessarily confer immunity on the person undertaking the conduct in question. It simply serves to avoid passing judgment on the sovereign acts of foreign nations as such.

LOOKING FOR EXTRA MARKS?

In 2012, the DC District Court ruled that, ordinarily, the nationalization of a foreign enterprise by the territorial State would not give rise to a civil suit before the courts of the investor's country of nationality because of the operation of act of State defence. However, the case was different where the nationalization was undertaken without a law or governmental action for the benefit of the local population (as is required for the legitimacy of expropriation). In the case at hand, the local government abused its position as majority shareholder, thus depriving its actions of a public character (*McKesson Corp v Islamic Republic of Iran* (2012)).

Functional and personal immunities

So far, we have looked at the immunities afforded to States or their instrumentalities, such as government departments, central banks, and government-run enterprises. All these cases concerned immunity from civil suit and attachment (of property). This section focuses on immunities afforded to natural persons exercising governmental functions and authority. While some pertain to civil suits, in many cases they also involve immunity from the criminal jurisdiction of national courts.

Personal immunities

Personal immunities (or **ratione personae**) shield a limited number of persons from the jurisdiction of foreign courts on the basis of their particular status, irrespective of whether the act which has given rise to the suit or the criminal prosecution is a governmental or a private act. Personal immunities are afforded to a very narrow list of persons; namely, heads of State, heads of government, foreign ministers, and ambassadors (or heads of diplomatic missions). Immunity *ratione personae* persists for as long as the office-holder maintains his or her status, following which the immunity is lost and the person may lawfully be sued or prosecuted. Once the person is no longer immune, he or she may be sued or prosecuted in respect of all acts done during his or her tenure in office. This type of immunity may help shield persons that have committed serious international crimes, but if the international community is willing to prosecute an accused head of State, it can lawfully refer him or her to the prosecutor of the International Criminal Court (ICC) or other tribunal. In fact, the United Nations Security Council (UNSC) has done exactly this in the case of the heads of State of Libya (SC Resolution 1970 (2011)) and Sudan (SC Resolution 1593 (2005)).

R v Bow Street Metropolitan Stipendiary Magistrate, ex parte Pinochet Ugarte (No 3) (1999) 2 All ER 97

Pinochet was a former head of State of Chile, who arrived in the UK for medical treatment. Spain sought his extradition on the basis of widespread crimes committed during his 20-year reign in Chile. The House of Lords held that, while the immunity of a current head of State is absolute and subject to no limitations, a former head of State enjoys immunity only in respect of acts performed while in office such that could be characterized as 'official'. Immunity for all other acts committed while in office ceases to exist.

Case Concerning the Arrest Warrant of 11 April 2000 (Congo v Belgium), ICJ Rep (2002), p 3

Pursuant to its universal jurisdiction law, the Belgian authorities indicted the incumbent foreign minister of the Congo, alleging that he was involved in the commission of serious international crimes, including crimes against humanity. Congo rebuked the legality of the indictment, arguing that the minister enjoyed immunity. The ICJ held that incumbent foreign ministers enjoy absolute immunity under international law, this being personal rather than functional immunity. This implies that the nature of the contested act as official or private is irrelevant.

Functional immunity

All acts of the State are afforded immunity from the jurisdiction of foreign courts, but only if they constitute governmental or official acts. Because States perform acts through their agents (ie the military, security forces, government employees, etc) the immunity covering said acts incidentally also covers the persons performing them. That is why this type of immunity is called functional—because its purpose is to provide immunity to the act/function, rather than the individual behind the act. As a result, even if the individual is removed from office, the immunity of the act itself persists.

It is not true that all acts performed by agents of the State constitute official acts. The House of Lords in the *Pinochet (No 3) case* observed that the UN Torture Convention could not possibly have afforded immunity to those accused of the offence. This is because the definition of torture in the Convention requires that the perpetrator be a State agent, in which case all acts of torture would be immune, a result which would be contrary to the elaborate 'prosecute or extradite' structure of the Convention. Despite some judgments to the contrary on the basis of the US Aliens Tort Claims Act, it is generally admitted that functional immunity shields States and their agents from the civil (not criminal) jurisdiction of foreign courts, even if the act complained of is an international crime (*Bouzari v Islamic Republic of Iran* (2004)).

Al-Adsani v United Kingdom (2001) 34 EHRR 273

The plaintiff was tortured in Kuwait by agents of that country. He subsequently went on to sue them in tort in England, but his suit was turned down because the defendants were found to enjoy immunity as agents of Kuwait. The plaintiff applied to the European Court of Human Rights (ECtHR), arguing that the privilege of immunity deprived him of the right to a fair trial. The ECtHR, with a thin majority, held that immunity, being a principle of international law, was not in conflict with the right to a fair trial, in particular the right to judicial remedies. The two principles were not in conflict because they were found to serve different objectives. Essentially, the operation of immunity in a particular case does not disproportionately affect the other party's human rights.

REVISION TIP

Immunities essentially belong to the State as such, but the effect and the privilege afforded by an immunity encompasses a State's property as well as the person of its agents. In the case of civil suits, the conferral of immunity will depend on the nature of the conduct as private/commercial or public/sovereign. In respect of criminal suits (or prosecution), the culprit will be covered by immunity whether by virtue of his or her status (**ratione personae**) or as a result of the sovereign function of the contested conduct (**ratione materiae**).

Diplomatic and consular immunities

Diplomatic immunities

The privileges and immunities of diplomatic personnel are explicitly provided in the 1961 Convention on Diplomatic Relations. Their nature may be considered similar to immunity *ratione personae*, given that they shield diplomatic agents from all possible action that can be undertaken by the receiving State. The basic rule is that the person of the diplomatic agent is inviolable (Art 29) and, moreover, that the premises, archives, and correspondence of the mission are equally inviolable. The receiving State is under an obligation to protect the agents, the premises, archives, and correspondence (Arts 22, 24, 27). Although in no case do the courts of the receiving State enjoy criminal jurisdiction over diplomatic agents, said courts may assume civil jurisdiction in three situations: law suits relating to immovable property in the receiving State; legal action relating to succession which is of a private nature; and legal action relating to any professional or commercial activity undertaken by a diplomatic agent outside his or her official functions (Art 31). If a diplomatic agent is thought by the receiving State to have violated its laws or prejudiced its public order, it can dismiss him or her from its territory without any justification as ***persona non grata*** (literally, as a non-welcome person) (Art 9).

US Diplomatic and Consular Staff in Iran (USA v Islamic Republic of Iran), ICJ Rep (1980), p 3

In 1979, Iranian students seized the US embassy in Tehran, under the direction, or at least with the tacit consent, of the then new Iranian government. A number of US diplomatic agents were held for well over a year. Iran argued that this was a spontaneous reaction by the people and that, in any event, US diplomatic staff had abused their position in the country by consciously suppressing the people's will and collaborating with the previous regime. The ICJ held that, even if this were indeed so, Iran could have expelled such persons from its territory. Moreover, it emphasized that the protection of diplomatic premises and the inviolability of the person of diplomats is a concrete obligation of the receiving State.

Immunities at the International Criminal Court

Under Art 27 ICC Statute, official capacity does not preclude the Court from exercising jurisdiction. Article 98(1), however, prevents the Court from proceeding with requests for surrender or assistance to a State party if the execution of such requests would force the requested State to breach existing obligations against a third state in the area of immunities, including personal immunities. This means that the requested State can entertain the Court's request only after it has obtained a waiver of immunities from the third State in question. This is unlikely in practice.

As explained, the UNSC may refer a situation to the Court in accordance with Art 13(b) ICC Statute. In Resolution 1593 (2005), the UNSC referred to the jurisdiction of the Court a sitting head of State, namely, the president of Sudan, Al-Bashir. Despite the indictment issued against him, Al-Bashir travelled to several African States, all of which were parties to the ICC Statute. The Court did not rely on Art 27(2), which makes personal immunities redundant, but instead argued that customary international law does not recognize any immunity for heads of State in respect of proceedings before international courts (*Decision Pursuant to Article 87(7) of the Rome Statute on the Failure of the Republic of Malawi to Comply with the Cooperation Request by the Court with Respect to the Arrest and Surrender of Omar Hassan Ahmad Al Bashir*, ICC-02/05-01/09 (12 December 2011)).

Immunities of international organizations

International organizations possess international legal personality and their charter or constituent instrument, which is a treaty, will spell out the range of privileges and immunities afforded. These will bind member States. Moreover, international organizations will enter into headquarters agreements, which too are treaties, with their host countries, which contain immunities provisions. Finally, most States have enacted legislation concerning the legal status of international organizations active on their territory, which too contain immunity privileges. In addition, the 1946 Convention on the Privileges and Immunities of the United Nations provides extensive immunities from civil and criminal jurisdiction to the staff of the UN.

The law in this area is rather complex. Italian courts, for example, have considered that matters relating to rents and immovable property undertaken by international organizations should be treated as commercial acts that do not attract immunity (*Food and Agriculture Organisation v INPDAI* (1995)). The Italian government later ratified the 1947 Convention on the Privileges and Immunities of Specialised Agencies and dismissed the distinction between public and private acts by providing immunity to all. It is generally agreed that national courts have no authority to inquire whether a particular immunity is functional in order to assess whether the function for which it was granted has been abused or overridden (*Manderlier v UN and Belgium* (1969)). Nonetheless, some national courts occasionally differ by arguing that only official acts of the staff of international organizations attract immunity, not private ones. In one case, this distinction was used to refuse immunity to an official involved in a bribe (*Arab Monetary Fund v Hashim (No 4)* (1996)).

In *Saramati v France and ors* (2007), the applicants claimed that the failure of European Convention on Human Rights (ECHR) member States participating in a UN Chapter VII operation to defuse cluster bombs which killed one child in Kosovo violated the right to life of the victim. The ECtHR held that the relevant acts were attributable to the UN and not to the participating States individually and concluded that States contributing troops to UN missions cannot be held responsible for their acts and omissions.

Immunities versus *jus cogens* norms

In cases such as *Al-Adsani*, but also increasingly most immunity cases, it is questioned whether the conferral of an immunity should be allowed to override an act that violates a *jus cogens* norm, in respect of which immunity is conferred. In *Al-Adsani*, this conundrum was resolved by distinguishing immunity as a substantive rule from the procedural nature of the victim's right of access to justice. This is an artificial construction that is out of touch with the limitations imposed on immunities in the context of multilateral treaties (such as the ICC Statute), as well as by State practice. In *Samantara v Yousuf* (2010), for example, the US Supreme Court held that Somali foreign officials accused of serious international crimes did not enjoy individual immunity under FSIA.

LOOKING FOR EXTRA MARKS?

Much like the *Al-Adsani* judgment, the ECtHR has accepted that the immunities afforded to international organizations may constitute a proportionate measure to restrict the application of the right of access to court, guaranteed under Art 6 ECHR (*Waite and Kennedy v Germany* (2000)).

KEY CASES

CASE	FACTS	PRINCIPLES
Germany v Italy (Jurisdictional Immunities of the State), ICJ Judgment of 3 February 2012	Italian courts had begun entertaining civil suits against Germany for crimes committed by members of its armed forces during World War II, as well as enforcing judgments of a similar nature issued by the courts of Greece. Italian courts accepted that Germany did not enjoy immunity from jurisdiction and attachment in respect of its assets in Italy. Interestingly, the Italian government disagreed with the view that Germany did not possess immunity, but could not interfere in the judicial sphere. The ICJ was asked to assess whether States enjoyed immunity from jurisdiction and **immunity from enforcement** in respect of criminal conduct attributed to their agents.	The ICJ held that there is no conflict between *jus cogens* rules and the principle of sovereign immunity. The latter is a procedural rule which does not extinguish the peremptory nature of the violated entitlement (ie the fact that immunity from civil suit persists does not mean that the underlying offences are extinguished). States enjoy immunity from the jurisdiction of the courts of other nations even in respect of serious offences. Moreover, immunity from enforcement against their assets is much broader because even if a State waives its immunity from jurisdiction it does not also waive its immunity from enforcement. Italian courts were wrong to enforce Greek judgments against German assets in Italy.

CASE	FACTS	PRINCIPLES
Jones v Ministry of Interior of the Kingdom of Saudi Arabia [2006] 2 WLR 1424	Several British nationals working in Saudi Arabia were tortured by the Saudi police, which believed they were involved in a bombing incident. The plaintiff, Jones, undertook legal action in the UK against both the Saudi Interior Ministry and the officer responsible for his torture. The action was civil in nature and no criminal prosecution was pursued.	The judgment by the House of Lords has been criticized as being very conservative. It held that, as regrettable as the conduct of the Saudi agents was, both the State and its agents continued to enjoy immunity in the UK, particularly since said conduct did not trigger any of the exceptions to immunity found in the UK's Sovereign Immunities Act. In line with the *Al-Adsani* judgment, the conferral of immunity under international law was found not to be disproportionate with the denial of the right to legal remedies which the accused would have otherwise enjoyed.

KEY DEBATES

Topic	The backlash of indicting sitting heads of state from the African Union
Author/academic	C Jalloh and I Bantekas
Viewpoint	The indictment of African leaders by the ICC, as well as the exercise of universal jurisdiction for the same purpose by European prosecutors, led the African Union to create a third (criminal) chamber in its regional human rights court. Several of its members withdrew from the ICC Statute and there was significant hostility against the ICC and international criminal justice institutions.
Source	*International Criminal Court and Africa* (Oxford University Press, 2017)

EXAM QUESTIONS

Problem question

The serving president of country X visited country Y for an official two-day visit. He is notorious worldwide for having committed gross human rights violations against his own people. During his stay, he became ill and remained in a private hospital to recover, following which he took a few days off work for his own leisure. The public prosecutor of country Y decided to bring criminal proceedings against the president by arguing that:

1. his immunity was no longer in operation because his official visit had expired and he was now in country Y on private business;

2. in any event, the crimes committed by the president were the worst possible offences, namely, genocide and crimes against humanity, and therefore whatever immunity he might otherwise enjoy, it did not shield him from these offences because they did not constitute public acts;
3. country Y enjoyed universal jurisdiction over these offences (irrespective of whether the president also enjoys immunity in the present instance);
4. the prosecutor declared that if the courts of his country were precluded by the operation of immunity, then the president's country may waive his immunity.

Which of these arguments is correct and why?

See the Outline answers section in the end matter for help with this question.

Essay question

Are former heads of State entitled to immunity under international law for criminal conduct committed while in office? If so, what kind of immunity is this, and is it only available to former heads or also to other State agents?

Online Resources

For an outline answer to this essay question, as well as interactive key cases and multiple-choice questions, please visit the online resources.

https://www.oup.com/he/bantekas-papastavridis-concentrate5e

8 The law of the sea

THE EXAMINATION

Typically, exam questions in this field concern jurisdiction of coastal or flag States, as well as the delimitation of maritime areas. They usually avoid theoretical issues involving the history of the evolution of the law of the sea. Common questions involve the right of port States to inspect and arrest foreign vessels and their crew members, as well as the right of coastal States to suppress or prevent infringements of their laws and regulations within their coastal zones. They may also involve questions on the sovereign rights of coastal States to explore and exploit natural resources on their continental shelves or within their **exclusive economic zones (EEZs)**. Equally, questions about interdiction of vessels on the high seas are frequent, particularly in respect of piracy.

KEY FACTS

- The key treaty on the law of the sea is the **UN Convention on the Law of the Sea 1982 (LOSC). LOSC** largely reflects customary international law.
- The regulation of the oceans reflects a compromise between, on the one hand, exclusive claims to maritime dominion on the part of coastal States and, on the other, inclusive claims to the reasonable use of the oceans on the part of the international community as a whole.
- The legal order of the oceans ascribes jurisdictional competences to coastal States and flag States. The countries where vessels are registered (flag States) possess a significant amount of competence over these and their crew in all maritime belts. Likewise, countries with maritime territory (coastal States) possess significant competences of regulation and enforcement therein.
- Coastal States enjoy broad competences in certain maritime belts, namely, internal and territorial waters, which is expressed with the term 'sovereignty'. In other maritime belts, including the continental shelf and the EEZ, they enjoy limited competences. These are denoted by the term 'sovereign rights'.

CHAPTER OVERVIEW

Maritime zones and the law of the sea

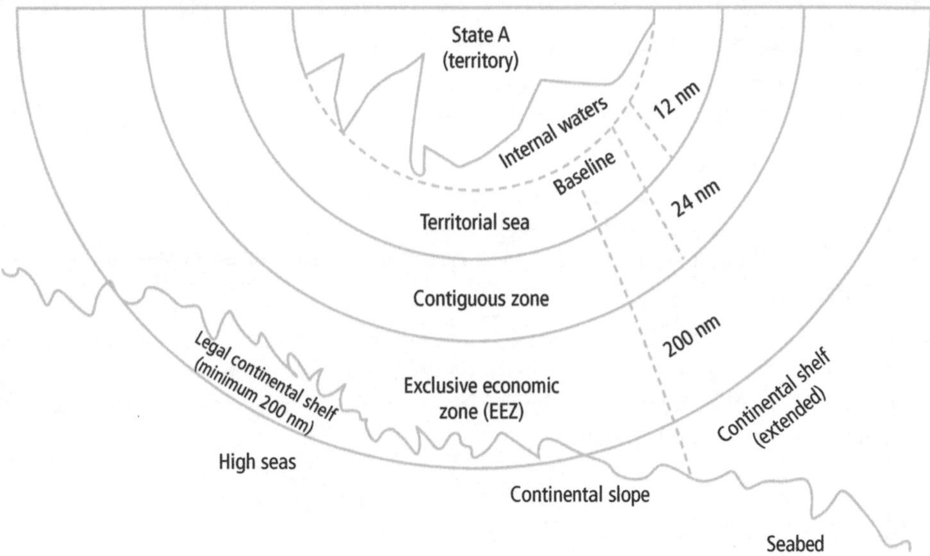

Determining baselines for maritime zones

The law of the sea fragments the sea into a series of zones in which States enjoy sovereign rights or jurisdictional competences. Instrumental to the establishment of such zones is the determination of **baselines**, which constitute the starting point for measuring the breadth of each zone. Anything landward of these baselines, such as harbours, river mouths, or bays, are designated as 'internal waters', and are fully subject to the sovereignty of the coastal State. On the other hand, all waters seaward of the baselines are subject to the sovereignty of the coastal State, namely, the territorial sea, or are otherwise encompassed under its sovereign rights or jurisdiction, ie contiguous zone, continental shelf, and EEZ.

It should be stressed that maritime zones are available to land territory proper, in addition to islands pursuant to Art 121(2). This means that islands are entitled to all maritime zones (territorial sea, contiguous zone, continental shelf, and EEZ). Exceptionally, under Art 121(3) LOSC: 'Rocks which cannot sustain human habitation or economic life of their own have no Exclusive

Economic Zone or continental shelf.' According to *Territorial and Maritime Dispute (Nicaragua v Colombia)* (2012), Art 121 as a whole reflects customary law.

LOOKING FOR EXTRA MARKS?

This provision was at the heart of the arbitration between the Philippines and China in the South China Sea Dispute. In its Award of 12 July 2016, the tribunal became the first ever judicial body to touch upon Art 121(3) and offer some very useful interpretative insights with respect to terms such as 'human habitation' and 'economic life of their own'. According to the tribunal, the status of a feature is to be determined on the basis of its natural capacity, without external additions or modifications intended to increase its capacity to sustain human habitation or an economic life of its own. Moreover, the term 'human habitation' should be understood to involve the inhabitation of the feature by a stable community of people for whom the feature constitutes a home and on which they can remain. On the other hand, the term 'economic life of their own' is linked to the requirement of human habitation, and it must be oriented around the feature itself and not focused solely on the waters or seabed of the surrounding territorial sea.

Normal and straight baselines

Normal baselines do not start from the beach, but from the low-water lines as depicted in official charts (Art 5 LOSC). However, exceptionally, when coastlines are deeply indented or cut into, or where there is a fringe of islands in the vicinity of the mainland coast, normal baselines may be avoided. Art 7 LOSC sets out a different method, ie the drawing of straight baselines. This method consists of drawing a series of artificial straight lines linking the outermost points of rocks, islands, and indents. Norway was the first to adopt and claim straight baselines in order to delimit its territorial sea. The UK challenged this claim in the *Fisheries case (UK v Norway)* (1951), but the International Court of Justice (ICJ) held that, because of the inconvenience in drawing normal baselines in such geographically complicated circumstances, it was permissible to draw straight baselines.

In order to avoid manipulation by coastal States, straight baselines 'must not depart to any appreciable extent from the general direction of the coast, and the sea areas lying within the lines must be sufficiently closely linked to the land domain to be subject to the regime of internal waters' (Art 7, para 4).

REVISION TIP

The drawing of baselines is of paramount importance because they constitute the starting point for measuring the breadth of all maritime zones. There are two major types of baselines, namely, normal and straight baselines. Whichever method is employed, the validity of a baseline and, consequently, the breadth of a maritime zone is contingent upon its consistency with international law (*Fisheries case (UK v Norway)* (1951)).

Sovereignty at sea: areas in which coastal States exercise sovereignty

Internal waters

Internal waters comprise waters situated landward (direction-wise) from the baselines, typically encompassing ports, bays, and rivers. States enjoy exclusive sovereignty in their internal waters. This means that no State is obligated to allow foreign vessels into its internal waters, and especially its ports, except in cases of distress or where this is provided for in a bilateral or multilateral treaty. Otherwise, coastal States are free to impose whatever conditions they wish upon entry into territorial waters, and especially their ports.

Once a foreign vessel has entered internal waters, it is subject to the domestic legislation of the coastal State which can, in principle, take enforcement action against delinquent vessels, and even prevent them from leaving port. That said, port States generally do not enforce their criminal jurisdiction over crimes that do not infringe their customs laws or disrupt peace and public order. Thus, incidents that pertain to the 'internal economy' of the foreign vessel will usually not be subject to the jurisdiction of the port State, unless the master of the vessel or the port consul requests intervention. As was reaffirmed in the *'ARA Libertad' case (Argentina v Ghana)* (2012), warships and other State vessels enjoy immunity in foreign ports both in respect of criminal and civil jurisdiction.

Territorial sea

The first maritime zone seaward (direction-wise) of the baselines is the territorial sea (or waters), which is subject to the sovereignty of the coastal State. Article 3 LOSC recognizes the right to establish a territorial sea of up to 12 nautical miles. The sovereignty of the coastal State extends also to the airspace above the territorial sea, in addition to its seabed and subsoil.

The coastal State exercises sovereignty over its territorial waters, subject, however, to certain restrictions, particularly the right of innocent passage. Ships of all States enjoy a right of 'innocent passage' through the territorial seas of coastal States. A vessel's passage is considered 'innocent' where it is not prejudicial to the peace, good order, or security of the coastal State (Art 19(1) LOSC). LOSC includes a long list of activities and circumstances whereby innocence is deemed lost, such as fishing, serious pollution, research, etc. If a foreign vessel engages in such activities, the coastal State may request its departure from the territorial sea, while arguably it may also exercise enforcement jurisdiction in respect of matters that have already enacted legislation pursuant to Art 21 LOSC. These include, among others, the safety of navigation, conservation of living resources, and violations of customs or immigration laws.

Straits

Less power to exert authority and jurisdiction is granted to the coastal State with respect to narrow straits wholly composed of territorial seas but linking one part of the high seas with another and used for international navigation, such as the straits of Dover, Gibraltar, and Hormuz.

Corfu Channel (United Kingdom of Great Britain and Northern Ireland v Albania), Judgment (Merits), ICJ Rep (1949), p 1

A British warship passing through the Corfu Channel and the territorial sea of Albania was hit by mines and sunk. The UK protested that innocent passage through straits is recognized by international law, whereas the Albanian government contended that foreign warships and merchant vessels had no right to pass through Albanian territorial waters without prior authorization. The ICJ held that warships were entitled to exercise a right of innocent passage through straits used for international navigation and that coastal States are not entitled to suspend innocent passage within such straits for any ship.

Transit passage

Under LOSC, the regime of 'non-suspendable innocent passage' through straits is supplemented by another entitlement, ie the right of transit passage. This right applies only to straits connecting high seas or EEZs with other areas of high seas or EEZs and as long as these are used for international navigation. There are also straits covered by particular treaty regimes (eg the Dardanelles). The main difference between the regime of innocent passage and the right of transit passage is that, under the latter, aircraft are accorded the right of overflight, whereas submarines may also proceed submerged.

LOOKING FOR EXTRA MARKS?

One of the most controversial aspects of innocent passage is whether it may be exercised by warships, given that their passage is ordinarily 'non-innocent'. Major maritime powers have generally favoured the enjoyment of innocent passage by warships. In a recent Provisional Measures Order, the International Tribunal for the Law of the Sea (ITLOS) clarified that all vessels, including warships, enjoy the right of innocent passage (*ITLOS, Case Concerning the Detention of Three Ukrainian Vessels (Ukraine v. Russia)* (2019)).

Maritime zones in which coastal States exercise certain sovereign rights and jurisdiction

Contiguous zone

It has long been accepted that coastal States may exercise certain police powers outside their territorial waters in relation to offences already committed there or in the process of being committed. Under Art 33 LOSC, the coastal State is permitted to exercise certain enforcement powers; namely, to prevent and punish infringements of customs, fiscal, immigration, or sanitary laws up to 24 miles from its baselines. This coastal belt is known as the contiguous zone.

Continental shelf

Art 76 LOSC stipulates that the continental shelf extends to: (a) 200 miles from the baselines; or (b) the outer edge of the continental margin, whichever of the two is further. The outer lines based on the latter option cannot be drawn more than 350 miles from the baselines or more than 100 miles from a point at which the depth of the water is 2,500 metres. Under LOSC, a coastal State may delineate the outer limits of its continental shelf beyond 200 nautical miles only on the basis of a recommendation by the Commission on the Limits of the Continental Shelf, which was established by the Convention.

Following relevant State practice and the work of the International Law Commission (ILC), the 1958 Geneva Convention on the Continental Shelf stipulated that 'the coastal State exercises over the continental shelf sovereign rights for the purpose of exploring it and exploiting its natural resources' (Art 2(1)). As was later accepted by the ICJ in the *North Sea Continental Shelf cases* (1969), this provision reflects customary law, and these rights exist independently of an express act or declaration. This was reiterated in Art 77 LOSC. Natural resources include both mineral and other non-living resources of the seabed and subsoil, as well as sedentary species (Art 77, para 4).

Exclusive economic zone (EEZ)

Under Art 57 LOSC and customary international law, States may claim an EEZ up to 200 miles (Art 57 LOSC). There, first and foremost, coastal States exercise sovereign rights for the purposes of 'exploring and exploiting, conserving and managing' both living and non-living resources (Art 56). Such exploitation includes also the harnessing of wind and wave power. In addition, coastal States enjoy jurisdiction over the establishment and use of artificial islands and installations, marine scientific research, and the preservation of the marine environment in the EEZ (Art 56(b) and (c) LOSC).

As to the juridical nature of the EEZ, it is cited as a *sui generis* zone, ie a zone subject to a distinct jurisdictional framework and composed of neither territorial seas nor high seas. Thus, Art 58 LOSC provides that three of the freedoms of the high seas—ie navigation, over-flight, and the laying of cables and pipelines—are exercisable by all States within the EEZ in accordance with the general framework governing the high seas. However, as was affirmed in *Philippines v China (South China Sea Award)*, third States should pay due regard to the rights of the coastal states in exercising these freedoms.

Conversely, the coastal State should equally pay due regard to the rights of other States therein (Art 56(2)). For example, in the *Chagos Marine Protected Area Arbitration (Mauritius v United Kingdom)* (2015), the tribunal, while rejecting all the territorially related claims of Mauritius due to the lack of jurisdiction to entertain them, still found that the UK, in establishing a Marine Protected Area in the EEZ of the Chagos Archipelago, was in violation of its procedural obligations, including under Art 56(2) to consult and give due regard to the legally binding rights of Mauritius.

LOOKING FOR EXTRA MARKS?

Although LOSC confers enforcement jurisdiction to the coastal State over illegal fishing within its EEZ, it also demands that vessels or crew arrested 'shall be promptly released upon the posting of reasonable bond or other securities' (Art 73). In addition, ITLOS enjoys automatic jurisdiction over claims concerning the prompt release of vessels and this has so far been the main judicial activity of the tribunal.

Areas beyond national jurisdiction

The high seas

Both the 1958 Geneva Convention on the High Seas and LOSC proclaim the high seas to be free and open to vessels of all States, all of which have a range of non-exhaustible freedoms. Under LOSC, these are: navigation, fishing, overflight, the laying of cables and the construction of artificial islands and other installations, and marine scientific research. All are to be enjoyed with 'due regard' to the interests of other States (Art 87).

The essential idea underlying the principle of freedom of the high seas is the peacetime prohibition of interference by the ships of one nation against those of another. This prohibition has given rise to the principle of exclusivity of flag State jurisdiction, namely, that ships on the high seas are, as a general rule, subject to the exclusive jurisdiction and authority of the State whose flag they lawfully fly (*ITLOS, M/V Norstar case (Panama v Italy)* (2019)).

Central to the application of the principle of exclusivity of flag State jurisdiction is the notion of 'nationality of vessels'. Under the law of the sea and, in particular, LOSC: 'every State shall fix the conditions for the grant of its nationality to ships, for the registration of ships in its territory, and for the right to fly its flag' (Art 91).

Exceptions to flag State jurisdiction on the high seas

The principle of exclusivity of flag State jurisdiction is not an absolute rule from which no derogation is permitted. On the contrary, international law has recognized certain instances where interference is permissible. The most notable exceptions are found in the general right of visit (Art 110 LOSC) and in the right of hot pursuit (Art 111 LOSC). Other exceptions are found in various law enforcement treaties which contemplate measures of visit, inspection, and arrest of vessels on the high seas in relation to particular subject matters.

Under Art 110 LOSC, the right of visit is accorded to warships only against those vessels on the high seas reasonably suspected of having engaged in certain proscribed activities. These activities include: (a) piracy; (b) the slave trade; (c) unauthorized broadcasting; (d) the absence of nationality; or (e) though flying a foreign flag or refusing to show its flag, the ship is in reality of the same nationality as the warship.

Furthermore, by virtue of Art 111 LOSC, coastal States may pursue outside of their maritime zones, into the high seas, and take enforcement action against a foreign ship that has violated the laws and regulations of that State, under certain cumulative conditions (ITLOS, *M/V 'SAIGA' (No 2)*, (1999)). First, the coastal State must have *good reason to believe* that the vessel being pursued has violated the laws or regulations of that State. Secondly, pursuit may only be commenced 'after a visual or auditory signal to stop has been given at a distance which enables it to be seen or heard by the foreign ship'. This provision was construed evolutively by the Arbitral Tribunal in the *Arctic Sunrise case (Netherlands v Russia)* (2015). Thirdly, pursuant to Art 111(1) and (4), the pursuit must be commenced when the foreign ship or its boats are within the relevant maritime zone of the coastal State. Fourthly, the pursuit must be *continuous and uninterrupted*, while the right of hot pursuit ceases as soon as the ship pursued enters the territorial sea of its own State or of a third State (Art 111 (3)).

Piracy

As regards piracy, it is defined in Art 101 LOSC as:

> any illegal acts of violence or detention, or any act of depredation, committed for private ends by the crew or the passengers of a private ship or a private aircraft, and directed: (i) on the high seas, against another ship or aircraft, or against persons or property on board such ship or aircraft.

The constituent elements of piracy *jure gentium* are, accordingly, the following: (a) the most salient and controversial requirement is that acts must be committed for 'private ends', as opposed to 'public or political ends'; (b) the two-ship requirement, which entails that situations in which only one vessel is involved, such as the crew seizure or passenger takeover of their own vessel, are explicitly excluded from the definition of international sea piracy; (c) piracy *jure gentium* should take place on the high seas or in the EEZ. Under LOSC and customary international law, every State may seize a pirate ship or aircraft and accordingly arrest the pirates and seize the property on board. This is an expression of the principle of universal jurisdiction (Art 105 LOSC).

LOOKING FOR EXTRA MARKS?

In the period between 2008 and 2013, there was an unprecedented growth of piratical attacks in Africa, in particular off the coast of Somalia and the West Indian Ocean, while more recently, piratical attacks have occurred mainly in the Gulf of Guinea. The North Atlantic Treaty Organization (NATO) and the European Union have launched maritime operations to protect international shipping from such attacks and the UN Security Council has adopted a series of resolutions under Chapter VII, starting with SC Resolution 1816/2008, authorizing entry into the territorial waters or even onto the mainland of Somalia for the purpose of arresting the suspect pirates.

REVISION TIP

On the high seas, the principle of exclusive jurisdiction of the flag State is paramount. Thus, interference with the vessels of other States is prohibited, save for a sound legal basis under treaty or customary law. The most common legal bases are the right of visit or the right of hot pursuit, but there are many bilateral and multilateral agreements conferring the right of visit in respect of illegal fishing, smuggling of migrants, drug trafficking, etc.

LOOKING FOR EXTRA MARKS?

Even if States are granted the right to board a suspect foreign vessel on the high seas, this does not automatically mean that they have the power to exercise enforcement jurisdiction over the suspects. They must have enacted prior domestic legislation and the flag State must consent to it. In *Medvedyev v France* (2010), the Grand Chamber of the European Court of Human Rights found a violation of the right to liberty of the crew members of a drug-trafficking vessel arrested on the high seas (Art 5 European Convention on Human Rights). This was because France had not proscribed drug trafficking on the high seas in a precise and foreseeable manner in its domestic legislation.

Delimitation of overlapping maritime zones

The most controversial question in international theory and practice of the law of the sea has been the delimitation of maritime zones between States with opposite or adjacent coastlines. It is often impossible for States to extend their jurisdiction as far seawards as international law permits, due to geographical constraints and overlapping claims of other neighbouring States. The problem of delimitation is therefore vexing and has given rise to more cases before the ICJ and other tribunals than any other single subject.

Treaty law

In respect of the delimitation of the territorial sea, Art 15 LOSC provides that, in the absence of agreement to the contrary, States may not extend their territorial seas beyond the median or equidistance line unless there are historic or other 'special' circumstances that dictate otherwise. On the other hand, Articles 74 and 83 LOSC, on the delimitation of the EEZ and the continental shelf respectively, set out that the delimitation shall be effected by agreement on the basis of international law, as referred to in Art 38 ICJ Statute, in order to achieve an equitable solution.

The delimitation process

In the aftermath of the adoption of LOSC, and mainly since *Maritime Delimitation in the Black Sea (Romania v Ukraine)* (2009), all international courts and tribunals have applied a three-stage approach by (a) drawing a provisional equidistance line; (b) conducting an examination as to whether the line should be adjusted by taking relevant circumstances into account; and (c) applying the (dis)proportionality test in order to achieve an equitable result. The purpose of this test is to ensure that the areas appertaining to each State are not disproportionate to the ratio between the lengths of their relevant coasts adjoining the area. All the recent cases of the ICJ (from *Territorial and Maritime Dispute (Nicaragua v Colombia)* (2012) to *Maritime Delimitation in the Caribbean Sea and the Pacific Ocean (Costa Rica v Nicaragua)* (2018)), of ITLOS (*Delimitation case between Bangladesh and Myanmar in the Bay of Bengal* (2012)), and of arbitral tribunals (*Bay of Bengal Boundary (Bangladesh v India)* (2014)) follow this three-stage approach ritually.

KEY CASES

CASE	FACTS	PRINCIPLES
North Sea Continental Shelf Case (Germany v Denmark/The Netherlands), ICJ Rep (1969), p 1	The dispute related to the delimitation of the continental shelf between the Federal Republic of Germany (FRG) and Denmark, on the one hand, and between the FRG and the Netherlands, on the other. The parties asked the Court to state the applicable delimitation principles and rules of international law.	The Court determined that were the rule enshrined in Art 6 Geneva Convention on the Continental Shelf (1958) to be applied mechanically to the concave German coastline, it would restrict Germany to a modest triangle of the continental shelf to the substantial benefit of its neighbours. It thus rejected the rule of Art 6 and found that the boundary lines in question were to be drawn by agreement between the parties and in accordance with equitable principles. It indicated certain factors to be taken into consideration for that purpose.
Territorial and Maritime Dispute between Nicaragua and Honduras in the Caribbean Sea (Nicaragua v Honduras), ICJ Rep (2007), p 659	Nicaragua filed an application instituting proceedings against Honduras in respect of a dispute relating to the delimitation of the maritime areas appertaining to each of those States in the Caribbean Sea.	In this exceptional case, the ICJ emphasized that equidistance remained the general rule. It held, however, that both the configuration and the unstable nature of the relevant coastal area made it impossible to identify base points and construct a provisional equidistance line at all. This amounted to a special circumstance justifying the use of an alternative method, namely, the use of a line that bisected two lines drawn along the coastal fronts of the two States.

KEY DEBATES

Topic	Novel threats to maritime security and the law of the sea
Author/academic	N Klein
Viewpoint	Whereas the protection of sovereignty and national interests remains fundamental to maritime security and the law of the sea, there is increasing acceptance of a common interest to respond to modern maritime security threats. It is argued that security interests should be given greater scope in our understanding of the law of the sea in light of the changing dynamics of exclusive and inclusive claims to ocean use. More flexibility may be required in the interpretation and application of LOSC if appropriate responses to ensure maritime security are to be allowed.
Source	*Maritime Security and the Law of the Sea* (Oxford: Oxford University Press, 2011)

Topic	The governance of areas beyond national jurisdiction
Author/academic	R Rayfuse and R Warner
Viewpoint	A global approach to further developing the high seas regime on the basis of an oceanic trust beyond national jurisdiction could foster environmentally responsible use of the high seas and their resources and ensure the application of modern conservation principles and management tools. In view of escalating threats to the oceans from existing and emerging uses and from the impacts of climate change, transformation to a legal regime better suited to integrated management and preservation of vital ocean ecosystem services and resilience may be a necessity.
Source	'Securing a Sustainable Future for the Oceans beyond National Jurisdiction', 23 *International Journal of Marine and Coastal Law* (2008) 399

EXAM QUESTIONS

Problem question

MV So San, a freighter flying the flag of Panama, was suspected of drug trafficking. While sailing on the high seas, it was approached by a UK warship with information that the *MV So San* carried more than 100kg of cocaine.

1. Does the UK have a right to halt, board, and search the vessel? On what legal basis can the UK exercise the right of visit?
2. Does the UK have a right to exercise enforcement jurisdiction over the alleged crime and seize the vessel, arrest the suspect crew members, bring them to port, and try them? What are the prerequisites for the exercise of enforcement jurisdiction on the high seas under international law?

See the Outline answers section in the end matter for help with this question.

Essay question

Critically analyse the differences between the continental shelf and the EEZ under the law of the sea and, in particular, LOSC.

Online Resources

For an outline answer to this essay question, as well as interactive key cases and multiple-choice questions, please visit the online resources.

https://www.oup.com/he/bantekas-papastavridis-concentrate5e

9

State responsibility

THE EXAMINATION

Exam questions in this field may concern the attribution of the wrongful conduct to States or the circumstances precluding wrongfulness, such as consent or necessity. Questions may also involve the role of non-State organs in bringing about the responsibility of States or the plea of countermeasures in international law. Equally, questions about the invocation of State responsibility and the notion of injured State or the forms of reparation, such as restitution and compensation, are frequent.

KEY FACTS

- The 2001 International Law Commission (ILC) **Articles on State Responsibility** is the key instrument in this field, despite the fact that it is not a treaty.
- State responsibility requires an existing obligation, a breach of this obligation, and attribution of the breach to a State.
- The responsibility of the State is engaged by both acts and omissions. These may be committed by government officials as well as by non-government agents if the act or omission may otherwise be attributed to a State.
- Responsibility gives rise to reparation claims by the injured State. These may take the form of restitution, compensation, and satisfaction.

CHAPTER OVERVIEW

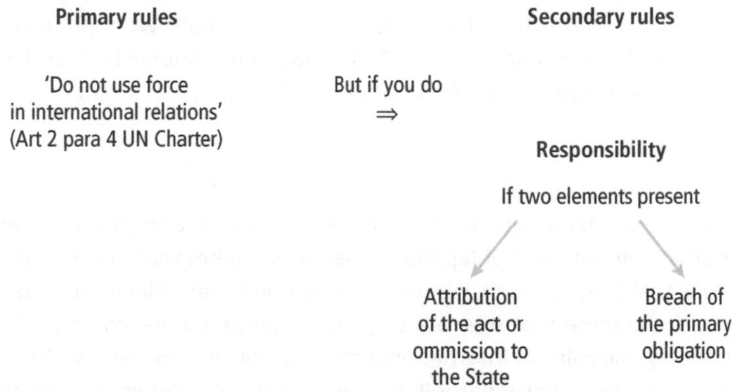
State responsibility
Primary rules
Secondary rules
'Do not use force
in international relations'
(Art 2 para 4 UN Charter)
But if you do
⇒
Responsibility
If two elements present
Attribution
of the act or
ommission to
the State
Breach of
the primary
obligation
Exceptions: circumstances precluding wrongfulness, eg consent,
self-defence, countermeasures, force measures, distress, necessity.

Introduction

Meaning of State responsibility

The rules of State responsibility describe what happens when there is a violation of an international obligation. International law sets out legal obligations and rights for States. However, it is almost certain that not all States comply with these obligations. Should a breach of an obligation occur, it is the law of international responsibility that explains the legal consequences of this breach.

This law of international (or State) responsibility has been developed and codified by the ILC. The main text and point of reference is the ILC Articles on Responsibility of States for Internationally Wrongful Acts (ARSIWA) (2001). The ARSIWA has not taken the form of a treaty, yet the majority of its provisions reflect customary international law. The ARSIWA was followed in 2011 by the ILC Articles on the Responsibility of International Organizations (ARIO). ARIO was based primarily on ARSIWA and it remains to be seen how international courts will react to it. It is not clear whether most of its provisions reflect customary law or constitute progressive development of the law.

Internationally wrongful act

The law of international responsibility is based on the notion of an '**internationally wrongful act**'; that is, a breach of an international obligation which may be attributed to a particular State. In accordance with the law of State responsibility, every internationally wrongful act gives rise to the liability of the State that caused it. Internationally wrongful conduct consists of an act or omission: (a) 'attributable to the State under international law'; and (b) that 'constitutes a breach of an international obligation of the State' (Art 2 ARSIWA).

The meaning of international obligations

The law of State responsibility sets out the rules that govern the legal consequences arising from a breach of an international obligation. What distinguishes these from other rules of international law is that they do not lay down primary rights and obligations upon States, but secondary ones, in the sense that they are triggered following a breach of a primary obligation. To put it simply, the rules of international responsibility would not say 'Do not use force in international law', but rather what will happen if a country defies this obligation and illegally uses force. In other words, the 'primary rules' impose particular obligations on States, whereas 'secondary rules' determine the consequences for failing to fulfil obligations established by 'primary rules'. It is true that this distinction is somewhat artificial, but it is central to our understanding of the law of international responsibility.

The general meaning of attribution

State responsibility arises from an internationally wrongful act. This wrongful act constitutes the breach of a primary obligation, which itself is attributed to the culprit State. The act may take the form of action or omission. Although numerous actions or omissions may in fact violate international law, responsibility only arises in respect of those that are linked to a State. This causal link between the unlawful conduct and the State is called *attribution*. Under the rules of State responsibility, the conduct will be attributed to the State if, inter alia, the act or omission was done by State organs or other private persons or entities under the direction or control of the State.

No requirement for damage

State responsibility is not based on the existence of damage or harm caused by the unlawful act. It arises even in the absence of material damage. The notion of damage may play a role in the compensation procedure, but it is not a prerequisite for the responsibility to arise in the first place. Moreover, responsibility does not require the existence of a tort in the municipal sense. Instead, international responsibility concerns breaches of treaty, custom, **unilateral acts,** and other international obligations.

LOOKING FOR EXTRA MARKS?

The ARSIWA deals only with the responsibility of States, not international organizations. Of course, as the International Court of Justice (ICJ) affirmed in *Reparation for Injuries Suffered in the Service of the United Nations* (1949), the United Nations 'is a subject of international law and capable of possessing international rights and duties . . . it has capacity to maintain its rights by bringing international claims'. Generally, the responsibility of international organizations is premised upon the two elements of Art 2 ARSIWA, namely, the attribution of the wrongful act or omission to the organization and the breach of an international obligation of the organization (Art 4 ARIO).

Attribution to the State

While the breach of a State's international obligation is a matter of fact, the element of attribution is a matter of law and thus merits closer scrutiny. As provided in the ARSIWA, the act or omission that constitutes the wrongful conduct should be attributable to the State concerned. Under international law, the only conduct attributed to the State at the international level is that of its organs or of persons and entities acting under the direction, instigation, or control of those organs, ie as agents of the State. As a direct consequence, the conduct of private persons in their private capacity is not attributable to their country of nationality or any other country.

The attribution of conduct to a State is based on criteria determined by international law and not on the mere recognition of a link of factual causality. In Arts 4–11 ARSIWA, the ILC sets out the conditions under which conduct is attributed to the State for the purposes of determining its international responsibility.

State organs

It is reasonable that the acts or omissions which by definition bring about State responsibility would be those of the organs of the State. Article 4(1) ARSIWA provides that the conduct of any State organ shall be considered an act of that State under international law. The reference to a 'State organ' encompasses all individuals or collective entities which make up the organization of the State and act on its behalf. The range of persons thus considered to be State organs may be ascertained by reference to a State's internal law (Art 4, para 2 ARSIWA). The acts of *de jure* State organs are attributable to that State, regardless of the character of the organ concerned and whatever function it exercises. For example, the acts of the head of State, as well as those of a foot soldier, would both be attributable to the State because they are an integral part of the official State apparatus.

In particular, it has been acknowledged that governmental action or omission by the executive gives rise to international responsibility. In addition, actions by the judiciary, as was recognized in the Advisory Opinion in ***Difference Relating to Immunity from Legal Process of*** *a Special Rapporteur of the Commission on Human Rights* (1999), as well as by the legislative (eg *Certain German Interests in Polish Upper Silesia* (1926)), may bring about the responsibility of the State. Equally, actions by organs of territorial communities that are subordinate to the State or federal units are attributable to the latter.

Interestingly, the ICJ recognized another form of organs, the 'de facto organs'—that is, organs acting in 'complete dependence' on the State without, however, having any official capacity under domestic law. Such organs are usually agents of the State, but the latter is unwilling to admit that they are part of its official machinery: a James Bond type of agent! It has been stressed that attribution in such cases 'must be exceptional, for it requires proof of a particularly great degree of State control' (*Application of the Convention for the Prevention and Punishment of the Crime of Genocide case (Bosnia and Herzegovina v Serbia and Montenegro)* (2007)).

It is often the case today that private institutions are called upon to exercise elements of governmental authority, for example, private persons acting as prison guards. Article 5 ARSIWA recognizes that the conduct of these 'parastatal entities' is to be attributed to the State. The justification lies in the fact that the internal law of the State has conferred on the entity in question the exercise of specific functions, which are akin to those normally exercised by organs of the State.

Finally, it has long been recognized that acts of public authorities which are unauthorized or *ultra vires* should not release the State from its wrongfulness. Accordingly, Art 7 ARSIWA sets forth that 'the conduct of an organ of a State or of a person or entity empowered to exercise elements of governmental authority shall be considered an act of the State if the organ, person or entity acts in that capacity, even if it exceeds its authority or contravenes instructions'.

Velásquez Rodríguez v Honduras, Inter-American Court of Human Rights, Series C, No 4 (1988) 95 ILR 232

Honduran citizens demonstrated a systematic policy of enforced disappearance by members of the country's security forces. The Honduran government argued, inter alia, that it had not ordered or sanctioned this policy. The Court emphatically held that a breach of the American Convention on Human Rights:

> is independent of whether the organ or official has contravened provisions of internal law or overstepped the limits of his authority: under international law a State is responsible for the acts of its agents undertaken in their official capacity and for their omissions, even when those agents act outside the sphere of their authority or violate internal law' (p 296).

Private persons

There has been no issue surrounded by so much controversy in the law of responsibility as that under which circumstances, acts, or omissions of persons or other entities, which have no official capacity are attributed to a particular State. In general terms, the approach of international courts and scholarly opinion is twofold and, as you will see, there are disagreements between the various international courts and tribunals on the matter.

1. The *stricto sensu* approach, which dictates that only the conduct of persons under the 'effective control' of the State, is attributable to the latter. The Nicaragua case exemplifies this approach:

Military and Paramilitary Activities in and against Nicaragua (Nicaragua v United States of America), Merits, Judgment, ICJ Rep (1986), p 14

The ICJ was asked to assess the responsibility of the USA for violations of international humanitarian law by the contras, an armed group in rebellion against the government of Nicaragua which was supported by the USA. As the contras were not *de jure* organs of the USA, the Court had to formulate a test for the attribution of the acts of the contras to the USA. It came up with two tests of attribution. Under the *complete control* test, which is of general application, attribution requires control by the State over the entire functioning of a group. The *effective control* test is subsidiary to its *complete control* test counterpart. It concerns a State's control over the conduct of a specific operation, in the course of which violations have been committed and applies when the conditions of the first test have not been met.

2. The *lato sensu* approach: it suffices to prove that there exists *overall control*, as there is no need to require a high threshold for the test of control:

Prosecutor v Duško Tadić, International Tribunal for the former Yugoslavia, Case IT-94-1-A (1999) 38 ILM 1518

The question was whether the financing and military support provided by Yugoslavia to a rebel group in Bosnia during that country's civil war rendered the rebels agents of Yugoslavia, with the consequence that the conflict had become international. The ICTY Appeals Chamber held the appropriate test was that of *overall control*, which went 'beyond the mere financing and equipping of such forces and involved also participation in the planning and supervision of military operations' (p 1541).

In the *Application of the Convention on the Prevention and Punishment of the Crime of Genocide (Bosnia and Herzegovina v Serbia and Montenegro)* (2007), the ICJ reaffirmed that the 'effective control', set out in the *Nicaragua case*, is the appropriate control test, rather than the ICTY's 'overall control' test, which the Court considered as non-applicable in the realm of state responsibility. On the other hand, the ILC eschewed taking a firm position. Article 8 ARSIWA provides in general terms that 'the conduct of a person or group of persons shall be considered an act of a State under international law, if the person or group of persons is in fact acting on the instructions of, or under the direction or control of, that State in carrying out the conduct'.

LOOKING FOR EXTRA MARKS?

In the *Nicaragua case*, the ICJ held that 'persons under the complete control of the State' were agents of the controlling State. Years later, in the *Bosnia–Serbia Genocide case*, it considered them (de facto) organs under Art 4 ARSIWA.

Conduct acknowledged and adopted by the State *ex post facto*

Article 11 ARSIWA envisages the attribution of conduct that was not, or may not have been, attributable to a State at the time of its commission, but which was subsequently acknowledged and adopted as its own. However, the conduct will not be attributable under Art 11, where a State merely acknowledges its existence or expresses its verbal approval in respect of it; the term 'acknowledges and adopts' in Art 11 makes it clear that what is required is something more than a general acknowledgement of a factual situation.

REVISION TIP

The attribution of particular conduct to a State, as an element of international responsibility, is governed by the rules set out in Arts 4–11 ARSIWA. Fundamental is the distinction between private persons that act or which are empowered by law to act in an official capacity and persons that are controlled or directed by the State. Attribution on the basis of 'control' remains controversial. International courts and tribunals adopt varying interpretations of the 'control' requirement, with the ICJ insisting on a high evidentiary threshold of 'effective control'.

Circumstances precluding wrongfulness

Circumstances precluding wrongfulness are 'excuses' and 'defences' that serve as justifications available to States for excluding responsibility in a particular case. The invocation of these circumstances has the function of 'a shield against an otherwise well-founded claim for the breach of an international obligation'. The ILC included in the ARSIWA six types of circumstances precluding wrongfulness:

1. **Consent** (Art 20): consent to particular conduct done by another State precludes the wrongfulness of that act in relation to the consenting State, provided the consent is valid and to the extent that the conduct remains within the limits of the consent given. Consent is very frequent in everyday State practice, for example, a coastal State consents to the otherwise illegal pursuit of a drug-trafficking vessel by a third State within its coastal waters. The requirements are that the consent should have been given prior to the wrongful conduct; *ex post facto* consent is rather a waiver of responsibility claim under Art 45 ARSIWA. In addition, the consent should be valid and clearly expressed, not tacit or presumed.

Armed Activities on the Territory of the Congo (Democratic Republic of Congo v Uganda), ICJ Rep (2005), p 168

The Court had to assess whether the consent of the Democratic Republic of Congo (DRC) to the presence of Ugandan troops on its territory had been withdrawn pursuant to a DRC statement of 28 July 1998. It concluded that:

> the consent that had been given to Uganda to place its forces in the DRC, and to engage in military operations, was not an open-ended consent. Even had consent to the Ugandan military presence extended much beyond the end of July 1998, the parameters of that consent, in terms of geographic location and objectives, would have remained thus restricted [para 52].

2. **Self-defence** (Art 21): here, self-defence does not operate as a 'primary norm', ie an individual or collective right enshrined in Art 51 UN Charter and customary law operating as exception to the prohibition of the use of force under Art 2 para 4 UN Charter, but as a 'secondary norm', namely, a circumstance precluding the wrongfulness of other breaches of international obligations of the defending State, which are excused because they occur in the context of self-defence.
3. **Countermeasures** (Art 22): as was stated in *Gabčíkovo-Nagymaros Project (Hungary/Slovakia)* (1997), countermeasures might justify otherwise unlawful conduct when 'taken in response to a previous international wrongful act of another State and . . . directed against that State', provided certain conditions are met. These conditions are set out in Arts 49–54 ARSIWA. Generally, before resorting to countermeasures, a State that finds itself injured must call upon the culprit State to cease the wrongful conduct and offer reparation for the injury. Article 52(1) adds the requirement to formally notify the responsible State of the decision to take countermeasures, as well as the need to negotiate.

   A central requirement is that countermeasures must be proportional to the wrongful conduct. In the *Gabčíkovo-Nagymaros case* (p 56), the Court found that the unilateral assumption of control over a large part of the waters of the Danube was not commensurate with the injury suffered, taking into account the rights in question. Finally, there are certain fundamental obligations which may not be subject to countermeasures, such as human rights law, the prohibition of **reprisals** under humanitarian law, and the prohibition of the use of force (Art 50 ARSIWA).

Air Service Agreement of 27 March 1946 between the United States of America and France (1978) 18 RIAA 417

In this case, the USA invoked countermeasures to justify measures adopted in response to the French interpretation of the 1946 agreement. The arbitral tribunal clarified that 'if a situation arises, which in one State's view results in the violation of an international obligation by another State, the first State is entitled, within the limits set by the general rules of international law pertaining to the use of armed force, to affirm its rights through counter-measures' (p 443). The tribunal placed emphasis on the requirement of proportionality and concluded that the countermeasures taken by the USA were lawful, as not being 'clearly disproportionate when compared to those taken by France' (p 444).

One issue is whether countermeasures may be taken by third States which are not themselves individually injured by the internationally wrongful act in question. Article 54 leaves open the question whether any State may adopt countermeasures to ensure compliance with an obligation *erga omnes*, as a matter of general interest, as opposed to personal interest as an injured State. State practice, however, supports the legality of such collective countermeasures.

Countermeasures under the World Trade Organization

When a World Trade Organization (WTO) dispute panel resolves a dispute in favour of a State party, satisfactory compensation must be agreed with the losing party within 20 days of the expiry of a reasonable period of time. If not, in accordance with Art 22.2 WTO Dispute Settlement Understanding (DSU), the complainant may ask the Dispute Settlement Body (DSB) for permission to impose trade sanctions against the respondent that has failed to implement. Technically, this is called 'suspending concessions or other obligations under the covered agreements', which are effectively countermeasures.

4. ***Force majeure*** (Art 23): *force majeure* involves a situation where a State is effectively compelled to act in a manner not in conformity with the requirements of an international obligation. A situation of *force majeure* precluding wrongfulness only arises where three elements are met: (a) the act in question must be brought about by an irresistible force or an unforeseen event; (b) the event is beyond the control of the State concerned; (c) which makes it materially impossible in the circumstances to perform the obligation. *Force majeure* situations may arise due to a natural or physical event (eg earthquakes, floods) or to human intervention (eg loss of control over a portion of the State's territory). The ongoing COVID-19 pandemic may well come under this heading.
5. **Distress** (Art 24): the Article precludes the wrongfulness of conduct adopted by the State agent in circumstances where the agent had no other reasonable way of saving life. Unlike situations of *force majeure* dealt with under Art 23, a person acting under distress is not acting involuntarily, even though the choice is effectively nullified by the situation of peril. In practice, cases of distress have mostly involved aircraft or ships entering State territory under stress of weather or following mechanical or navigational failure.

Case Concerning the Difference between New Zealand and France Arising from the Rainbow Warrior Affair (1990) XX RIAA 215

France removed two French officers from the island of Hao following their direct involvement in the death of environmental activists in New Zealand. It justified their removal on the ground of 'circumstances of distress in a case of extreme urgency involving elementary humanitarian considerations affecting the acting organs of the State'. The tribunal unanimously accepted that this plea was admissible in principle, and by majority that it was applicable to the facts of one of the two officers, who was under serious health risk.

6. **Necessity** (Art 25): necessity denotes those exceptional cases where the only way a State can safeguard an essential interest threatened by a grave and imminent peril, for example, public health by the COVID-19 pandemic, is, for the time being, to avoid performing some other international obligation of lesser weight or urgency. Under conditions narrowly defined in Art 25, such a plea is recognized as a circumstance precluding wrongfulness.

   In the *Gabčíkovo-Nagymaros Project (Hungary/Slovakia)* (1997) judgment, paras 51–2, the ICJ carefully considered an argument based on the ILC's draft article, expressly accepting the principle while, at the same time, rejecting its invocation in the circumstances of that case.

LOOKING FOR EXTRA MARKS?

In accordance with Art 26 ARSIWA, circumstances precluding wrongfulness cannot justify or excuse a breach of a State's obligations under a peremptory rule of general international law. Thus, for example, one State cannot, through consent, dispense with its obligation to comply with a peremptory norm, for example, in relation to genocide or torture, whether by treaty or otherwise.

Consequences of an internationally wrongful act

In the event of an internationally wrongful act by a State, other States may be entitled to respond. This may be done by invoking the responsibility of the wrongdoer, by seeking cessation and/or reparation, or possibly by taking countermeasures. We have already referred to countermeasures. Cessation and reparation are dealt with in Part Two ARSIWA. It must be stressed from the outset that international responsibility is undifferentiated: there is no difference in principle between responsibility arising from the breach of a treaty (*ex contractu*) or from breach of general international law (*ex delicto*).

Cessation

Cessation refers to the basic obligation of compliance with international law, irrespective of a continuing violation committed by another State. It is true that, as a result of the internationally wrongful act, a new set of legal relations is established between the responsible State and the State or States to whom the international obligation is owed. But this does not mean that the pre-existing legal relation established by the primary obligation disappears. As Art 29 states, the legal consequences of an internationally wrongful act do not affect the continued duty of the State to perform the obligation it has breached. Thus, it becomes important that the responsible State ceases the wrongful conduct and assures—if circumstances so require—its non-repetition in the future (Art 30 ARSIWA).

Reparation

The obligation to make full reparation, ie to wipe out all the consequences of the wrongfulness, as has been famously enunciated by the Permanent Court of International Justice in the *Factory at Chorzow case* (1928), is the second general obligation of the State that committed the wrongful act. It is used to refer to all measures which may be expected from the responsible State, over and above cessation: it includes restitution, compensation, and satisfaction, either alone or alongside the other forms of reparation (Art 34 ARSIWA).

Restitution

In accordance with Art 34, restitution is the first of the forms of reparation available to a State injured by an internationally wrongful act. Restitution involves the re-establishment, as far as is possible, of the situation which existed prior to the commission of the wrongful act. In its simplest form, this involves the release of persons wrongly detained or the return of property wrongly seized. Besides the *Factory at Chorzow case* (1928), in which restitution was considered as the natural redress for violation of or failure to observe the 1922 Geneva Convention, *Pulp Mills on the River Uruguay (Argentina v Uruguay)* (2010) is also relevant: the ICJ reaffirmed that 'customary international law provides for restitution as one form of reparation for injury, restitution being the re-establishment of the situation which existed before the occurrence of the wrongful act' (para 273).

Compensation

Pecuniary compensation is usually an appropriate—and often the only—remedy for injury caused by an unlawful act. Under Art 36 ARSIWA, whenever restitution is not possible, compensation becomes the standard consequence for injury. It covers 'any financially assessable damage including loss and profits'. This is consistent with the jurisprudence of international courts and tribunals, such as the *Corfu Channel case (UK/Albania)* (1949), *Ahmadou Sadio Diallo (Republic of Guinea/Democratic Republic of the Congo)* (2010), and *Compensation Owed for Certain Activities Carried Out by Nicaragua in the Border Area (Costa Rica v Nicaragua)* (2018).

Satisfaction

This is any measure that the responsible State is bound to take, apart from restitution or compensation. Satisfaction may take many forms, which may be cumulative: apologies or other acknowledgement of wrongdoing by means of a payment or indemnity; the trial and punishment of the physical perpetrators and others. In *Corfu Channel* (1949), Albania requested the Court to simply declare that the British Navy had violated its sovereignty by means of an unlawful minesweeping operation.

REVISION TIP

In cases of a breach of international obligation which is attributed to a particular State, the latter has to do the following under the rules of State responsibility: first, if the violation is continuing, it must cease and, if so requested, provide assurances of non-repetition; secondly, it has to make reparation to the injured State, which may take the form of restitution, compensation, and/or satisfaction.

Invocation of responsibility

Central to the invocation of responsibility is the concept of the injured State. Central to the concept of the injured State is the nature of the obligation breached. This concept is set out in Art 42 and takes a twofold form. Under Art 42(a) ARSIWA, the key is the existence of an individual obligation: a State is 'injured' if the obligation breached was owed to it individually. The expression 'individually' indicates that, in the circumstances, performance of the obligation was owed to that State, for example, pursuant to a bilateral treaty.

Under Art 42(b), the key is the violation of collective obligations; these are obligations that exist between more than two States and whose performance is not owed to one State individually, but to a group of States, or even the multilateral or international community as a whole. The violation of these obligations only injures a particular State if additional requirements are met, for example, the breach specifically affects that State, or it is of such a character as to radically alter the position of all other States to which the same obligation is owed. An example provided by the ILC is the following: 'if one State party to the Antarctic Treaty claims sovereignty over an unclaimed area of Antarctica contrary to article 4 of that Treaty, the other States parties should be considered as injured thereby and as entitled to seek cessation, restitution'.

What about the other 'non-injured' States to whom collective obligations are owed? Are they entitled to invoke the responsibility of the culprit State? This is addressed by Art 48, which is based on the idea that, in case of breaches of specific obligations protecting the collective interests of a group of States (obligations *erga omnes partes*) or the interests of the international community as a whole (obligations *erga omnes*), responsibility may be invoked by States which are not themselves injured in the sense of Art 42. Under Art 48(2), these States:

> may claim from the responsible State: (a) cessation of the internationally wrongful act, and assurances and guarantees of non-repetition in accordance with article 30; and (b) performance of the obligation of reparation in accordance with the preceding articles, in the interest of the injured State or of the beneficiaries of the obligation breached.

Questions Relating to the Obligation to Prosecute or Extradite (Belgium v Senegal), Judgment, ICJ Rep (2012), p 422
In this case, Belgium instituted proceedings against Senegal in respect of a dispute concerning 'Senegal's compliance with its obligation to prosecute Mr Habré for acts including crimes of torture or to extradite him to Belgium pursuant to the UN Convention against Torture'. Senegal disputed the existence of any specific legal interest on the part of Belgium to invoke the responsibility of Senegal. The Court held that all the State parties to the Convention against Torture (CAT) 'have a legal interest' in the protection of the rights involved and that these obligations may be defined as 'obligations *erga omnes partes*' in the sense that each State party has an interest in compliance with them in any given case.

The most recent judicial example of the application of Article 48 is the *Application of the Genocide Convention (Gambia v Myanmar)* (2020), in which the ICJ found that any State party to the Genocide Convention, and not only a specially affected State, may invoke the responsibility of another State party with a view to ascertaining the alleged failure to comply with its obligations *erga omnes partes* and to bringing that failure to an end. The Court concluded that the Gambia had prima facie standing to submit to it the dispute with Myanmar on the basis of alleged violations of obligations under the Genocide Convention with respect to the Rohingya group.

LOOKING FOR EXTRA MARKS?

Under the law of State responsibility, there exists the possibility of joint/multiple responsibility: this may take the form of multiple States being responsible for the same wrongful conduct. Article 47 states the general principle that, in such cases, each State is separately responsible for the conduct attributable to it. In addition, there may be responsibility of a State in connection with an act of another State; for example, Art 16 provides for responsibility in cases where one State aids or assists another in the commission of a wrongful act.

KEY CASES

CASE	FACTS	PRINCIPLES
Application of the Convention for the Prevention and Punishment of the Crime of Genocide case (Bosnia and Herzegovina v Serbia and Montenegro), Merits, ICJ Rep (2007), p 43	Bosnia initiated proceedings against the then Former Republic of Yugoslavia (FRY) in March 1993 concerning the application of the Genocide Convention to the events in and around Srebrenica. Bosnia claimed that the FRY was responsible for the acts of genocide perpetrated by the rebel Bosnian-Serb Army.	The Court found that Serbia was neither directly responsible for the Srebrenica genocide nor complicit. However, it did rule that Serbia had breached the Genocide Convention by failing to prevent the Srebrenica genocide. The Court based its conclusion on the rules of attribution under the ARSIWA (Arts 4–11), which were considered as reflective of customary law. It also referred to the customary rule of complicity under Art 16 ARSIWA. However, according to the Court, the genocide as such was not attributable to the FRY.

CASE	FACTS	PRINCIPLES
US Diplomatic and Consular Staff in Tehran (US v Iran), ICJ Rep (1980), p 3	On 29 November 1979, the USA had instituted proceedings against Iran for the seizure and detention of US diplomatic and consular staff in Tehran and other Iranian cities.	The ICJ drew a clear distinction between the legal situation immediately following the seizure of the US embassy and its personnel by the militants and that created by a decree of the Iranian State, which expressly approved and maintained the situation. In the words of the Court: 'The approval given to these facts by the Ayatollah Khomeini and other organs of the Iranian State, and the decision to perpetuate them, translated continuing occupation of the Embassy and detention of the hostages into acts of that State' (para 74).

KEY DEBATES

Topic	Circumstances precluding wrongfulness
Author/academic	AV Lowe
Viewpoint	The author takes the view that the ILC could have characterized the conduct for which circumstances precluding wrongfulness exist as wrongful but excused. This article explores the theoretical differences between those alternatives and, in particular, the distinction between the right of an injured State to waive its entitlement to reparation and the right of an injured State to release other States from their obligation to obey the law. It argues that, even if the creation of international legal obligations is, by virtue of the principle of opposability, an essentially bilateral matter, violation of those obligations engages a wider community interest and is not a matter of concern to the law-breaker and the injured State alone.
Source	'Precluding Wrongfulness or Responsibility: A Plea for Excuses', 10 *European Journal of International Law* (1999) 405

Topic	Countermeasures
Author/academic	LA Sicilianos
Viewpoint	The author critically discusses the ambivalent provision of the ARSIWA concerning the possibility of collective countermeasures (Art 54). The controversies inherent in this chapter concern, on the one hand, the circle of States that are entitled to take such measures and, on the other, the fear that there will be an overlap with the institutional powers of the Security Council under Chapter VII UN Charter.
Source	'Countermeasures in Response to Grave Violations of Obligation Owed to the International Community' in J Crawford et al (eds), *The Law of International Responsibility* (Oxford: Oxford University Press, 2010)

EXAM QUESTIONS

Problem question

State A entered into a bilateral agreement with State B, which provided for the joint exploration and exploitation of resources within their continental shelf. After several years, State A faced an unprecedented and unforeseen economic crisis; its government decided that it should retain, for the survival of its population, the profits from the exploitation of the joint continental shelf. In response, State B, without any warning, froze all the assets of the nationals of State A within its territory; it also forcibly invaded and occupied a small island belonging to State A.

1. Does State A have a right to stop sharing the profits of the joint venture on its continental shelf in light of the economic crisis?
2. Does State B have the right to freeze the assets and to occupy the island of State A?

See the Outline answers section in the end matter for help with this question.

Essay question

Discuss the notion of 'injured State' in the law of international responsibility.

Online Resources

For an outline answer to this essay question, as well as interactive key cases and multiple choice questions, please visit the online resources.

https://www.oup.com/he/bantekas-papastavridis-concentrate5e

10 Peaceful settlement of disputes

THE EXAMINATION

Exam questions will almost certainly revolve around the International Court of Justice (ICJ) and concern the jurisdiction of the Court, the issuance of provisional measures, and intervention by third States. In addition, questions concerning the advisory proceedings of the ICJ, as well as the difference between international adjudication and arbitration, are frequent. Moreover, there may be questions regarding diplomatic means of dispute settlement.

KEY FACTS

- States are obliged to resolve their disputes by peaceful means. The principle of peaceful settlement of disputes, enshrined in **Art 2(3) UN Charter**, is the other side of the coin regarding the prohibition of the use of force in international relations.
- A range of dispute settlement methods have been developed, many of which are enumerated in **Art 33 UN Charter** and the **1982 Manila Declaration**. The basic distinction is that between diplomatic means of settlement (negotiation, mediation, inquiry, and conciliation) and legal means, namely, arbitration and judicial settlement. States, however, are free to choose their own means of dispute settlement, including resorting to regional arrangements or good offices of the United Nations (UN).
- The ICJ, the principal judicial organ of the UN, is a standing court to which States may bring their legal disputes. The Court's jurisdiction is based upon the consent of the parties to the dispute. This consent may be expressed either directly in respect of a specific dispute or in advance of future disputes. The Court is also empowered to provide advisory opinions to UN organs and specialized agencies.

CHAPTER OVERVIEW

Dispute settlement

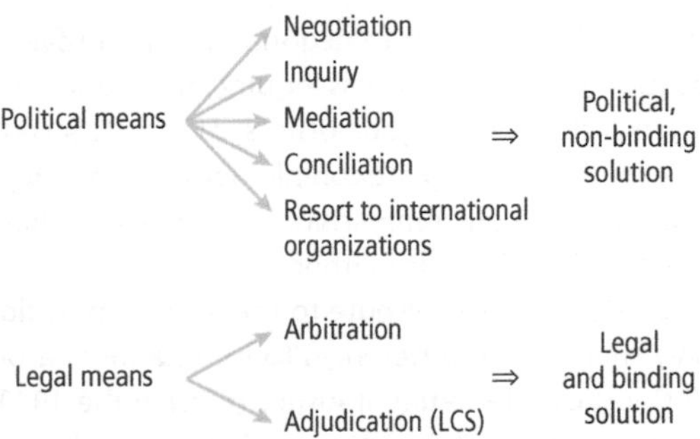

Introduction

The principle that international disputes should be settled by peaceful means, rather than by the use of force, has been the cornerstone of the UN era and is enshrined in Art 2(3) UN Charter. It complements the other fundamental principle of the UN Charter, namely, the prohibition of the use of force under Art 2(4).

These provisions essentially oblige States, whenever a dispute arises amongst them, to endeavour to resolve it peacefully and, in any event, not to use force. They have an obligation of conduct, namely, to try to resolve their disputes through peaceful means. This does not entail an obligation to resolve their disputes. Disputes may well linger without giving rise to the international responsibility of the States concerned.

A 'dispute' under international law is a disagreement on a point of law or fact, typically—but not exclusively—between States, with consequences on the international plane. However, as was affirmed in the judgment of the ICJ in the Preliminary Objections filed by the UK in the *Obligations Concerning Negotiations Relating to Cessation of the Nuclear Arms Race and to Nuclear Disarmament case (Marshal Islands/UK)* (2016), for a '**justiciable** dispute' to exist, it must be shown that the claim of one party is positively opposed by the other (para 37) (see also *South West Africa (Ethiopia v South Africa; Liberia v South Africa)*, Preliminary Objections, Judgment (1962)).

International law sets out various means of dispute settlement, both diplomatic and legal. These are set out in Art 33 UN Charter, as well as in an important resolution of the UN General Assembly, the 1982 Manila Declaration on the Peaceful Settlement of Disputes. There is no hierarchy among these methods and the choice belongs to the disputing States.

In general terms, States initially attempt to negotiate. If this proves unsuccessful, they will try other methods of political resolution, such as inquiry, mediation, or conciliation, as well as resorting to regional organizations or the 'good offices' of the UN Secretary General. These are the political or diplomatic methods, which are complemented by the legal methods, ie arbitration or adjudication by the ICJ. The outcome arising from legal methods is final and binding, whereas this is not the case with diplomatic methods.

Legal methods entail a referral of the dispute to the ICJ or arbitration. Until the twentieth century, States could only submit their differences to international arbitration. The establishment of the Permanent Court of International Justice (PCIJ) in the 1920s and its successor the ICJ in 1945, as the main judicial organ of the UN, provided States with a standing forum for the adjudication of their disputes. This forum, however, is open only to States that have given their consent. This is the most significant difference from national courts, in which the applicant can submit his or her case unilaterally.

The ICJ functions on the basis of a set of detailed rules set out in the UN Charter, the ICJ Statute, and, finally, the Rules of the Court. The Court's decisions are final and binding upon the parties. In the overwhelming majority of the cases, States do comply with the decisions of the Court. If they fail to do so, there is the possibility of the Security Council taking action (Art 94 (2) UN Charter).

Diplomatic methods

Negotiation

Negotiation is the most widely used means of dispute settlement in international law. It is the first diplomatic method that is applied when a dispute arises and it is often the only one if it proves successful. As the ICJ acknowledged in the *Obligation to Negotiate Access to the Pacific Ocean case (Bolivia v Chile)* (2018), there is no self-standing obligation to negotiate; 'States are free to resort to negotiations or put an end to them' (para 86). Since negotiation allows the disputants to retain control of their dispute without involving third parties, it is not surprising that governments find it attractive. Nonetheless, the decision to negotiate is sometimes controversial, as it implies an acknowledgement of the other party's standing and the legitimacy of its claims.

Negotiation is so fundamental that it must not be thought of as only a first stage in the settlement of all disputes, but rather as an option available to parties throughout a dispute. It may exist alongside other processes. For example, in the *Aegean Continental Shelf case (Greece v Turkey)* (1978), the Court indicated that the initiation of negotiations during litigation is not a bar to the exercise of its powers and vice versa.

North Sea Continental Shelf cases (Germany v Denmark/Netherlands), Judgment, ICJ Rep (1969), p 3

The Court decided that, according to customary international law, the delimitation of continental shelf boundaries between neighbouring States must be effected by agreement in accordance with equitable principles. On specifically how the negotiations must be conducted, the Court held that:

> the parties are under an obligation to enter into negotiations with a view to arriving at an agreement; they are under an obligation so to conduct themselves that the negotiations are meaningful, which will not be the case when either of them insists upon its own position without contemplating any modification of it [para 85].

Mediation

When negotiation fails, a third party may be involved upon invitation. If the invitee does no more than encourage the protagonists to resume negotiations, or simply acts as a channel of communication, the role is described as 'good offices'. The mediator is expected to do more, in the sense of being an active participant, authorized to advance fresh ideas and transmit the parties' proposals to each other.

Mediation can only take place if the parties to a dispute consent and a mediator is available. In fact, the UN, especially the Secretary General, and other regional organizations commonly act as 'mediators' or provide 'good offices'. Once mediation has been accepted, the task of the mediator is to devise or promote solutions that are acceptable to both parties. Much can be achieved by simply facilitating communication, especially if the parties are unable to deal with each other directly. This was the case with the Diplomatic Hostages dispute between Iran and the USA in 1980, in which Algeria acted as an intermediary. The success of mediation ultimately depends on the parties' readiness to compromise.

Inquiry

Inquiry relates to the resolution of a disputed issue of fact; it can be a process performed either in the course of another dispute settlement procedure—for example, in the context of arbitration or adjudication—or as a distinct and autonomous fact-finding process. In this case, it will take the form of a specific institutional arrangement, which may be selected in lieu of arbitration or other means. A commission of inquiry will be established to ascertain the conditions under which a specific situation occurred. Such commissions of inquiry were envisaged by the 1899 Hague Convention. They are rarely used in practice and resemble arbitration.

Red Crusader case (1962) 35 ILR 485

A Scottish trawler, the *Red Crusader*, was arrested in 1961 off the coast of the Faroe Islands by Danish authorities. Through the exchange of notes between the governments of the UK and Denmark, a commission of inquiry was set up to investigate the circumstances surrounding the arrest. In addition to written memorials, there was also oral evidence and cross-examination of witnesses. Based on the report of the Commission, the two States decided to waive their claims.

Report of the Secretary General's Panel of Inquiry on the 31 May 2010 Flotilla Incident (September 2011)

A very interesting commission of inquiry was set up by the UN to investigate the events surrounding the interdiction and killing of Turkish activists on board the Turkish-flagged *MV Marmara* by Israeli forces on 31 May 2010. The UN Secretary General established a Panel of Inquiry, which issued its report in September 2011. The report took the view that the blockade of Gaza was legal; however, Israel was found to have used 'excessive and unreasonable' measures in boarding the *MV Marmara*, resulting in 'unacceptable' loss of life.

Conciliation

If mediation is essentially a continuation of negotiation, conciliation is a continuation of mediation in a formal or institutionalized sense. It involves a commission set up by the parties, either on a permanent or an ad hoc basis, which proceeds to an impartial examination of the dispute and proposes settlement terms. However, this settlement will not be binding upon the parties. Although conciliation is regularly included in provisions on dispute settlement, the number of cases in which it has actually been used remains very small (eg *Conciliation Commission on the Continental Shelf Area between Iceland and Jan Mayen: Report and Recommendations to the Governments of Iceland and Norway,* Decision of June 1981 **(1981)** XXVII RIAA 1–34).

REVISION TIP

States are under an obligation to resolve their disputes in a peaceful manner. International law distinguishes between political and legal means. Political means are not binding upon the disputants, who are free to follow the outcome or pursue other means of settlement. Amongst these, the primary role is ascribed to negotiation, which is usually the starting point for any dispute settlement, whereas mediation, conciliation, and inquiry encompass the involvement of a third party. This third party, or the relevant commission, is activated upon the consent of the parties to the dispute.

Legal methods

Arbitration

The origins of arbitration in the modern era can be traced back to the 1794 Jay Treaty between Great Britain and the USA. The parties to a dispute on legal matters set up a tribunal on the basis of international law and agree to treat its decisions as binding. Each party selects one or two members of the arbitral tribunal, while the president of the tribunal, the umpire, is selected by consent, the arbitrators, or the president of the ICJ. States also select the applicable law and other procedural matters and rules, such as the public character of the proceedings.

Frequently, they will resort to an established arbitral institution, such as the Permanent Court of Arbitration (PCA), otherwise it is considered ad hoc.

Arbitration, like conciliation, can be employed when a dispute arises, or can be stipulated in advance in a treaty. Arbitration clauses are found in the dispute settlement provisions of multilateral and bilateral conventions as either an optional or a compulsory procedure and often in combination with other methods. The textbook example is the 1982 UN Convention on the Law of the Sea, which provides for compulsory settlement of disputes and which gives a prominent role to arbitration as the default rule.

Settlement of investment and trade disputes

Investment disputes arise between host States and foreign investors (entities with a nationality different to the host State). While the two parties may settle disputes through national courts and commercial arbitration, investment arbitration is also available, where the dispute in question concerns an 'investment' activity. What constitutes an investment is determined with precision in bilateral investment (BITs) or multilateral investment treaties (MITs). An example of the latter is the North American Free Trade Agreement (NAFTA). An investment may also be defined by domestic law or the parties' agreement. All three (BITs/MITs, domestic laws, and agreements) prescribe when the investor may have recourse to investment arbitration. The most common forum for entertaining investment disputes is the International Centre for the Settlement of Investment Disputes (ICSID), which was set up by the 1967 Washington ICSID Convention. Investment tribunals assess whether the host State has undertaken an unlawful expropriation or violated guarantees afforded to investors under customary law or BITs/MITs. They also assess violations of investment laws and the parties' agreement. For the applicable law, see *Wena Hotels v Egypt* (2002) covered in 'Key cases' in chapter 4. Investment awards are binding and not subject to appeal.

The most popular multilateral international trade/trade liberalization regime is that established under the various World Trade Organization (WTO) agreements. Unlike investment arbitration, disputes concerning the violation of such agreements are inter-State in nature. Three procedures exist, namely: (a) arbitration under Art 25 Dispute Settlement Understanding (DSU), which is rarely applied; (b) arbitration under Art 21 DSU, which concerns whether a 'reasonable period of time' has passed within which States must comply with the rulings and recommendations of a WTO Dispute Settlement Body (DSB), which may lead to a binding decision; and finally (c) the adjudication of complaints by WTO panels and the WTO Appellate Body. The procedures share many commonalities with classical arbitration and option (c) involves an inter-State complaint alleging a breach of an obligation under any of the WTO agreements. If the parties fail to resolve the dispute by consultation, a three-person panel is constituted, whose decision is subject to two forms of review: (a) an appeal to the WTO Appellate Body, whose review power concerns law not facts; and (b) panel and appellate body reports, which are only binding when they are formally adopted by the DSB.

The International Court of Justice

Introduction

The ICJ (or the 'Court') is the 'principal judicial organ' of the UN (Art 92 UN Charter). It is the successor to the PCIJ.

The ICJ is a standing mechanism for the judicial settlement of disputes between States, should they wish to make use of it. **No dispute can be the subject of a decision in the merits unless the disputing parties have consented to the Court's jurisdiction**. Access to the Court is enjoyed by all member States of the UN. It is not open to international organizations or individuals. It is also empowered to provide advisory opinions to questions referred to it by UN organs or other competent agencies. The legal framework of the Court is set out by the UN Charter, the ICJ Statute, and Rules.

Structure and composition

The Court consists of 15 judges, elected by the Security Council and the General Assembly for terms of 9 years. Judges can be re-elected and this is frequent, but care is taken that the membership of the Court is regularly renewed. Judges are elected in their individual capacity and not as representatives of their States and undertake a solemn oath of impartiality in the exercise of their functions. The disqualification or withdrawal of a judge from a case is provided in the ICJ Statute; the most common ground for exclusion is prior involvement in a case, for example, as counsel of a State.

The presence on the bench of a judge with the nationality of one of the parties was not seen as a ground for withdrawal; on the contrary, this ensures that the Court will fully understand the circumstances of the case. Accordingly, the ICJ Statute ensures equality by enabling the other party (ie which does not have a national sitting as judge) to nominate someone as a judge solely for that case, with the title of judge ad hoc. Moreover, in cases where neither party has a judge of its nationality, each party may choose a judge ad hoc.

Procedure

The proceedings in contentious cases are set in motion by the conclusion of an agreement (*compromis*) or by the filing of an application from one State instituting proceedings against another. The proceedings as such are divided as follows: in a first stage, the parties exchange written pleadings (Memorial by the applicant and Counter-Memorial by the respondent, followed by a Reply and a Rejoinder). There then follows a hearing, at which the parties address their arguments to the Court.

Evidence is normally submitted in the form of documents or other forms; witnesses may provide written evidence or appear at the hearing instead. The burden of proof rests with the party alleging the fact or making a claim (*onus probandi incumbit actori*). In line with the principle *iura novit curia* ('the law is known to the Court'), the parties are not required to prove the existence of the rules of international law they invoke. The sources of international law are enumerated in Art 38 ICJ Statute.

Jurisdiction

It has already been emphasized that the jurisdiction of the Court, like that of any international judicial or arbitral body, is based upon the consent of States. Such consent is usually expressed in particular ways. Before enumerating these, it should be recalled that 'only States may be parties to cases before the Court' (Art 38 ICJ Statute). To be a party to a case, a State must also be one of those to which the Court is open under Art 35—that is, parties to the ICJ Statute (and UN members) or non-State parties upon the recommendation of the Security Council.

The Court's jurisdiction is triggered as follows.

Special agreements or 'compromis'

The easiest way for two States that wish to have their dispute settled by the ICJ is for them to express their consent by entering into an agreement to that effect. This is the classic *compromis*, also used in order to submit a case to arbitration. Such an agreement will define the dispute and record the agreement of the parties in accepting the Court's decision as binding. Few cases have been submitted to the Court by *compromis*; one example is *Continental Shelf (Libyan Arab Jamahiriya/Malta)* (1985).

Compromissory clauses

There are numerous cases whereby States have already given their consent to submit future disputes to the Court. This is achieved by concluding a treaty providing that all disputes relating to its interpretation or application may be referred by any party to the Court by a unilateral act. Such a clause, known as a *compromissory clause*, is frequent and is found either in the final clauses of a treaty or optional protocols. The submission to the Court may be preceded by negotiations, but the existence of such a clause suffices as a jurisdictional basis. Compromissory clauses triggered the Court's jurisdiction in *US Diplomatic and Consular Staff in Tehran (US v Iran)* (1980), specifically the Optional Protocol to the 1961 Vienna Convention on Diplomatic Relations. The same instrument was utilized in *Application of the Interim Accord of 13 September 1995 (the former Yugoslavian Republic of Macedonia v Greece)* (2011).

Case Concerning Application of the International Convention on the Elimination of All Forms of Racial Discrimination (Georgia v Russian Federation), Preliminary Objections, Judgment of 1 April 2011
Georgia instituted proceedings against the Russian Federation in respect of a dispute concerning 'actions on and around the territory of Georgia' in breach of the 1965 International Convention on the Elimination of All Forms of Racial Discrimination (CERD). Jurisdiction was claimed on the basis of Art 22 CERD, which contained a compromissory clause. However, the Court upheld the preliminary objections of Russia on the basis that the two disputants had not negotiated prior to the Georgian application, as dictated by Art 22 CERD.

Such contractual consent to the jurisdiction of the Court may be given not only through a *compromissory clause*, but also by a treaty that has been concluded for the purpose of making advance provision for the settlement by the Court of all or some of the disputes that may subsequently arise between the parties. One such treaty was the 1928 General Act for Pacific Settlement of International Disputes, unsuccessfully used in the *Aegean Sea Continental Shelf case* (1978), as well as the 1957 European Convention for the Peaceful Settlement of Disputes, successfully used in *Jurisdictional Immunities of the State (Germany v Italy: Greece intervening)* (2012).

Optional clause

Under Art 36(2) ICJ Statute, a State may deposit with the UN Secretary General a declaration whereby it accepts the jurisdiction of the Court in respect of international legal disputes in relation to any other State accepting the same obligation. States making such declarations accept the jurisdiction of the Court as compulsory. Nonetheless, a reservation to an optional clause declaration is possible. This is linked with the idea of 'reciprocity' enshrined in Art 36(2) ICJ Statute, namely, that the acceptance of jurisdiction is contingent on any other State accepting the *same* obligation. Of the limited group of States that have made such a declaration (around 60), many have appended reservations. The effect of these reservations is that one needs to find the lowest common denominator of the jurisdiction not excluded by reservations on each side and consider whether the particular dispute falls within this. If such a common denominator exists, the Court enjoys jurisdiction.

Reservations to optional clause declarations vary from: (a) *ratione temporis* reservations, ie the Court would have jurisdiction over all disputes arising from a particular date onwards (eg declaration by the former Republic of Yugoslavia in 1999 in *Legality of Use of Force (Yugoslavia v Belgium)* (1999)); (b) *ratione personae* reservations, for example, the 'Commonwealth' reservation excluding disputes among Commonwealth States; and (c) *ratione materiae* reservations, namely, that a State excludes particular disputes from the jurisdiction of the Court (eg declaration of Greece excluding, among others, disputes concerning sovereignty and State boundaries).

Forum prorogatum

As the ICJ affirmed in the very recent Judgment in the *Arbitral Award case (Guyana v Venezuela)* (2020), the parties to a dispute are not bound to express their consent to the Court's jurisdiction in any particular form. Accordingly, international jurisprudence has accepted that the jurisdiction of an international court or tribunal may be broadened by the conduct of parties in the proceedings (*forum prorogatum*). The ICJ, in the *Armed Activities on the Territory of the Congo case* (2005), summarized the relevant jurisprudence on *forum prorogatum* as follows: 'The attitude of the respondent State must . . . be capable of being regarded as "an unequivocal indication" of the desire of that State to accept the Court's jurisdiction in a "voluntary and indisputable' manner"' (see *Corfu Channel case (UK v. Albania, Preliminary Objections* (1948)).

In view of the potential abuse in applications inviting the State named as respondent to consent to jurisdiction simply for the purposes of that particular case, despite the absence of any of the previous jurisdictional bases, a special provision was included in Art 38(5) Rules of the Court: an application of this kind is treated for procedural purposes as ineffective until the consent of the named respondent is expressed in writing. Such means of establishing jurisdiction were used in the case of *Certain Questions of Mutual Assistance in Criminal Matters (Djibouti v France)* (2008).

Jurisdiction and admissibility: preliminary objections

A well-established principle of the law relating to international arbitral and judicial proceedings is that a tribunal or court has power to decide, with binding effect for the parties, any question as to the existence or scope of its own jurisdiction (the principle of *compétence de la compétence* enshrined in Art 36(6) ICJ Statute). The Court must exercise this power in any case in which the existence of its jurisdiction is disputed. It would do so either *proprio motu* or after a 'preliminary objection' raised by the respondent. If the respondent considers that the Court lacks jurisdiction, it may normally raise an objection at an early stage. This may include an objection to the jurisdiction of the Court or to the admissibility of the application, ie whether it would be judicially appropriate for the Court to issue a judgment in that particular case.

Objections against admissibility include: (a) claims that the applicant lacks ***locus standi***, ie absence of a particular legal interest (see, eg *South-Western African cases (Ethiopia/Liberia v South Africa)* (1966)); (b) that local remedies have not been exhausted (eg *Interhandel case* (*Switzerland v USA*) (1959)); (c) that the case is, or has become, 'without object' or moot (eg *Northern Cameroons* (1963)); and (d) that the presence as a party of a third State is essential to the proceedings because its rights or obligations would form the very subject matter of the decision, namely, the *Monetary Gold* principle.

Provisional measures

According to Art 41 ICJ Statute, the Court has 'the power to indicate, if it considers that circumstances so require, any provisional measures which ought to be taken to preserve the respective rights of either party'. For a long time, it was debated whether the measures so indicated created an obligation of respect, binding on the States addressed. This was fuelled by the wording of Art 41, which uses the terms 'indicate' or 'measures to be taken'. The question long remained unsettled. The matter was addressed in the following case:

LaGrand (Germany v USA), Merits, Judgment, ICJ Rep (2001), p 466

The Court decided that the provisional measures addressed to the USA, ie the non-execution of Walter LaGrand, which had not been complied with (the person was executed, despite the provisional measures order of the Court), had created a legal obligation, the breach of which gave rise to a duty of reparation. The Court warranted its conclusion on an interpretation of Art 41 as having been intended to achieve that result (paras 98 et seq).

When dealing with a request for the indication of provisional measures, the Court begins by examining whether there is prima facie jurisdiction, ie the Court has to satisfy itself that the provisions relied on by the applicant appear, prima facie, to afford a basis on which its jurisdiction could be founded. The Court has the power to indicate provisional measures only if there is urgency, in the sense that there is a *real and imminent risk* that irreparable prejudice may be caused to those rights. After ascertaining the existence of that risk, the Court will assess whether the proposed provisional measures are adequate and effective.

This three-stage test sufficed for the Court to order provisional measures. However, recently the Court has added another requirement, namely, that *the rights asserted by a party are at least plausible* and that a link exists between the rights which form the subject of the proceedings before the Court on the merits of the case and the provisional measures being sought (see eg *Certain Activities carried out by Nicaragua in the Border Area (Costa Rica v Nicaragua)* (2011) and *Request for Interpretation of the Judgment concerning the Temple of Preah Vihear (Cambodia v Thailand)* (2011)).

Intervention

On what grounds may a third State be involved in a case in which it is neither respondent nor applicant? The ICJ Statute provides two possibilities: under Art 62, a State may request the Court to permit it to intervene in a pending case if it 'considers that it has an interest of a legal nature that may be affected by the decision in the case', while, under Art 63, it may request to intervene in cases where the subject matter is the interpretation of a treaty to which the requesting State is also a party. The possibility of intervening under Art 63 had been of virtually no use until it came to the fore in *Whaling in the Antarctic (Australia v Japan), Request of New Zealand to intervene* (2013), which concerned an interpretation of Art VIII International Convention for the Regulation of Whaling.

Jurisdictional Immunities of the State (Germany v Italy: Greece Intervening), Judgment of 3 February 2012

The case concerned a dispute originating in the violations allegedly committed by Italy through its judicial practice 'in that it has failed to respect the jurisdictional immunity which Germany enjoys under international law'. Among this judicial practice were the recognition and the declaration of enforceability in Italy of judgments of Greek courts against Germany concerning the reparation for war crimes committed during the German occupation of Greece during World War II. In view of this, Greece requested to intervene pursuant to Art 62, as it had a legal interest in the outcome of the Greek cases in Italy. By an Order of 4 July 2011, the Court authorized Greece to intervene in the case as a non-party, insofar as this intervention was limited to the decisions of Greek courts which were declared by Italian courts as enforceable in Italy.

LOOKING FOR EXTRA MARKS?

What about the enforcement of judgments? What would happen if a State party to a contentious case does not comply with the decision of the Court? The only relevant provision is Art 94(2) UN Charter, stating that 'if any party to a case fails to perform the obligations on it under a judgment . . . the other party may have recourse to the Security Council, which may, if it deems necessary, make recommendations or decide upon measures to be taken to give effect to the judgment'. It is apparent that the Security Council has discretion in respect of enforcement measures, which would, of course, be subject to the veto of its permanent members. Nicaragua actually claimed that the USA had not complied with the 1986 decision of the Court. Nonetheless, the overwhelming majority of States do comply with ICJ decisions.

Revision and interpretation

The judgments of the Court in contentious cases are final, binding on the parties to the case (Art 59 ICJ Statute) and without appeal. Thus, after the Court delivers its judgment the case cannot re-open. This is subject to two limited exceptions. The first is the interpretation that a party may request. Under Art 60 ICJ Statute, in the event of dispute as to the meaning or scope of the judgment, in particular the operative part of it, the Court shall construe it upon the request of any party. Such request was accepted by the Court in *Request for Interpretation of the Judgment Concerning the Temple of Preah Vihear (Cambodia v Thailand)* (2013). The second is the application for revision that a party may submit under the strict circumstances of Art 61 ICJ Statute, namely, when a fact has been discovered which is of such nature as to be a decisive factor for the judgment and which had been unknown to the Court at the time of the judgment. The application for revision must be made at the latest within six months of the discovery of the new fact. This fact, however, should have existed at the time of the judgment, which was not the case in *Application for Revision of the Judgment concerning the Preliminary Objections in the Genocide Case (Yugoslavia v Bosnia-Herzegovina)* (2003), since the crucial 'fact', ie admission to the UN in 2000, was subsequent to the relevant judgment of the Court in 1996.

Advisory proceedings

In addition to settling contentious cases, the Court is empowered to provide advisory opinions. The Court is to give opinions that are advisory and not determinative; the opinion, in principle, does not oblige any State, not even the organ or agency that requested it, to take or refrain from particular action. It merely expresses the view of the Court on a specific legal matter. In practice, the advisory opinions of the Court hold great juridical value as authoritative statements of international law.

Under Art 96(1) UN Charter, the General Assembly or the Security Council may request advisory opinions on any legal question, as well as 'other organs of the United Nations and specialized agencies, which may at any time be so authorized by the General Assembly, may also request advisory opinions of the Court on legal questions arising within the scope of their activities'. Such authorizations have, in fact, been given to the Economic and Social Council (ECOSOC) and other specialized agencies; however, the key fact is that such requests must be relevant to their powers. This became evident in *Legality of the Use by a State of Nuclear Weapons in Armed Conflict* (1996), which involved a request by the World Health Organization (WHO). The Court held that, under the 'principle of speciality', the WHO could not deal with matters beyond what was authorized by its constitution; in the case at hand, this was the legality of the use of nuclear weapons.

REVISION TIP

The ICJ has both the power to settle disputes between States and the power to give advisory opinions to legal questions posed by the organs and specialized agencies of the UN. As regards the power to settle contentious cases, of paramount importance is the prerequisite that States that are party to a dispute should have expressed their consent. This consent, which forms the jurisdiction of the Court, is expressed by the following means: (a) a special agreement; (b) a compromissory clause within a treaty; (c) an optional clause declaration; and (d) *forum prorogatum*. The Court has the inherent power to examine its jurisdiction over a case, as well as the admissibility of the application in question.

KEY CASES

CASE	FACTS	PRINCIPLES
Legal Consequences of the Construction of the Wall in the Occupied Palestine Territory, Advisory Opinion, ICJ Rep (2004), p 136	The Court had to address the following question posed by the General Assembly: 'What are the legal consequences arising from the construction of the wall being built by Israel, the occupying Power?' Due to the increased political character of the subject matter of the request, there were calls that the Court should have abstained from giving an advisory opinion.	The Court held that it could not accept the view that it has no jurisdiction because of the 'political' character of the question posed. The Court considers that because a legal question encompasses political aspects, this 'does not suffice to deprive it of its character as a "legal question" and to "deprive the Court of a competence expressly conferred on it by its Statute", and the Court cannot refuse to admit the legal character of a question which invites it to discharge an essentially judicial task'. Moreover, with regard to the argument concerning the discretionary power to decline to give an advisory opinion, the Court held that the request for an advisory opinion 'represents its participation in the activities of the Organization, and, in principle, should not be refused'.

CASE	FACTS	PRINCIPLES
Monetary Gold Removed from Rome in 1943 (Italy v UK, France and Germany), Judgment, ICJ Rep (1954), p 19	The disputed gold had been removed from Rome by Germany during World War II, but was subsequently found by an arbitrator to have belonged to Albania. Italy and the USA, however, each claimed the disputed gold on the basis of legal claims against Albania.	The Court found that, in order to determine the validity of Italy's claim, it would have to 'determine whether Albania has committed any international wrong against Italy, and thus to decide a dispute between Italy and Albania'. Nonetheless, Albania was not before the Court as a party to the proceedings and had not consented to the dispute being settled by the Court (p 32).

KEY DEBATES

Topic	Intervention of third States
Author/academic	B Bonafé
Viewpoint	The interest of a legal nature is a crucial requirement under Art 62 and the scope of intervention largely depends on the definition of such a requirement. In light of the recent case law of the Court, the author explores the different types of legal interests that could justify permitting a third State to intervene before the ICJ.
Source	'Interests of Legal Nature Justifying Intervention before the ICJ', 25 *Leiden Journal of International Law* (2012) 739–57

Topic	International adjudication
Author/academic	C Brown
Viewpoint	This book makes a significant contribution to understanding the impact of the proliferation of international courts by addressing one important question, namely, whether international courts and tribunals are increasingly adopting common approaches to issues of procedure and remedies. This book's central argument is that there is an increasing commonality in the practice of international courts to the application of rules concerning these issues and that this amounts to the emergence of a common law of international adjudication.
Source	*A Common Law of International Adjudication* (Oxford: Oxford University Press, 2007)

EXAM QUESTIONS

Problem question

State A had concluded a bilateral agreement with State B which provided for the joint exploitation of part of their respective continental shelf. The agreement envisaged the establishment of a joint venture encompassing oil platforms and drilling. However, after a short period, the relationship between the two States deteriorated to the extent that they started threatening each other with the use of armed force. State A decided to denounce the agreement and cease its part of the joint venture. It proceeded to expel all the nationals of State B from its territory. In response, State B initiated proceedings before the ICJ with the claim that State A had violated the bilateral treaty and the prohibition against the threat of the use of force under Art 2(4) UN Charter, as well as the customary law concerning the treatment of its nationals in State A. State B also requested the Court to order provisional measures concerning the cessation of the allegedly illegal acts of State A.

State A declared that it recognizes as compulsory the jurisdiction of the Court under Art 36(2) ICJ Statute in respect of all disputes, save for those that relate to military measures for national defence. State B has made a similar declaration recognizing the jurisdiction of the Court in all disputes, without exception.

1. Does the Court have jurisdiction to hear the present case?
2. Supposing that the Court does have jurisdiction, can it order provisional measures and will State A be obliged to comply with them?

See the Outline answers section in the end matter for help with this question.

Essay question

Discuss the differences between political and legal means of dispute settlement.

Online Resources

For an outline answer to this essay question, as well as interactive key cases and multiple choice questions, please visit the online resources.

https://www.oup.com/he/bantekas-papastavridis-concentrate5e

11

Use of force

THE EXAMINATION

There are some key cases concerning the use of force which you should ensure familiarity with. They are all International Court of Justice (ICJ) cases; namely, the ***Nicaragua case, Oil Platforms***, the ***Nuclear Weapons*** Advisory Opinion, the ***Palestine Wall*** Advisory Opinion, the ***DRC v Uganda case***, and ***Serbia & Montenegro v Belgium (Case Concerning the Legality of Use of Force)***. It is also useful to have a good understanding of the ***Caroline case***. Examination questions will often focus on one of two areas, namely: (a) the prohibition of force and self-defence (**Arts 2(4)** and **51 UN Charter**); and (b) **collective security** and the role of the United Nations Security Council (UNSC) under **Chapter VII UN Charter**.

KEY FACTS

- The law on the use of force concerns the lawful preconditions for the use of armed (military) force by States and the UN through the UNSC. This is regulated in **Arts 2(4)** and **51** and **Chapter VII UN Charter**.
- The UN is the only international body with the power to authorize the use of force, outside cases of self-defence. The UN does not possess its own armed forces and necessarily relies on coalitions willing to contribute their forces.
- Collective security concerns the power of the UNSC to authorize the use of armed force against States or non-State entities, such as pirates.
- States are only entitled to use armed force in situations of self-defence. Self-defence arises only where the target State is under an 'armed attack'. An armed attack is a very significant use of armed force against the target nation.
- Whereas an 'armed attack' is a necessary precondition for self-defence, it is not a precondition in the context of collective security.
- The legality of some types of force is not clear. This is particularly true in respect of **humanitarian intervention**, **pre-emptive self-defence**, **anticipatory self-defence**, and extraterritorial action to save nationals abroad.

CHAPTER OVERVIEW

Rules regarding use of force

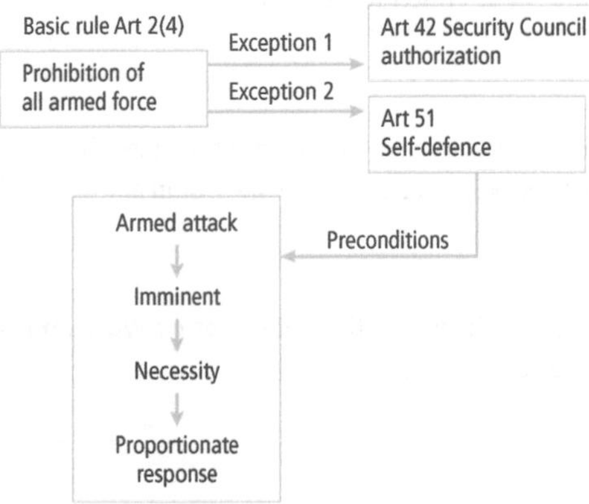

The prohibition of force before 1945

At the end of World War I, in 1918, the international community attempted to limit recourse to war as a means of settling inter-State disputes. Article 12 League of Nations Covenant (the predecessor to the UN) introduced a very weak provision stipulating that, if a dispute arose between two or more nations, they were to seek peaceful settlement, failing which they agreed to a cooling-off period of three months before resorting to war. The Covenant did not prohibit war as a matter of international law and did not impose any kind of liability on aggressor States.

In 1928, the so-called Kellogg–Briand Pact (or Treaty of Paris) was adopted. Although its wording is stronger than the League Covenant, the signatories merely 'condemned recourse to war' and 'renounced it as an instrument of national policy'.

Thus, right up to the beginning of World War II in 1939, recourse to war was not totally prohibited, at least under treaty law. This is confirmed by the fact that various nations prior to 1939 entered into bilateral non-aggression agreements, the majority of which were subsequently violated. At the end of World War II, in 1945, it became apparent that the reorganization of the international community would need to be grounded on an express and concrete prohibition of war and other forms of armed force in order to prevent the proliferation of protracted and destructive international conflicts.

The general prohibition of force in the UN Charter

The principal provision is Art 2(4), which states that:

> UN Charter Art 2(4)
>
> All members shall refrain in their international relations from the threat or use of force against the territorial integrity or political independence of any State, or in any manner inconsistent with the purposes of the United Nations.

This is a 'loaded' provision, which means that each set of words has a deeper meaning than may immediately be apparent.

Threat or use of force

Article 2(4) prohibits all threats to use force, as well as the actual use of force. Threats are now uncommon, but they do still exist. Turkey has issued a long-standing threat to Greece that it will treat any extension of the latter's territorial sea as an act of war. A threat is unlawful, even if it is not followed by armed force.

The term 'force' in Art 2(4) refers to armed or military force and hence does not encompass economic or political sanctions and measures. This is confirmed by the fact that, when the matter was discussed in 1945, the delegates to the UN Charter conference excluded economic sanctions from Art 2(4).

Article 2(4) prohibits all types of armed force, from the lowest-intensity skirmishes to the highest-intensity armed conflicts. The rationale is that, by containing even the slightest potential for military force, the international community is preventing the potential for an escalation of conflict.

Against the territorial integrity or political independence of other States

Since all instances of armed force are prohibited, the cause for which they are undertaken (save for self-defence) is irrelevant. Military force is illegal, even if it is not aimed at disrupting the territorial integrity or political independence of other nations. In the *Corfu Channel case (Albania v UK)* (1949), a British warship entered Albanian waters with the aim of removing mines that impeded international navigation and which had earlier been responsible for the destruction of passing British ships. The removal of the mines was undertaken without Albanian approval. The British government argued that it had not violated Art 2(4) because its actions intended to remove the mines and had no effect on the territorial integrity or political

REVISION TIP

Article 2(4) UN Charter prohibits all types of armed force, from the slightest (ie removal of mines) to the most severe. It does not encompass economic or political sanctions. However, some authors, such as Dinstein and Brownlie, have argued that 'armed force' requires the use of a weapon that causes physical damage. This, of course, goes against the *Corfu Channel* judgment.

LOOKING FOR EXTRA MARKS?

The unilateral imposition of political and economic measures or sanctions is prohibited under customary international law, save for lawful countermeasures. This is attested to in UN General Assembly (UNGA) Resolution 2625 (XXV) of 24 October 1970. This is one of the most important resolutions adopted by the UNGA and is known as the Friendly Relations Declaration. It is generally agreed that it represents customary international law. The very essence of the declaration is that all kinds of external interference in the domestic affairs of other nations are prohibited. The rule against **non-interference** is stipulated in Art 2(7) UN Charter. The only exception to this rule concerns actions and interventions authorized or undertaken by the UNSC acting under Chapter VII UN Charter.

independence of Albania. The ICJ disagreed, holding that a violation of Albanian territorial integrity had taken place, irrespective of whether the action was temporary and had limited objectives.

This also means that unilateral actions (ie action not authorized by the UNSC) with the aim of restoring democracy or for the purposes of regime change constitute violations of Art 2(4).

Exceptions to the prohibition of force

- Use of force in self-defence.
- Authorization of armed force by the UNSC, also known as collective security.

Self-defence

Self-defence is regulated under customary international law, as well as under Art 51 UN Charter. This is another loaded provision, which we shall explain in more detail. It reads:

Article 51 UN Charter

Nothing in the present Charter shall impair the inherent right of individual or collective self-defence if an armed attack occurs against a member of the United Nations, until the Security Council has taken measures necessary to maintain international peace and security.

Key terms in this Article are *'inherent right'*, *'armed attack'*, and *'occurs'*. Another issue that has traditionally been taken for granted in Art 51, but which is now in dispute, is whether non-State actors, particularly terrorists, can (in strict legal terms) commit an armed attack.

The meaning of 'armed attack'

This term is not defined. However, given that Art 2(4) prohibits even the slightest use of armed force, it is assumed that, in order for a State to be entitled to respond with force against an armed attack, the attack must be of considerable gravity. If the attack is not of considerable gravity, then the defending State does not have the right to use armed force in retaliation and must employ peaceful methods. The French version of Art 2(4) speaks of *'aggression armée'*, which raises the question whether aggression and armed attack are in fact synonymous. UNGA Resolution 3314 (1974) provides a definition of aggression.

USA v Nicaragua (Military and Paramilitary Activities in and against Nicaragua or Nicaragua case), ICJ Rep (1986), p 14

The ICJ distinguished between the 'most grave forms' (ie armed attacks) and 'less grave forms' of the use of force on the basis of the UN Declaration on Friendly Relations. An 'armed attack' was found to encompass 'certain scale and effects', which was distinguishable from a 'mere frontier incident'.

In this case, the ICJ provided an indication of its 'scale and effects' test, as follows:

> not merely action by regular armed forces across an international border, but also the sending by or on behalf of a State of armed bands, groups, irregulars or mercenaries, which carry out acts of armed force against another State of such gravity as to amount to an actual armed attack conducted by regular forces, or its substantial involvement therein.

The mere provision of assistance or logistical support to rebels (eg arms supply, financial and logistical support) by a third State was not found by the ICJ to constitute an armed attack, but may be considered as a threat of force or otherwise a form of unlawful intervention.

Iran v USA (Oil Platforms case), ICJ Rep (2003), p 161

In a later case, US warships attacked Iranian commercial oil installations as a response to an alleged armed attack by Iran. This alleged armed attack consisted of laying sea mines and the firing of missiles against commercial vessels flying a US flag. The ICJ was asked to decide whether a single attack against a warship amounted to an armed attack and whether cumulative, but small, incidents of armed force also amount to an armed attack.

With regard to the first question, the Court did 'not exclude the possibility that the mining of a single military vessel might be sufficient to bring into play the inherent right of self-defence', but the matter will depend on the existence of appropriate gravity and attribution. As to the *accumulation approach*, although the ICJ did not directly address its validity, its judgment does suggest that it is not hostile to the idea if appropriate cases arise in the future.

Proportionality and necessity

When an armed attack takes place, the response of the defending State is not unlimited. Article 51 does not address what is an appropriate response to an armed attack. This is regulated by customary law and encompasses the principles of proportionality and necessity (the latter may also be viewed as an element of proportionality). Self-defence must be proportionate to the armed attack. This does not mean that it must necessarily be the same. It should be of such gravity as to dissuade the attacking State and prevent any further strikes. Proportionality is therefore assessed on a case-by-case basis. Necessity refers to the measures adopted for self-defence. These must be necessary to respond to the armed attack (Advisory Opinion on *Legality of the Threat or Use of Nuclear Weapons* (1996)). For example, the aerial bombardment of heavily populated cities is both disproportionate and unnecessary as a response to an exchange of fire between two naval warships on the high seas. In *DRC v Congo* (2005), the ICJ held that targets deep in the aggressor's territory cannot be 'necessary' or 'proportionate' as a response to an initial transborder attack.

In each case, the defending state has the burden of proof to demonstrate that the target of its defensive force committed the initial armed attack (*Oil Platforms case*).

The *Caroline* case

In 1837, Britain was (and remains) the sovereign of Canada. The steamship *Caroline* was used by Canadian rebels in the USA to send troops and arms into Canada to fight the British. At the time of the incident, it was moored in US waters, where the British army destroyed it, killed its crew, and sent the boat over the Niagara Falls. The case never went to court or international arbitration and was instead negotiated (although perhaps not resolved) through an exchange of letters between the US and British foreign ministers. The letter of the US Secretary of State is cited as the definitive statement on necessity and implicitly on the right of anticipatory self-defence. He stipulated that necessity must be:

> instant, leaving no choice of means, and no moment for deliberation . . . It must be [shown] that admonition or remonstrance to the persons on board the Caroline was impracticable, or would have been unavailing . . . but that there was a necessity, present and inevitable, for attacking her, in the darkness of the night, while moored to the shore, and while unarmed men were asleep on board . . .

Inherent right of individual or collective self-defence

The term 'inherent' signifies that pre-UN Charter customary law pertinent to self-defence continues to apply following the adoption of the UN Charter. The problem is that certain pre-UN Charter justifications for self-defence are incompatible with the high-gravity threshold for an armed attack established by Art 51. For example, prior to 1945, it was lawful to use armed force as a reprisal against what might have been a small-scale attack. A reprisal is a limited and intentional violation of international law in order to 'punish' another state for its prior violation of said law. Reprisals involving armed force are no longer permitted under Art 51. Two schools of thought have emerged on the issue. The restrictive school (Brownlie and Franck) renders the threshold of armed attacks the only yardstick, thus restricting the application of self-defence. The expansive school (Bowett and Reisman) takes the opposite view by relying on pre-UN Charter practices as being valid today. The likelihood of complementary or equal rules in both treaty and customary law on the use of force was emphasized in approval by the ICJ in its *Nicaragua* judgment, paras 183–201.

These pre-UN Charter practices, although it is by no means clear that they ever constituted customary law, include: anticipatory self-defence (ie use of force in anticipation of an imminent or anticipated armed attack); humanitarian intervention; armed force to rescue nationals abroad; reprisals; and pre-emptive force against an enemy that is preparing to strike, although said strike is not necessarily imminent but rather remote.

Self-defence is primarily individual, ie by one State against another. Article 51, however, allows collective instances of self-defence. This includes armed responses to an armed attack by more than one nation against the aggressor. In order for collective self-defence to be lawful, it is required that: (a) the target country is indeed under an armed attack; (b) its government has specifically called other States to its assistance; (c) the assisting States have consented; and (d) their response is proportionate and necessary.

The timing of self-defence

The verb 'occurs' in Art 51 seems to suggest that self-defence is lawful only after an armed attack (or an accumulation of smaller attacks) has taken place. As a result, pre-emptive force would be unlawful because the threat is remote. Where the threat is imminent, however, a good number of nations, particularly Israel and the USA, argue that it is absurd to wait for the enemy to strike first when there is ample evidence that it is preparing to attack. They have used this argument to justify defensive action against States that are in the process of building up their nuclear arsenal, as is the case with Iran and North Korea, but such cases are best described as pre-emptive defence, rather than anticipatory. We have already explained that the *Caroline case* is employed to demonstrate that anticipatory self-defence has traditionally been recognized under customary international law. This is not the case for pre-emptive self-defence because the right to self-defence arises only in response to an *existing* armed attack and its purpose is, or must be, to promptly put an end to said attack. In the absence of an attack, force is not necessary.

LOOKING FOR EXTRA MARKS?

Besides Art 51, self-defence exists also under customary law. This was amply explained by the ICJ in the *Nicaragua case*. The two sources carry the same normative value, ie no hierarchy of sources exists. Scholars argue for a broader customary self-defence, but the ICJ has only employed the customary nature of self-defence to complement and further narrow Art 51.

Can non-State actors commit an armed attack and can States lawfully use force under self-defence?

In 1945, the drafters of the UN Charter clearly did not envisage that entities other than States would be physically capable of carrying out anything close to an armed attack against States. The terrorist operations of 9/11 in 2001 seem to have changed the dynamics of the law of self-defence. In the aftermath of 9/11, the UNSC adopted Resolution 1368 (2001), which linked the right of self-defence to terrorism and threats to international peace and security. Implicitly, this seems to suggest that an operation of the scale and the number of victims inflicted by the 9/11 terrorist attacks will meet the criteria of armed attack under Art 51.

Commentators, although not dismissing this line of thinking, have identified some serious practical problems. The most poignant concerns proportionality and necessity. Terrorist attacks, large or small, raise the issue of possible attribution to the State wherein they operate, particularly if the latter is capable of exercising due diligence and preventive action, as well as the reaction of the target State in a manner that does not violate the sovereignty of the country from which the attack originated. Whatever the answer to this question, one should not forget that in the *Caroline case* the incident which gave rise to the self-defence claim was committed by a rebel group, ie a non-State actor. Thus, it may be assumed that under customary or natural law (expressed by the word 'inherent'), non-State actors have traditionally been deemed capable of committing an armed attack (see chapter 9 'State responsibility' for a discussion of attribution to a State of acts undertaken by non-State actors). Overall, it should be stressed that, in accordance with Art 4 ILC Articles on State Responsibility, the conduct of non-State actors may, under certain conditions, be attributable to a State and if such conduct amounts to an 'armed attack', then the defending State may use force in self-defence against the attributable State (*Nicaragua case* (1986) and *DRC v Uganda* (2005)). Where terrorist action is not attributable to a State, then self-defence should be limited against the non-State actors, with as little interference as possible to the sovereignty of the State from which it is operating.

Legal Consequences of the Construction of a Wall in the Occupied Palestinian Territory (*Palestinian Wall*), Advisory Opinion, ICJ Rep (2004), p 136

Israel justified the construction of a wall to prevent Palestinians from occupied territories freely entering its territory on security grounds. Palestine is not formally recognized by all countries as a State and any attacks against Israel come from groups of individuals engaged in a war of liberation or terrorism. The ICJ admitted that terrorist attacks of the gravity and nature encompassed under SC Resolution 1368 and originating outside the attacked country give rise to a right of self-defence. In the case at hand, the threat originates from territory occupied by Israel given the latter's occupation of Palestine and therefore Art 51 UN Charter is inapplicable.

The requirement to inform the Security Council

The relevant part of Art 51 is somewhat misleading. The right of self-defence is by no means dependent on informing the UNSC and waiting for it to take action first. It is an independent entitlement. However, once the UNSC undertakes military measures itself and specifically demands that the target State terminate its defensive action, in theory the target State must terminate such action. In practice, the UNSC's measures may be deemed inadequate by the defending State, in which case it can choose to ignore the UNSC's demands, but risk violating the UNSC's express terms.

Collective security

Collective security refers to the power of the UNSC to authorize the use of armed force and actions below the use of force (eg sanctions) against States that threaten international peace and security, as well as to demand that a target State cease its defensive action. Collective security is different from the right of collective self-defence in Art 51 because the latter refers to a decentralized process, whereas collective security is centralized and institutional (ie it depends on UNSC approval). It is merely an expression of individual self-defence undertaken by more than one nation acting together (separate opinions of Judges Higgins, Buergenthal, Kooijmans, and Simma in *Palestine Wall* **Advisory Opinion** and ***DRC v Uganda* (2005)**.

However, collective security does not only concern the use of armed force by the UNSC. Rather, it generally concerns the UNSC's principal mandate and power to maintain and restore international peace and security. This may well entail action that falls short of the use of armed force, as well as measures intended to restore peace and justice to a country that has emerged from a war. Given that the UN does not possess a standing army, collective security also involves delicate questions of authorizing other actors, namely, States and coalitions thereof, to maintain international peace and security on behalf of the UNSC.

Collective security is principally contained in Chapter VII UN Charter, whereas Chapter VIII discusses regional arrangements which the Council may use to respond to threats or breaches of the peace. The key provisions in Chapter VII are Arts 39, 41, and 42.

Measures not involving the use of armed force

The UNSC is charged with primary authority—above other States and international organizations—to determine the 'existence of any threat to the peace, breach of the peace, or act of aggression' and accordingly make recommendations and decide what measures are to be taken to maintain and restore international peace and security (Art 39). The UNSC is thus charged with an important preventative role. Whereas traditionally, the UNSC has considered threats to the peace to primarily arise from inter-State conflicts, since the end of the Cold War and beginning with the conflict in the former Yugoslavia, it has made it clear that international peace and security are equally threatened by internal conflicts and gross human rights violations (SC Resolution 827 (1993)). This is important because such an interpretation expands the ambit of Art 2(7) UN Charter, which would not otherwise permit the UNSC to intervene in the internal affairs of a country if said affairs did not also threaten international peace and security.

Once the UNSC determines the existence of a threat or a breach under Art 39, it will seek a peaceful solution with the parties concerned, by means of negotiation, mediation, adjudication, or other. If the situation persists, it may then impose measures not involving the use of armed force, such as interruption of communications, embargoes, severance of diplomatic relations, sanctions, and others, in accordance with Art 41. The list of measures in Art 41 is merely indicative, not exhaustive. If these measures are of no avail, the UNSC may then authorize the use of armed force under Art 42. Chapter VII does not establish an obligatory sequence between Arts 41 and 42. As a result, the SC may impose measures under Art 42 without first exploring action not involving the use of armed force, although this is unlikely in practice.

REVISION TIP

Resolution 827 (1993), which set up the International Criminal Tribunal for the former Yugoslavia (ICTY) was implicitly based on Art 41 UN Charter.

LOOKING FOR EXTRA MARKS?

The imposition of naval or other blockades and sanctions, although strictly encompassed under Art 41, requires, in most cases, an element of force against those who attempt to violate them. This may be implicit or explicit in the relevant resolutions and hence these measures are known informally as Art 41-and-a-half measures.

The authorization of armed force by the Security Council

Article 42 does not mention the term 'armed force'. In fact, all relevant UNSC resolutions refrain from using this term altogether and do not even cite Art 42 as their basis. Instead, the UNSC authorizes the use of 'all necessary means' in place of 'armed force' in all its resolutions, grounding said authorization on Chapter VII UN Charter, rather than Art 42 thereof. Although resolutions authorizing the use of armed force are clearly more important than resolutions on other matters, they are adopted with the same majority (ie all UNSC permanent members, in addition to the four non-permanent members).

Although the language is the same in all resolutions (ie 'use all necessary means'), the mandate in each resolution may, in fact, be very different. Resolution 794 (1992) authorized nations making up the UN Mission to Somalia (UNOSOM) to use all necessary means to ensure a secure environment for humanitarian relief operations. Resolution 1816 (2008) authorized States to employ force in order to deter and prevent piracy off the coast of Somalia. Resolution 678 (1990), on the other hand, authorized States participating in the liberation of Kuwait to use all necessary means to not only restore Kuwaiti sovereignty, but moreover to 'restore international peace and security in the region'. The mandates in the three resolutions differ significantly geographically, spatially, and quantitatively. It should have become clear from the analysis that the UNSC may authorize States to employ force also against non-State actors, whether these are collaborating with States or not. Besides Somali pirates, the SC in Resolution 2240 (2015) authorized the interception of vessels by non-flag States in order to stem the practice of human trafficking and smuggling.

Delegation of collective security

Although Chapter VII originally envisaged the contribution of troops under the military authority of the UNSC (Art 43), this never materialized. Moreover, there is nothing in the UN Charter that suggests that the UNSC can oblige member States to use armed force. This is only undertaken voluntarily. In practice, the country that tables a resolution of this nature, typically a permanent member of the UNSC, will have already assembled a coalition of willing States.

Given that the UNSC is physically unable to undertake enforcement action, it delegates this function. Chapter VIII UN Charter envisages delegation to regional organizations dealing with peaceful settlement, as would be the case with the Economic Community of West African States (ECOWAS) or the African Union (AU). Any operations undertaken as a result remain under the authority of the UNSC and require an express mandate by it. The UNSC may retract its mandate at any time.

Besides regional organizations, enforcement action may be delegated to informal alliances or coalitions of like-minded States. Although the military units that make up these coalitions answer to their national authorities, they are nonetheless under unified command and control and the mandate of the coalition is prescribed by the terms of the UNSC's resolution. Coalitions of this nature include those that participated in the liberation of Kuwait in 1990 and the deposition of the Iraqi regime in 2003.

Collective security against Iraq: 1990 and 2003

Following the invasion of Kuwait by Iraq in 1990, the UNSC adopted a series of resolutions encompassing non-forcible measures. These did not deter Iraq and so the UNSC adopted Resolution 678 (1990), which authorized a coalition to liberate Kuwait in order to 'restore international peace and security in the region'. This latter part of the mandate is very broad because it does not have a termination date and the security of the entire region may be interpreted to include States other than Iraq. As a result, Resolution 678 was used by the coalition for over a decade to establish no-fly zones and to justify anew the invasion of Iraq in 2003. Another justification for the 2003 invasion was the alleged failure of Iraq to comply with the SC's nuclear disarmament demands (Resolution 1441 (2002)).

Collective security without the Council: the doctrine of implied authorization

Collective security without the UNSC's express permission cannot exist. Yet, certain powerful nations have argued that, where a country consistently fails to ensure the maintenance of peace in material breach of UNSC resolutions, there is an implied authorization to use all necessary means to compel that country to comply with its international obligations. Resolution 1441 (2002) was one of the bases for implied authorization in the campaign against Iraq in 2003. This resolution called for a 'final opportunity to comply'. The doctrine is not supported in the majority of scholarly writings and was rejected by those countries sitting in the UNSC that would have refused to adopt a resolution authorizing the use of force in the particular case.

UNSC Resolution 2249 and 'unable or unwilling'

Paragraph 5 UNSC Resolution 2249 (2015) authorized UN member States to 'take all necessary measures' to prevent and suppress terrorist acts committed by Islamic State (IS) and associated entities in Syria and Iraq. UNSC resolutions authorizing collective security are explicitly adopted under Chapter VII UN Charter and use the phrase 'all necessary means'. This is not the case with Resolution 2249 and this is largely the result of the permanent UNSC members' varying interests in the ongoing conflict. Russia relies, for its intervention, on an invitation by the incumbent Syrian government, and the US-led coalition equally relies on consent from Iraq. External intervention in Syria has been justified on the basis of additional debatable arguments. The USA, Canada, Australia, and Turkey have introduced the so-called 'unable-or-unwilling' test, which posits that, when the government of the State where the threat is located is unwilling or unable to prevent the use of its territory for such attacks, then other States may use force against terrorists as a matter of self-defence under Art 51. Deeks (2012) suggests that an appropriate test may be ascertained by reference to customary law. In the case at hand, self-defence under the 'unable-or-unwilling' test arises because IS undertakes attacks against the aforementioned countries or against their allies (eg Iraq) (Letter by the US Permanent Representative to the UN, UN Doc S/2014/695 (2014)). The UK, Germany, and France, on the other hand, rely for their interventions on broad interpretations of self-defence.

LOOKING FOR EXTRA MARKS?

In 1990, the military coalition acting for the liberation of Kuwait could have relied on collective self-defence under Art 51 and taken action sooner. Instead, it waited for a UNSC authorization because the USA wanted the broad mandate of Resolution 678, which it was not entitled to under the terms of collective self-defence.

Humanitarian intervention

Humanitarian intervention (HI) involves the use of military force by one or more States against another State violating the human rights of its people on a gross and systematic scale. Modern examples include the invasion of East Pakistan (now Bangladesh) by India in 1971 and that of the North Atlantic Treaty Organization (NATO) against Yugoslavia in 1999 in respect of the latter's alleged repression of its Kosovar minority. HI does not find a legal basis in the UN Charter. Thus, a precondition for lawful use of force for humanitarian purposes is the authorization of the UNSC. In *Serbia v Belgium (Case Concerning the Legality of Use of Force)* (2004), involving the legality of the NATO bombing of Serbia, Belgium was the only NATO member that pleaded HI. Even so, and irrespective of the emergence of the global political responsibility to protect, (R2P 2005), several authors, such as Téson, argue that HI does, in fact, find support in state practice, even if superpowers do not make it available to all States.

Responsibility to protect (R2P)

R2P was initially coined by scholars. Because of the legal and moral ambiguity surrounding HI, the UNGA endorsed it. It rests on three pillars:

1. Every State has a primary responsibility to protect its people from mass atrocity crimes.
2. The international community is responsible for assisting States to protect their people.
3. If the target State manifestly fails to protect its people, the international community may assume that role and take collective action involving the use of force in conformity with the UN Charter.

R2P was endorsed in the 2005 World Summit Outcome Document, adopted as GA Resolution 60/1 (2005). The difference is that unlike HI, R2P has been delineated and endorsed at UN level and hence lacks arbitrariness. Moreover, R2P requires authorization by the UNSC. The key difference is that R2P is significantly broader and encompasses non-forcible means. In the course of the 2011 Libyan uprising, the UNSC adopted Resolution 1973 (2011), which specifically invoked the principles underlying R2P. This does not mean, however, that R2P is free of ambiguity, and several critics argue that it is an attempt to legitimize otherwise forbidden interventions for purposes that are foreign to the values underpinning R2P and which rather serve the interests of individual States.

LOOKING FOR EXTRA MARKS?

Article 4(h) African Union's Constitutive Act stipulates that the AU may intervene in a State in Africa pursuant to a decision of its Assembly 'in respect of grave circumstances, namely: genocide, war crimes and crimes against humanity'. This is an exceptional provision that is inconsistent with Chapter VII UN Charter, but it is argued that it constitutes a reflection of the R2P principle in a regional context.

KEY CASES

CASE	FACTS	PRINCIPLES
Advisory Opinion on Legality of the Threat or Use of Nuclear Weapons, ICJ Rep (1996), p 226	The UN and the WHO requested an advisory opinion from the ICJ as to whether the threat or use of nuclear weapons would in any circumstance be permitted under international law.	The ICJ's opinion is not entirely clear. What is clear is that the use of nuclear weapons other than for self-defence is always unlawful. However, under treaty and customary law it is not unlawful to possess nuclear weapons. The Court noted that nuclear weapons are incapable of discriminating between military and civilian objectives and, as such, are contrary to the laws of war. Nonetheless, in urgent situations where the very existence of a nation is under threat from a nuclear attack, the use of similar weapons as a means of self-defence may not be unlawful. The opinion has been criticized because it approached its subject matter from a very legalistic viewpoint.
USA v Nicaragua (Military and Paramilitary Activities in and against Nicaragua or Nicaragua case), ICJ Rep (1986), p 14	Nicaragua claimed that the USA had financed and supplied arms to a rebel group, the *contras*, in order to launch attacks against its legitimate government. It also claimed that US agents had trained the *contras*. The USA argued that it was merely acting in collective self-defence in favour of Nicaragua's three neighbouring States, which Nicaragua had attacked. The basic question before the Court, for the purposes of this chapter, was whether this level of assistance amounted to an armed attack.	The Court's assessment as to the criteria for an armed attack was provided earlier in the chapter ('The meaning of armed attack'). In relation to the specific circumstances of this case, the ICJ held that the mere delivery of assistance to rebels in the form of weapons or logistical support does not amount to an armed attack. This was in line with the Court's requirement of gravity, which is essential for an attack to be classified as an armed attack. This gravity test seems to have been slightly watered down in the ***Oil Platforms* case**.

KEY DEBATES

Topic	Use of force in modern contexts
Author/academic	UN and other documents
Viewpoint	Modern debates focus on use of force and cyber-war/aggression (Tallinn Manual); use of force by private military companies (Montreux document); use of force by peacekeeping operations (and the Brahimi report); and the implications of the Bush doctrine (2002 United States National Security Strategy document).
Source	www.icrc.org/eng/assets/files/other/icrc_002_0996.pdf; www.un.org/en/events/pastevents/brahimi_report.shtml

EXAM QUESTIONS

Problem question

Country X was experiencing a civil conflict on its territory with an ethnic minority that sought independence. The minority received logistical support and arms from country Y, whose army, however, never entered the territory of X and did not control the military operations of the minority. Critically examine the following issues:

1. Does country X possess the right to self-defence under Art 51 against country Y?
2. Would the SC be entitled to regulate the civil conflict, assuming that country Y did not provide any support to the minority?
3. If country X had sufficient and credible information that neighbouring country XX was preparing to make a land invasion against it, would it be entitled to use military force against XX as a means of pre-emptive self-defence?

See the Outline answers section in the end matter for help with this question.

Essay question

What does the term 'armed attack' encompass under Art 51 UN Charter?

Online Resources

For an outline answer to this essay question, as well as interactive key cases and multiple-choice questions, please visit the online resources.

https://www.oup.com/he/bantekas-papastavridis-concentrate5e

Human rights and humanitarian law

12

THE EXAMINATION

Typically, exam questions in this field avoid theoretical issues involving the philosophical nature of rights and focus generally on how rights are construed and implemented by the international community. Themes such as **cultural relativism** versus **universalism, indivisibility,** interdependence, and **progressive realization**, however, are often mentioned. Equally, questions about individual complaint mechanisms are frequent, particularly the European Court of Human Rights (ECtHR) and **UN Charter**-based mechanisms, as well as their general admissibility criteria.

KEY FACTS

- The key human rights provisions in the **UN Charter** are **Arts 1(3), 55, 56, 62**, and **103**. Note that these carry few, if any, obligations for UN member States. The language they employ is mostly aspirational and framed in non-obligatory terms. Nonetheless, their importance cannot be underestimated, as they clearly suggest that the protection of human rights is a means of achieving international peace and security.
- Only States are burdened with human rights obligations against rights-holders (ie individuals and legal persons). Individuals/natural persons, including terrorists and multinational corporations, do not possess human rights obligations, although a small number of cases argue otherwise. Rather, if they are responsible for the killing or torture of another person, they are liable under ordinary criminal law.
- The ECtHR was established not by the European Union (EU), but by the Council of Europe. The Court enforces the **European Convention on Human Rights and Fundamental Freedoms (ECHR)** and its additional protocols.
- For ordinary people to enjoy international human rights, the relevant treaties in which these rights are embodied must first be implemented in domestic law and subjected to the jurisdiction of local courts. When implemented, the addressees of rights acquire legal standing (*locus standi*) to bring claims and local courts assume jurisdiction.
- The (UN) Bill of Rights is composed of three instruments: the **1948 Universal Declaration of Human Rights (UDHR)** (which is not a treaty, but a resolution of the UN General Assembly), the **1966 International Covenant on Civil and Political Rights (ICCPR)**, and the **1966 International Covenant on Economic, Social and Cultural Rights (ICESCR)**. The **ICCPR** and **ICESCR** are multilateral treaties.
- Charter-based mechanisms receive their mandate directly from the **UN Charter** or its principal organs. The most important **UN Charter**-based mechanism is the Human Rights Council, although both the United Nations General Assembly (UNGA) and the United Nations Security Council (UNSC) undertake significant human rights work. Charter-based mechanisms are generally distinguished from human rights treaty bodies. The latter are quasi-judicial entities that monitor and enforce the provisions of the pertinent human rights treaties that establish them, such as the **ICCPR**.
- International humanitarian law (IHL) (known also as laws of war or *jus in bello*) is applicable only when an armed conflict is deemed to have commenced and during such time as it persists. It does not apply in times of peace. There, general international human rights law usually regulates the conduct of States.

CHAPTER OVERVIEW

Brief overview of global human rights institutions

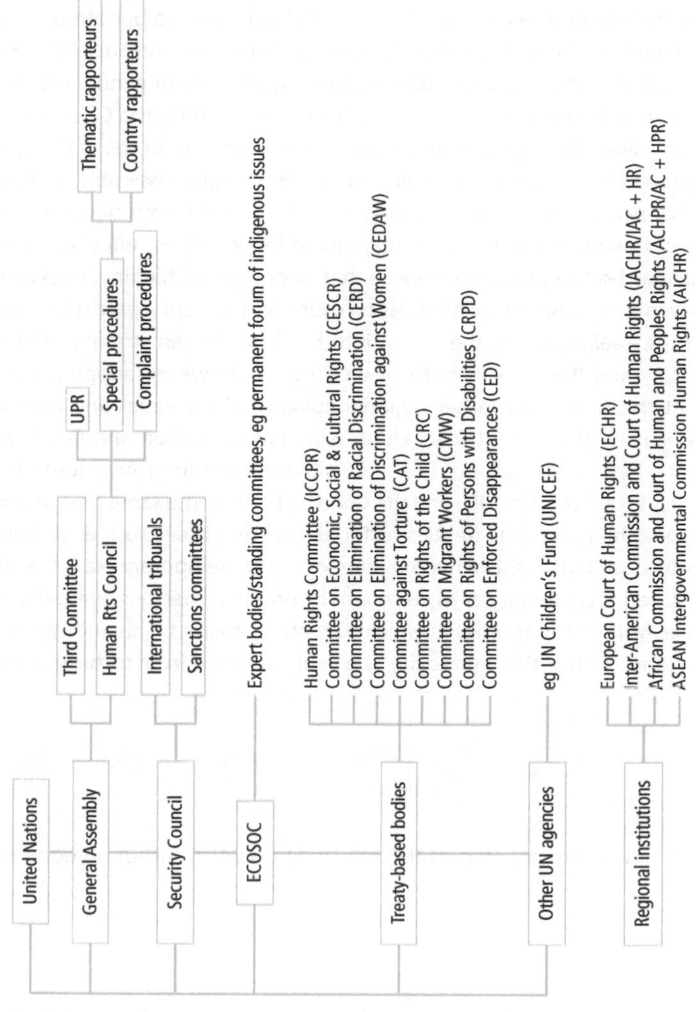

Origins of human rights

The contemporary manifestation of human rights starts with the adoption of the UN Charter, which is an international treaty. The obligations addressed to States therein use very weak language, such as 'promote' and 'cooperate', in the pursuit of human rights (Arts 55 and 56). This clearly suggests that the drafters of the UN Charter did not aspire to burdensome human rights obligations at the international level. Nonetheless, the Economic and Social Council (ECOSOC), a principal organ of the UN, whose mandate involves making recommendations for the promotion and protection of human rights (Art 62(2)), immediately set up the Commission on Human Rights. The Commission, although a political body, was responsible for the drafting of the UDHR, which was approved by means of a resolution by the General Assembly in 1948. Although General Assembly resolutions are not binding, the UDHR is still considered an instrument of immense legal and political value and the majority of its provisions reflect customary law. The UDHR was a **standard-setting** tool, in the sense that, although not binding, it sets out a platform for future achievement without placing stress on countries to adopt a particular treaty.

Attempts at the realization of the UDHR into hard law began straight after its adoption through the ICCPR and the ICESCR, both of which were, however, adopted almost 20 years later, in 1966. At the same time, other regional human rights treaties and institutions began to emerge, particularly the ECHR (1950), along with its Commission and Court, and later the American Convention on Human Rights (1969), although the Inter-American Commission on Human Rights was established in 1959 and the Court in 1979. At the same time, many specialized regional and global human rights treaties surfaced, covering issues such as children, racial discrimination, torture, and others. The main feature of the contemporary era is that those human rights acknowledged as customary or as *jus cogens* belong to all persons, irrespective of whether one's country has ratified the treaties in which they are contained. This encompasses all fundamental human rights, such as the right to life, the right to be free from torture, and many others.

The nature and qualities of international human rights

Human rights are meant to encompass the following qualities, although none are free from difficulty.

Indivisibility

This is based on the idea that there exists no hierarchy among rights and that none are more important than others. If a formal hierarchy were put in place, then policymakers would, in principle, be free to choose the implementation of one right over another and thus justify the violation of other rights.

Interdependence

This follows from indivisibility and underlines the fact that no right is realizable in isolation from others. For example, the right to self-determination requires the freedom to elect, a certain degree of education, freedom of expression, and others.

Universalism versus cultural relativism

Human rights apply to all people and are enjoyed by all under the same terms ('everyone shall . . .'). This is in contrast to the antithetical notion of *cultural relativism*, which posits that rights can only be validated by a particular society's cultural, religious, or other values and if a particular right is in conflict with a cultural value, it may be set aside. Examples of relativism constitute the practice of female genital mutilation in parts of rural Africa, as well as the denial of the right to convert from Islam to a religion of one's choice. The Cairo Declaration on Human Rights in Islam (1990), which is non-binding, exemplifies a relativist perspective by subjecting all rights therein to a test of compatibility with the *Sharia* (which itself is not always compatible with international human rights standards).

The nature of State obligations

Rights and freedoms in international treaties entail obligations of *conduct* and obligations of *result* on State parties. These further encompass three additional sub-layers of obligations; namely, to *respect, protect*, and *fulfil*. The obligation to respect requires States to refrain from interfering directly or indirectly with the enjoyment of rights (ie discrimination). The obligation to protect requires measures that prevent third parties from interfering with the right, as is the case with terrorist acts or privatization of public goods, such as water, which the poor can no longer afford. The obligation to fulfil requires the adoption of appropriate legislative, administrative, judicial, budgetary, or other action in order to implement the right in question.

As a result of these classifications, it is clear that human rights obligations are both *negative* in nature (ie to avoid interference, to refrain from torture, etc) and *positive* (ie to provide education or to maintain an effective police to safeguard the right to life). The jurisprudence of international human rights treaty bodies confirms that States are under a positive obligation to protect their citizens' right to life when threatened by terrorist or other violence committed by private actors (*Osman v UK* (1998); Human Rights Committee General Comment 31 (2004)). The positive dimension necessarily requires material resources from States and many often declare their inability to fulfil a particular right due to lack of resources. As a result, some treaties, such as ICESCR, entertain the distinction between progressive and immediate realization. In order to overcome such claims, human rights treaties, such as Art 2(1) ICESCR, stress that States are obliged to realize socio-economic rights by making the 'maximum use of their available resources'.

Justiciability

Justiciability means that a particular right or rights are susceptible to judicial protection. In reality, the formal recognition of a right and its justiciable character are indistinguishable. In most cases, this is self-evident. The victim of a policy that denies him the freedom to publish artistic works is entitled to challenge the restriction against freedom of expression. It is acknowledged that progressively realizable rights are also justiciable, as are rights subject to resource scarcity. The lack of resources is relevant only to the substance of the right, whereas justiciability refers to procedure (ie the ability to challenge the infringement), to which resource scarcity and progressive realization are irrelevant. Nonetheless, most third-generation solidarity rights are viewed by States as non-justiciable, principally because there is no global consensus on the substance of the right, let alone an agreement that their collective rights-holders possess judicial remedies. The South African Constitutional Court in the *Treatment Action Campaign case* decided that the absence of public availability of a drug preventing the transmission of HIV from mothers to babies was unreasonable and breached the right of poor mothers and their newborns to effective health care (*South African Minister of Health v Treatment Action Campaign* (2002)).

Derogations

Certain human rights treaties stipulate that, in exceptional circumstances threatening the life of a nation, a State party may temporarily suspend the full applicability of certain rights or adjust its implementation of those rights. This is the essence of derogations. Such public emergencies include armed conflicts, civil and violent unrest, natural disasters, and others. The validity of the restrictions imposed is subject to the severity of the threatening circumstances, their temporariness, the issuance of a proclamation, proportionality, their non-discriminatory character, and their legality under general international law. More significantly, fundamental human rights may never be subject to derogation. Non-derogable rights include the right to life, freedom from torture and slavery, and prohibition of retroactive penal measures.

Derogation clauses are provided in Art 4 ICCPR, Art 15 ECHR, and Art 27 American Convention on Human Rights.

A and ors v UK (2009) 49 EHRR 29

In response to the 9/11 attacks in 2001, the ECtHR held that the threat of international terrorism constituted a public emergency within the meaning of Art 15 ECHR. It added that a broad range of factors determine the nature and degree of *imminent threat* to a nation and that it was not necessary for the institutions of the State under terrorist threat to be in immediate danger.

Reservations

Article 2(1)(d) Vienna Convention on the Law of Treaties (1969) defines reservations as unilateral statements by which a State purports to exclude or modify the legal effects of certain provisions of a treaty in their application to itself. While reservations are generally acceptable under international law, subject to their approval by the other parties to a treaty, there is a great debate as to whether they should be permitted at all in respect of human rights treaties. The reason is that each right contained in a treaty is essentially a mini-treaty and any reservations thereto would render the particular right meaningless and ineffective. Imagine a scenario where a State accepts to respect the right to life but enters a reservation to the ICCPR that allows it to kidnap, torture, and incarcerate without trial those it suspects of undermining its authority.

Reservations to the Genocide Convention, Advisory Opinion, ICJ Rep (1951), p 15

Contrary to the practice that prevailed in the early 1950s, the ICJ held that the validity of a reservation should be measured by its compatibility with the *object and purpose* of the treaty to which it is addressed. Since the object and purpose of the Genocide Convention and other humanizing treaties was to protect populations from crimes and human rights violations, such treaties were not susceptible to individual advantages and disadvantages. As a result, reservations that tended to obfuscate the object and purpose of the crime of genocide were deemed invalid.

REVISION TIP

Do not confuse reservations with derogations. The object of the former is to exclude the legal effects of particular treaty provisions for the reserving State, whereas derogations are made after the treaty has been ratified. Their objective is to restrict the application of certain rights on grounds of public emergency.

International courts and institutions devoted to human rights

One may point to four types of bodies, depending on membership and the legal basis upon which they were established.

UN Charter-based bodies

These are typically subsidiary bodies created by the principal organs of the UN (ie the General Assembly, the Security Council, and ECOSOC). The most significant is the Human Rights Council, which replaced the Commission on Human Rights in 2005. It was established by the General Assembly and, although it is a political body, its member States should possess a good human rights record; a requirement departing from past UN practice. It performs three main functions related to human rights. The first is the Universal Periodic Review (UPR), on the basis of which all States are required to periodically submit a brief report on the status of all rights on their territory, to which the Council, with the participation of other States and non-State actors, responds in a non-confrontational manner. The UPR procedure is public and is meant to engage States with a view to offering concrete recommendations and capacity-building assistance. The second function involves a complaint mechanism. This is a confidential procedure (formerly known as a 1503 ECOSOC procedure) that is triggered only when there are credible reports of gross human rights violations. The final function concerns the appointment of special rapporteurs to deal with the implementation of particular rights (eg the right to water or food) or to assess the human rights situation of specific countries.

Treaty-based human rights committees

The most prominent is the Human Rights Committee, the watchdog of the ICCPR. All of these bodies are considered quasi-judicial (ie not fully judicial) and are open to universal membership. Experts appointed thereto are independent from any government. All the major universal human rights treaties make provision for such bodies, in order to avoid rendering the treaties a mere contractual arrangement between States with no overseeing authority.

The creation of the Human Rights Committee is stipulated in Arts 2, 28–45 ICCPR. Its job is to ascertain whether member States adhere to their obligations. It undertakes this role in four ways: (a) through the consideration of periodic reports submitted by member States; (b) by issuing General Comments, with the purpose of identifying and addressing common themes arising from the member States' periodic reports, which essentially take the form of a commentary; (c) by their competence to hear inter-State disputes, albeit none have yet been submitted; and (d) through consideration of individual communications by those victims and their families whose country has ratified the 1976 Optional Protocol allowing individual communications. Its decisions in such contentious cases are not binding on the parties, but the member States must report to the Committee how they have implemented such decisions.

LOOKING FOR EXTRA MARKS?

The ICJ considered that Qatari nationals forced to leave the UAE were potentially subject to 'a serious risk of irreparable prejudice' as regards the rights protected in the International Convention on the Elimination of All Forms of Racial Discrimination (ICERD). It ordered the UAE to end its policy of collective expulsion and avoid any further 'aggravating' measures (*Qatar v UAE*, Order for Provisional Measures (2018)).

Extraterritorial reach of human rights treaties

As a general rule, treaty-based human rights obligations are territorial in nature and are addressed as such to States. This should be distinguished from the extraterritorial competence of national courts and institutions to arrest and prosecute persons charged with crimes under international law. Where a State effectively occupies the territory of another State, the human rights obligations of the occupier are transferred to the persons residing in the occupied territory. This is dictated by the law of occupation under IHL and has also been confirmed by international human rights courts, as in *Al-Skeini and ors v UK* and *Al Jeddah and ors v UK* (2011), where the Grand Chamber of the ECtHR held that the ECHR is applicable extraterritorially where a State exercises control or authority over an individual through its agents, as well as where it exercises effective control over territory.

Loizidou v Turkey (1997) 23 EHRR 513

The applicant lost control of her property when the northern part of Cyprus was occupied by Turkish forces, which then proceeded to claim that northern Cyprus had become an independent country and was thus outside the jurisdictional reach of the ECHR. The ECtHR held that its jurisdiction may be triggered through acts undertaken by the authorities of member States, whether performed within or outside national boundaries, which produce effects outside their own territory, as well as 'when as a consequence of military action—whether lawful or unlawful—a member State exercises *effective control* of an area outside its national territory'.

LOOKING FOR EXTRA MARKS?

Paragraph 9 Maastricht Principles on Extraterritorial Obligations of States in the Area of Economic, Social and Cultural (ESC) Rights (2011) states that such an obligation arises in:

1. situations over which [a state] exercises authority or effective control, whether or not such control is exercised in accordance with international law;
2. situations over which state acts or omissions bring about foreseeable effects on the enjoyment of ESC rights, whether within or outside its territory;
3. situations in which the state, acting separately or jointly, whether through its executive, legislative or judicial branches, is in a position to exercise decisive influence or to take measures to realize ESC rights extraterritorially, in accordance with international law.

International humanitarian law (IHL)

IHL is concerned with the protection of civilians and those not taking part in conflict from the effects of armed conflict, and in addition it aims to humanize warfare by setting out rules for combatants. Two large codifications of IHL took place during the course of the twentieth century, namely, the 1907 Hague Conventions and the 1949 Geneva Conventions. The former were chiefly concerned with warfare as such, whereas the latter sought to protect civilians and combatants no longer taking an active part in hostilities. Subsequent codifications include, among others, the two 1977 Additional Protocols to the Geneva Conventions (the first dealing with international armed conflicts, the second concerning non-international armed conflicts). In addition, the proliferation of international criminal tribunals since 1990 has entailed the adoption of statutes that have either codified the criminal dimension of customary IHL (as is the case with the International Criminal Tribunal for the former Yugoslavia (ICTY) and International Criminal Tribunal for Rwanda (ICTR) Statutes concerning crimes against humanity) or reinforced IHL principles enunciated by previous international tribunals or treaty law, as is the case with the 1998 Rome Statute of the ICC.

Fundamental principles and distinctions in IHL

IHL is applicable only in times of armed conflict (the term 'war' is no longer apt), not in times of peace or in times of unrest. The application of IHL (or *jus in bello*) may coincide in time with the *jus ad bellum* (eg where a threat to the peace is, at the same time, a violation of the *jus ad bellum* (use of force rules) and the starting point of an international armed conflict), but in practice the use of force by States precedes the application of IHL. These two regimes produce distinct legal consequences, as will become clear later on.

A distinction should be made between *international* and *non-international armed conflicts*. An international armed conflict commences, in accordance with Common Art 2 Geneva Conventions, when any of the following three circumstances exists:

1. declaration of war (even if not followed by armed hostilities);
2. armed hostilities between two or more states (even if of low intensity);
3. occupation, defined objectively as actual control over foreign territory.

Article 1(4) Protocol I of 1977 creates an additional category, whose aim in 1977 was to render the struggles of black South Africans and Palestinians as international conflicts, despite the fact that they were fought within those countries' borders. Article 1(4) stipulates that a self-determination struggle of peoples against colonial or alien occupation or a racist regime is tantamount to an international armed conflict.

Once an international armed conflict is deemed to have commenced, one needs to distinguish between *combatants* and *non-combatants*. Combatants are defined under Art 4 Geneva Convention III, which sets out four criteria, irrespective of whether the person is part of a regular or an irregular army, provided, however, that the group and its members satisfy the following requirements:

1. being commanded by a person responsible for his subordinates (essentially, the existence of hierarchy and internal discipline);
2. bearing a fixed distinctive sign recognizable at a distance;
3. carrying arms openly (ie treacherous tactics are deplored, but not secretive commando operations);
4. the group and its operations must comply with IHL (terrorist groups, eg even if they satisfy criteria (a)–(c), do not wish to comply with IHL, and openly target civilians).

Non-combatants include not only *civilians* or the civilian population, but also all those persons that are not taking an active part in hostilities, such as former combatants. The latter category includes those who have laid down their arms (surrendered), those who have been incapacitated by wounds or other impairments (known as *hors de combat*), and those who have been captured. Exceptionally, persons who would otherwise be classified as civilians and who spontaneously take up arms to defend against an advancing foreign enemy are regarded by Art 2 Hague Regulations annexed to Hague Convention IV (1907) as combatants, provided they carry their arms openly and conform to IHL. These types of combatants are known as *levée en masse*, for which international law allows the absence of criteria (1) and (2) above as a result of purely practical considerations.

Legal consequences of fundamental distinctions

Once an international armed conflict is deemed to have commenced as per the criteria set out above, civilians and civilian objects cannot be made the object of an attack. Only combatants and military objects can be targeted by the enemy (Art 48 Protocol I (1977)). This is known as the *principle of distinction*. Even so, Art 35 Protocol I (1977) sets out the general rule that the means and methods of warfare are not unlimited and that it is prohibited to use weapons or methods causing 'superfluous injury or unnecessary suffering' or 'widespread, long-term and severe damage to the natural environment'. It should be made clear that not every member of the armed forces of a regular or irregular group is considered a combatant. Chaplains and medical personnel are excluded (Art 33 Geneva Convention III), as are all those contributing to the war effort, but not taking a direct part in hostilities (DPH). There is fierce debate among IHL lawyers as to the range of persons actually taking DPH and, although the issue is complex, it is clear, for example, that civilian munitions factory workers can be targeted by the enemy, as their work makes a significant contribution to the military capacity of the armed forces, but only when engaged in such work and not at other times (eg at home with their families).

Combatants have the right to take DPH, whereas non-combatants do not (Art 43(2) Protocol I (1977)). This means that a civilian not part of an organized armed group who spontaneously and alone kills or injures personnel of an occupying power (even a brutal occupier) would be committing a war crime and would not be entitled to the protection afforded to combatants under IHL. Under such circumstances, the civilian foregoes the protection afforded to civilians. Combatants, unlike civilians, can target other combatants, whether to kill or to injure them. This is lawful under IHL and, if captured by the enemy, combatants are entitled to prisoner-of-war (POW) status, which means they are not liable for having killed or injured enemy combatants and are only liable for war crimes. Other than that, a POW is detained by the enemy for the duration of the armed conflict.

It is now clear that IHL is *lex specialis* in relation to international human rights law, this having been confirmed by the ICJ in the *Legality of the Threat or Use of Nuclear Weapons case* (1996). Despite the primacy of IHL, it is complementary and not mutually exclusive with human rights (*Legal Consequences of the Construction of a Wall in the Occupied Palestinian Territory* (2004)). Practically, this means that the right to life, which is otherwise an absolute right under international human rights law, is qualified under IHL when involving one combatant lawfully taking the life of another combatant. The complementary character of the two regimes is exemplified in situations of occupation where IHL is generally silent on the implementation of civil and political rights, let alone socio-economic rights, or other emerging rights, such as the right to development.

KEY CASES

CASE	FACTS	PRINCIPLES
SAS v France, ECtHR judgment (1 July 2014)	France adopted a law which provided a blanket (ie irrespective of circumstances) ban on the Muslim full-head veil (so-called 'burqa ban'). This was challenged on several human rights grounds. France argued that freedom of religion may be restricted on grounds of public safety and 'respect for the minimum set of values of an open and democratic society'. This set of values encompasses gender equality, human dignity, and 'respect for the minimum requirements of life in society' or 'living together', a fundamental principle of French constitutional law.	The ECtHR focused on the right to freedom of religion. It accepted that the restriction pursued a legitimate aim, namely the need for a State 'to be able to identify individuals in order to prevent danger for the safety of persons and property and to combat identity fraud'. However, the burqa ban itself was not necessary in a democratic society and, absent 'a general threat to public safety', it was held to be disproportionate. Although the ECtHR was not prepared to accept that religious freedom restrictions were justified on gender equality and public safety grounds, it did go on to note that the burqa ban ultimately satisfied the legitimate aim of 'living together' under 'the protection of the rights and freedoms of others', despite the fact that this is not listed in Arts 8(2) and 9(2) ECHR as a legitimate restriction.

KEY DEBATES

Topic	The legality of targeted killings
Author/academic	D Kretzmer
Viewpoint	Targeted killings like those of Osama bin Laden and other known terrorists do not necessarily contravene the right to life, nor do they constitute extrajudicial killings, because the targets are lawful combatants and they pose an imminent security threat.
Source	'Targeted Killing of Suspected Terrorists: Extra-Judicial Executions or Legitimate Means of Defence', 16 *European Journal of International Law* (2005) 171

EXAM QUESTIONS

Problem question

Country X, which is poor and underdeveloped, adopted the ICCPR and entered two reservations, as follows:

1. The first suggested that because its rural population had traditionally relied on a family model that prevented women from working outside the family unit, country X could not provide full equality to its female population, as this would risk destroying family cohesion.
2. The second stipulated that because it did not have enough money to employ a sufficient number of judges, it was forced to conduct expedited trials without due process guarantees. Therefore it entered a reservation against the right to a fair trial.

Moreover, three years from the adoption of the ICCPR, country X experienced a wave of industrial strikes from disgruntled workers who demanded better working conditions and salaries. Country X declared a state of emergency and immediately declared that it would derogate from all non-fundamental rights.

Discuss whether any one of the two reservations is valid and also whether the derogation is legitimate.

See the Outline answers section in the end matter for help with this question.

Essay question

Critically analyse the circumstances under which an aggrieved applicant may bypass the requirement that he or she must first exhaust all domestic remedies before applying to an international human rights body.

Online Resources

For an outline answer to this essay question, as well as interactive key cases and multiple-choice questions, please visit the online resources.

https://www.oup.com/he/bantekas-papastavridis-concentrate5e

13 International criminal law

THE EXAMINATION

International criminal law is linked to other key areas of international law, particularly human rights, international humanitarian law (IHL), immunities, and jurisdiction. It is important to have a good understanding of individual responsibility and a good understanding of the four core international crimes. The elements of these crimes may form a question in and of themselves, but you may also be asked to address the legal nature of international criminal tribunals and compare their key characteristics. You need to possess a good understanding of the difference between United Nations Security Council (UNSC)-based tribunals, treaty-based tribunals, and hybrid tribunals.

KEY FACTS

- Individual criminal liability is independent from the responsibility of States, even if the cause of action is the same.
- The four core international crimes are grave breaches (which are the most serious types of war crimes), crimes against humanity, genocide, and aggression.
- Transnational crimes differ from crimes under international law in that, although the source is a multilateral treaty, liability arises from implementing domestic laws, whereas liability for international crimes arises directly from treaties or custom and irrespective of domestic laws.
- Just like domestic crimes, international crimes comprise a material act (*actus reus*) and a volitional element (*mens rea*). Some crimes additionally require a particular context or a particular degree of knowledge.
- International crimes can be committed through ordinary forms of direct and accessorial liability, or by means of particular forms of participation in crime, including joint criminal enterprise (JCE) and command responsibility.
- The International Criminal Tribunal for the former Yugoslavia (ICTY) and the International Criminal Tribunal for Rwanda (ICTR) derive their authority from the UNSC, whereas the International Criminal Court (ICC) is a treaty-based judicial institution, as well as an intergovernmental organization.

Individual criminal responsibility

By requiring that States refrain from and prevent violations of human rights and IHL against all persons under their authority, both IHL and human rights emphasize the preventative obligation of States. Their emphasis is on the protection of victims. An equally important dimension of human rights and IHL consists of punishing the perpetrators of violations, which typically correspond to both domestic and international crimes. For example, the prohibition against torture as a human rights violation naturally corresponds to a physical act or torture committed by an individual (perpetrator) against a victim. The criminal law then expands the human rights violation by the State to encompass an additional dimension in the form of a discrete crime, which culminates in the criminal liability of the perpetrator. Where the crime is set out in a treaty or customary law, it is an international crime and the liability of the perpetrator arises under international law. Where the crime is defined and set out in a domestic statute, it is a crime under domestic law and liability arises only therein. The difference is significant. Crimes under international law give rise to individual criminal liability irrespective of whether the conduct in question is a crime under the law of the country where it was committed. As a result, the courts of other countries may exercise extraterritorial jurisdiction over such international crimes in accordance with the principles analysed in chapter 6 'Sovereignty and jurisdiction'.

Not all crimes set out in treaties give rise to individual criminal responsibility under international law and a distinction should be made between international crimes (or core crimes) and transnational crimes. The latter consist of crimes set out in treaties that allow domestic law to adapt the definition and forms of liability in accordance with domestic law (eg whether the penalty should be criminal or also administrative and whether corporations incur criminal liability). In this case, liability arises only as a result of domestic law and hence may vary from one country to another. A typical transnational crime is that contained in the 1997 Organisation for Economic Co-operation and Development (OECD) Convention on Combating Bribery of Foreign Public Officials. There is debate as to whether certain crimes are international or transnational in nature, particularly terrorism.

Core international crimes

Although every treaty may set out particular conduct as being criminal in nature, four crimes stand out as so-called 'core crimes'. Their regulation may be found in treaties, as well as customary international law. These generally consist of the following.

Grave breaches of IHL

Their contemporary manifestation may be traced in the 1949 Geneva Conventions and Protocol I (1977), as well as Art 8 ICC Statute (1988), and also the statutes of international criminal courts and tribunals, such as the ICTY, ICTR, Sierra Leone Special Court, and others. Grave breaches are particularly serious violations of IHL, committed in international armed conflicts, such as the killing or torture of prisoners of war. Grave breaches are typically distinguished from less serious infractions, which are given the more generic name of 'war crimes'. The difference is significant. While grave breaches are subject to universal jurisdiction, war crimes are not. However, this distinction is only important in the context of the Geneva Conventions. Customary international law treats all violations of IHL as war crimes.

War crimes in non-international armed conflicts

The occurrence of war crimes in the context of non-international armed conflicts has always challenged the international community because these conflicts were, until the early 1990s, considered as precluding external 'intervention', whether military or otherwise. In fact, prior to the 1990s, Common Article 3 of the 1949 Geneva Conventions was not viewed as a criminal law provision, but only as obliging states to protect victims of domestic conflicts, including captured combatants. The situation is further complicated by the fact that the State is under no obligation to treat captured rebels as combatants and hence as prisoners of war (POWs) (see discussion in chapter 12 'Human rights and humanitarian law') and may try them as common criminals under its domestic criminal law. Equally, States could treat serious crimes committed by their own armed forces as common crimes and ascribe immunity or pardon to the perpetrators. This state of affairs changed with the involvement of the UNSC in the non-international conflicts in Yugoslavia and Rwanda and the setting up of the ICTY and ICTR. The Appeals Chamber of the ICTY in *Prosecutor v Tadić* (1996) emphasized that, while States are free not to consider rebels as combatants, crimes committed in non-international armed conflicts are crimes under international law (not domestic law) and hence the liability of the perpetrators is international in nature. This means that any country may indict and try the alleged perpetrators, even if they have been acquitted or amnestied by the territorial state.

LOOKING FOR EXTRA MARKS?

The South African Truth and Reconciliation Commission (TRC) was set up in 1993 on the basis of the 1993 interim Constitution. One of the mandates of the TRC was to investigate human rights abuses that took place between 1960 and 1994, based on statements made to the TRC. An amnesty was granted only in those cases where the culprit made a full disclosure of his or her conduct during this period, and as long as such conduct related to omissions or offences associated with political objectives. The UN took the view that amnesties conferred in respect of international crimes during the apartheid era, while valid under South African law, did not extinguish the liability of offenders under international law.

Crimes against humanity

Crimes against humanity (CAH) first appeared in Art 6(c) of the Charter of the Nuremberg Tribunal (1945). The aim of the drafters then was to criminalize under international law mass crimes committed against (mainly) Jewish and other civilian populations in Germany, which were not grave breaches, but at best common crimes under German law; in fact, conduct otherwise reprehensible was legal under Nazi legislation. While most elements of the definition in Art 6(c) have survived today, the link/nexus to an armed conflict has disappeared. A detailed definition of CAH is set out in Art 7 ICC Statute, which itself is the result of the practice of the ICTY and ICTR, both of which dealt with this crime at length. CAH consist of: (a) an *attack*; (b) against a civilian population; (c) where the attack must be widespread or systematic; and (d) the perpetrator must have been aware of the overall context of the attack and intended to be part of it (*mens rea*).

The concept of 'attack' is an umbrella term, which encompasses one or more discrete offences (such as murder, extermination, rape, torture, and others) as long as the material conduct (*actus reus*) and subjective element (*mens rea*) of these discrete offences is satisfied. An attack is 'widespread' if it encompasses a large number of victims, whereas it is 'systematic' where the acts in question reflect a pattern. A pattern may, or may not, exhibit a policy. If a policy is found, it helps establish 'systematicity'. Prosecutors need only prove either the widespread or systematic element, but not both, depending on the evidence available to them. Concrete proof of a policy to commit CAH suffices for liability, even in the absence of a significant number of victims.

CAH typically involve some degree of organization and a plan/policy. As a result, several people, at various levels, are involved. Liability arises only where a perpetrator was aware of the overall context and his or her act intended to further the aims of the plan. If a perpetrator is unaware of the plan/context liability arises only for the particular crime committed and not for CAH.

Genocide

Genocide consists of criminal conduct committed with intent to destroy a group in whole or in part. The concept of a 'group' is limited to racial, religious, national, or ethnic, although certain courts have expanded the definition to include groups with a permanent status (eg a political group, such as communists). The list of criminal conduct is set out in Art II Genocide Convention (1948) and Art 6 ICC Statute. Genocide and CAH slightly overlap, but key differences are that: CAH are directed against *any* civilian population, while the object of genocide can only be a particular group; and CAH requires an intentional attack, whereas genocide necessitates an intention to destroy the targeted group in whole or in part.

The ICTR in *Prosecutor v Akayesu*, Trial Chamber Judgment (1998) was confronted with a delicate situation where victims and perpetrators shared racial, religious, national, and ethnic identities. It, therefore, determined that, as long as the perpetrators perceive their victims as being distinct, even if strictly speaking they are not, it suffices to trigger the crime of genocide. The 'in part' element does not characterize the destruction of the group, but refers instead to the intent of the perpetrator in destroying the group within the confines of a limited geographical area (*Prosecutor v Krstić*, Trial Chamber Judgment (2001), paras 582–4). Thus, if an individual possesses the intent to destroy a distinct part of a group within a limited geographical area, as opposed to an accumulation of isolated individuals within it, that person would be liable for genocide. Thus, genocide does not require that the perpetrator must intend to kill each and every member of the group.

Unlike common crimes, and even some grave breaches, genocide cannot be the result of spontaneous conduct and involves a significant degree of planning. In the context of the ICC Statute, the existence of a plan as a constitutive element of the crime is expressly required. This requirement is evident in the 'Elements of Crimes' pertinent to genocide, as set out in Art 9 ICC Statute, which require that said acts take place 'in the context of a manifest pattern of similar conduct directed against that group or conduct that could itself effect such destruction'.

Genocide is distinguished from other mass crimes by the fact that the selection of the victims by the perpetrator aims to destroy the group 'as such'. Just like CAH, therefore, liability for genocide arises where a perpetrator was aware of the overall genocidal plan and intended (in whatever capacity) to target members of the group in order to destroy the group, in whole or in part. This is the *dolus specialis* (specific intent) of genocide.

The Genocide Convention gives rise to an *erga omnes* obligation (Art IX), in the sense that all State parties have an enforceable interest in the prevention and cessation of genocide taking place in another State. In *Gambia v Myanmar (Application of the Convention on the Prevention and Punishment of the Crime of Genocide)*, although the plaintiff was completely unrelated to the alleged genocide against the Rohingya minority in Myanmar, it was justified in requesting that the International Court of Justice (ICJ) issue a provisional order against the defendant, until such time as the ICJ determined whether or not genocide had taken place. The Court, in fact, did so, chiefly on the basis of official UN reports (Order for Provisional Measures, (2020)).

LOOKING FOR EXTRA MARKS?

Since genocide is a mass-victim offence, the part targeted must be a substantial part of the group. In terms of victim numbers, ICTY and ICTR jurisprudence suggest that the intent to destroy a part of the group must affect a considerable number of individuals that make up a 'substantial' part of that group (*Prosecutor v Krstić*, Appeals Chamber Judgment (2004), paras 8–12).

Aggression

Aggression straddles between the State responsibility to refrain from illegal uses of force, as dictated by the UN Charter and customary international law (see chapter 11 'Use of force') and the criminal liability of the perpetrators. While the first is well regulated, the second is not. Aggression, as an international crime, first appeared in Art 6(a) Nuremberg Charter (1945), but subsequently became politically sensitive and fell out of use. It was revived at the Kampala review conference to the ICC Statute in 2010, in the form of a new Art 8*bis*. The definition of aggression is predicated on the UN Charter and customary law on the use of force. Article 8*bis* defines aggression in accordance with UNGA Resolution 3314 (which itself defines aggression) and it must, by its character, gravity, and scale, constitute a manifest violation of the UN Charter. This implies that only the most serious forms of unlawful use of force between States can be subject to ICC jurisdiction.

Forms of international criminal liability

Just like crimes under domestic laws, international crimes require a material act (*actus reus*) and an element of volition (*mens rea*). Certain international crimes require additional elements. These may include: (a) *general circumstances*, whereby grave breaches can only be committed in the context of an international armed conflict; (b) *circumstances pertinent to either the actus reus or mens rea*, such as the widespread occurrence of CAH; (c) *knowledge of a particular context*, such as knowledge of a genocidal policy or the overall context of CAH in order for a perpetrator to be charged with committing these crimes as opposed to ordinary crimes; or (d) special intent (*dolus specialis*). The special intent in genocide consists of committing these crimes with the intent of destroying the group, in whole or in part. Equally, the crime of apartheid requires a special intent to sustain an institutionalized system of racial domination (Art 7(2)(h) ICC Statute) and the definition of torture necessitates the existence of an additional prohibited purpose, consisting of obtaining a confession, punishment, coercion, intimidation, or discrimination against the victim (Art 1(1) 1984 Convention against Torture).

The organizational complexity typically associated with international crimes has given rise to several forms of criminal liability that are not generally encountered in domestic legal systems. Here, we will examine the two most unique forms, taking it for granted that direct perpetration (such as killing or ordering that a crime be committed), as well as all forms of accessorial/accomplice liability (eg aiding and abetting) and conspiracy are common to all legal systems and are applied consistently to international crimes with some degree of sensible analogy.

Command/superior responsibility

The latest codification of command responsibility is found in Art 28 ICC Statute. Persons in control of others may order or incite those under their authority to commit crimes. In such situations, the liability of the commander is direct and both ordering and inciting crimes entail the commander's direct perpetration. Command responsibility is omission-based liability. It involves the failure to prevent or punish crimes committed by persons under one's effective command or control, in circumstances where the commander knew, or should have known, that those under his or her command were about to commit, or had committed, crimes.

Given that command responsibility is a form of liability, it is generally applicable to all international crimes, whether committed in peacetime or armed conflict. Moreover, it is not restricted to those in the military, but to any person, particularly civilian leaders, as well as business executives. The necessary element is that of 'control', which is broader than the term 'command'. A person may assume control over others without any entity having conferred him or her any sort of command (so called *de facto* command). Hence, the element of control may be the subject of an objective evaluation, particularly where the accused is a member of a paramilitary or rebel group.

Under general international law, besides actual knowledge of crimes taking place by one's subordinates, knowledge may be inferred circumstantially. Given the duties inherent in command, commanders are required to be appraised at all times, and to the best of their ability under their particular circumstances, of the discipline and movement of their subordinates. This is a duty in and of itself, from which commanders cannot escape. Hence, a failure to be appraised as explained above is sufficient to infer that the commander either knew or chose not to know. Knowledge, whether actual or circumstantial, is a crucial element in the doctrine of command responsibility. It should be highlighted that the commander need not share the *mens rea* of his subordinates. In fact, the commander may not desire the commission of any crimes. Liability arises only because he or she knew of the crimes and failed to take remedial action. In *ICC Prosecutor v Bemba*, Appeals Judgment (2018), a divided ICC concluded that command responsibility requires 'effective control', which is difficult to substantiate where a commander's forces are scattered beyond his or her physical control.

Finally, despite the fact that the commander knew, or should have known, of his or her subordinate's crimes, he nonetheless omitted and took no effective measures to prevent or punish said crimes. Command responsibility is an important tool for prosecuting superior figures for which there is little, or no, direct evidence that they ordered or incited serious crimes.

Joint criminal enterprise (JCE)

Although JCE exists in a variety of forms in domestic criminal justice systems, its application to international crimes is unique and subject to significant disputes and contestation. The need for JCE liability in the criminal law arose from the need to attribute liability to a plethora of persons involved in a criminal scheme involving a multitude of offences. Whereas the leaders and organizers of such common purpose may be charged by reason of the orders they transmitted down the chain of command or on account of their failure to prevent or punish subordinate criminality (command responsibility), it is not clear what type of liability, if at all, may be attributed to those who participate in more minor roles in the implementation of such criminal schemes. The ICTY Appeals Chamber (*Prosecutor v Tadic*, Appeals Judgment (1999), para 188) held that a JCE consists of a common plan, design or purpose, the participation of a plurality of persons therein, all of which are acting with the aim of committing one or more international crimes. The Appeals Chamber distinguished between three JCE categories. The first (JCE I), and more general, consists of cases where a group of persons possesses a shared intent to commit a crime and a common design is accordingly formulated. JCE liability arises even for those participants that do not directly contribute to the execution of the crime, as long as they are found to enjoy a significant contribution in the formulation and perpetration of the common design. In terms of *mens rea*, the participant must willingly contribute to at least one element of the common design and intend the result of the ultimate crime(s) undertaken by his or her co-perpetrators (*Tadic* Appeals Judgment, para 196).

The second category (JCE II) involves concentration/POW camps and is also known as 'systemic', covering all cases 'relating to an organised system with a common criminal purpose perpetrated against the detainees. These consist of a common design, in which multiple persons participate in a 'system of ill-treatment' of detainees in camps. The participants must be aware of the system and intend to contribute to it (*Prosecutor v Kvočka*, Appeals Judgment (2005), 184–202).

The third category (JCE III) refers to common plans or designs in which the actions of one or more participants exceed the aim of the original design and, as such, the excessive action no longer coincides with the intention of them all (so-called 'extended JCE'). For liability to arise, a participant must have foreseen that a crime could be perpetrated even as a 'possible consequence' of the execution of the common purpose. This standard requires that the possibility of a crime being committed must be sufficiently substantial as to be foreseeable to an accused (*Prosecutor v Karadžić*, Appeal Decision on JCE III Foreseeability (2009), para 18).

From JCE in the ICTY to co-perpetratorship in the ICC

The JCE doctrine is not incorporated into the ICC Statute and the only comparable provision is Art 25(3)(d), but it is generally argued that JCE II and III are not encompassed therein and in fact ICC chambers are hostile to this doctrine. The ICC chambers elaborated, on the basis of general principles (chiefly found in civil law jurisdictions), so-called 'co-perpetrator liability'. This form of participation in crime arises in those circumstances where more than one perpetrator executes a criminal offence, not simply jointly, but in such a manner that the actions of each one make a significant contribution to the commission of the crime, on the basis of a functional cooperation. Any other contribution that does not have such a potent effect on the conclusion of the crime will render a participant merely an accomplice, not a perpetrator. The intent required for co-perpetration (and not merely 'knowledge' demanded in JCE) leads to 'joint control of the crime' (*ICC Prosecutor v Lubanga*, Pre-Trial Chamber Judgment (2007), para 420).

The rationale behind the various strands of co-perpetration is to set out an appropriate mode by which to counter instances of mass criminality, in which, although a criminal conduct or consequence comes about as a result of the actions of one person, it could just as well have been perpetrated by any other member of the group that was with him or her. As a result, the presumption that any one among ten persons could have thrown the fatal punch is not irrebuttable. If one demonstrates that he or she did not share the will or the proclivity of their comrades and was at the scene of the crime unwillingly, said person will certainly not be counted as a co-perpetrator. This form of attribution is well recognized in domestic criminal justice systems and is incorporated in Article 25(3)(a) of the ICC Statute as committing a crime 'jointly with another'. In the ICC context, co-perpetratorship is grounded on the 'control over the crime' test (ICC Prosecutor v Lubanga, Trial (2007), paras 331–42, 338).

Co-perpetration liability requires proof of both objective and subjective elements. The objective element necessitates the existence of a mutually coordinated agreement or common plan between two or more persons, thus excluding opportunistic collaborations. Not every member of a common plan can be charged as a principal, but only those persons to whom essential tasks have been assigned and who can at any time frustrate the offence. What this means is that co-perpetratorship requires an essential—as opposed to merely a substantial—contribution to the execution of the common plan.

REVISION TIP

JCE requires that the offence be completed, whereas co-perpetration does not. Moreover, regarding *mens rea*, JCE requires knowledge of the pertinent crimes, whereas co-perpetration requires intent to commit such crimes.

Enforcement of international criminal law

Enforcement is generally possible through the incorporation of international treaties and customary law in domestic legal orders and the conferral of broad jurisdiction (including extraterritorial) to national courts (see chapter 6 'Sovereignty and jurisdiction' on the various forms of jurisdiction). At the same time, international treaties prescribe a broad range of mutual legal assistance (MLA) procedures, which involve extradition of suspects, as well as exchange of information, joint investigations, and prisoner transfers. In the absence of a multilateral agreement, states typically enter into bilateral extradition agreements that are subject to mutually agreed limitations.

Since the early 1990s, a number of international criminal courts have been set up, whose jurisdiction is supplementary to that of national courts. These will be examined by reference to their legal nature.

UNSC-based tribunals

The ICTY and ICTR were set up by the UNSC on the basis of resolutions 827 (1993) and 955 (1994), respectively. Their statutes were incorporated in these resolutions. As a result, the ICTY and ICTR override any jurisdiction enjoyed by national courts and, because they were conferred with authority to compel the surrender of accused persons and evidence, all UN member States are bound to adhere to such orders by these tribunals (Art 29 ICTY Statute). This authority is derived from Art 40 UN Charter. The Lebanon Special Tribunal, while not a UNSC-based entity, is predicated on an agreement between the UN and Lebanon and ratified by UNSC resolution 1757 (2007). Its jurisdiction encompasses a single (terrorist) incident, to which Lebanese criminal law was only applicable.

Hybrid tribunals

The ICTY and ICTR caused political and financial fatigue to the international community, despite generally being considered successful experiments. However, the UNSC was not prepared to proliferate such tribunals, nor was it clear that States suffering from mass crimes were prepared to cooperate with the ICC. As a result, an intermediate solution surfaced, involving tribunals operating in the victim State, which were to be partially funded by the UN (typically UNGA) and whose statutes would involve a fusion of both international and domestic criminal laws. The agreement between the UN and the host State typically stipulates that half of the judges and prosecutors are local and the rest international. As these are not UNSC-mandated tribunals, they do not enjoy primacy over the courts of other nations, which may still exercise their jurisdiction over persons prosecuted by hybrid tribunals. Hybrid tribunals' budgets are tiny compared to the ICC and their UNSC-based counterparts and because of their proximity to the places where crimes occurred, they offer some degree of *local ownership* and provide authority and capacity-building to local justice institutions. Key hybrid tribunals are: the Sierra Leone Special Court (SLSC), the East Timor Special Panels, and the Extraordinary Chambers of Cambodia. It is not uncommon for some tribunals to operate alongside national truth commissions and local courts, as is the case with the SLSC.

The International Criminal Court

The ICC is the result of the Rome Statute of the International Criminal Court (1998). The adoption of the Statute was based on a multilateral treaty, which additionally rendered the ICC an inter-governmental organization, with its own distinct legal personality (Art 4(1)). As a result, it would not ordinarily be subject to the authority of the UNSC because, unlike its founding and member States, it is not a party to the UN Charter. Such eventuality, however, risked serious conflicts between the UNSC's mandate to maintain international peace and security and the ICC's jurisdiction, as well as possible inconsistencies in the treatment of aggressive acts.

This thorny issue was initially resolved through Art 13(b) ICC Statute, which authorizes the UNSC, acting under Chapter VII UN Charter, to refer a situation to the Court. One such referral under UNSC resolution 1593 (2005) concerned widespread crimes committed by the government of Sudan in Darfur. Following the Kampala review conference of 2010, the UNSC's role in the prosecution of the crime of aggression in Arts 15*bis*(7) and 15*ter* ICC Statute is supplementary, but in no way constrains the judicial determination of the Court in a particular case concerning aggression.

In addition to the UNSC, the jurisdiction of the Court may be triggered also by States parties (Arts 13(a) and 14), as long as the situation or offence takes place in the territory of, or by a national of a State party (Arts 12(1) and 14(1)), in which case, either the territorial State or the State of the nationality of the accused must be parties to the Statute and choose to refer the situation to the Court.

The third referral mechanism is by the ICC Prosecutor acting on his or her own motion (*proprio motu*) on the basis of credible information and subject to the approval of an ICC trial chamber (Arts 13(c) and 15).

Unlike UNSC-based tribunals, which enjoy primacy, the ICC's jurisdiction is *complementary* with respect to national courts. The principle of complementarity, which is found in the Statute's tenth preambular paragraph, as well as in Arts 1 and 17, stipulates that the Court's jurisdiction may be seized only in those situations in which State parties choose not to prosecute themselves, or are otherwise unable or unwilling.

The Court has jurisdiction over four core crimes; namely, war crimes and grave breaches, genocide, CAH, and aggression (Art 5). A document known as 'Elements of Crimes', as set out in Art 9 ICC Statute, provides detailed definitions of offences to avoid arbitrariness. Unlike its predecessors, Art 75 envisages a process of reparations for victims, further aided by the establishment of a dedicated trust fund.

Persons arraigned before the ICC are typically senior figures of government, or the army, all of whom generally (but not always) enjoy immunity from prosecution before national courts. For an analysis of the absence of such immunity at the ICC, see chapter 7 'Immunities'.

EXAM QUESTIONS

Problem question

John, a national of Y, was accused of having committed genocide in country X. Y was not a party to the ICC Statute, but X was. X was reluctant to transfer John to the ICC and its courts assumed jurisdiction. While the case was ongoing, the UNSC referred the situation (and John) to the ICC.

1. Can the UNSC refer a situation to the ICC in violation of the principle of complementarity?
2. In the event that X was willing to surrender John, to which Y is opposed, could X lawfully surrender John to the ICC?

Discuss.

See the Outline answers section in the end matter for help with this question.

Essay question

Critically discuss the elements in the definition of crimes against humanity.

Online Resources

For an outline answer to this essay question, as well as multiple-choice questions, please visit the online resources.

https://www.oup.com/he/bantekas-papastavridis-concentrate5e

Exam essentials

Identifying and analysing sources

Unlike other areas of law, where the various topics are somewhat relevant to each other, an international law exam may encompass a variety of fields that are not visibly connected. The thread that unites these disparate fields is, first and foremost, the sources of international law.

Before you begin to discuss an exam question, make sure you have identified those sources pertinent to your field of inquiry. These may consist of particular treaties, soft law instruments such as UN General Assembly resolutions, leading judgments from domestic or international courts, and customary law in the form of State practice. Once you identify these sources, you will have a generally good idea as to the subject matter of your inquiry.

International law is a rational discipline, whose various fields are interlinked by their common sources, as well as by common principles. By way of illustration, the rules on treaties, responsibility, legal personality, and others apply equally to all areas of international law. Hence, if you possess a good understanding of these, you can apply them everywhere.

The key to a good exam answer is the depth of the analysis and the sources one utilizes in order to put across one's argument. This will comprise the sources identified above. However, it is important to make a qualitative observation at this point. Whereas the sources used in other areas of law possess a more-or-less definite value, in international law a soft law instrument may possess greater value than a treaty which has not been widely ratified. Equally, a judgment by the courts of one nation may carry significant precedential value with the courts of other nations or the practices of international organizations. Hence, it is important to be aware of the qualitative value of the instruments or cases you mention in your analysis. In this sense, international law often seems vague, fluffy, and ultimately indeterminate to many students because of the approach they are familiar with in other areas of law. It is therefore crucial that you are able to appraise correctly the weight of each source you are referring to.

Using case law

Case law, both domestic and international, is an excellent way of demonstrating knowledge of a particular topic, given that you will have access to a treaty book anyway. So, make sure you are familiar with key cases. When penning your answers, do not simply refer to judgments. Make sure you provide some analysis and, most importantly, ensure that you link the cases to the specific point demanded in the exam question. Markers will be frustrated with responses containing all the available cases in a particular field without any attempt to link the cases to the question at hand.

Preparation strategy

When preparing for your international law exam:

1. Ensure that you are familiar with the treaties and other instruments in your statute book.
2. Practice beforehand so that you are confident that you can trace any issue in the relevant treaties and instruments without getting lost in the process.
3. It is important that you have a fairly good idea of the basic principles enunciated in key International Court of Justice cases. You will need to understand these well before you can rely on judgments from domestic courts. Do not become lost, confused, or despairing in a web of intricate cases. Make sure you understand the basic principles of all the areas examined in this book. If you are confident that you have a solid comprehension of these, you will, at the very least, be able to respond to the exam question, even if you cannot provide any case law.

Final tip

Do not provide verbatim redactions of treaty provisions found in your statute books. This is a waste of valuable time and carries no weight with the examiners!

Outline answers

CHAPTER 1

Problem answer

The question here concerns the conflict of norms in international law and, more specifically, the apparent conflict between *jus cogens* norms. It is inevitable that you will enter into a theoretical discussion over this issue. You will have to produce arguments in favour of the intervention to protect a *jus cogens* norm (ie, the protection of the population) and, at the same time, you have to find arguments in favour of the sanctity of the prohibition of the use of force, even in cases where the objective is to 'avert a humanitarian catastrophe'. This precise debate took place at the House of Commons in the context of the Kosovo intervention in 1999 and also underpins the whole discourse over the 'responsibility to protect' doctrine.

Under international law, there is no clear provision of how to resolve a conflict between *jus cogens* norms. Moreover, it seems difficult to use the usual maxims, *lex specialis* and *lex posterior*, in such cases. Both sides have to put forward jurisprudential arguments that would engage well-known theories on the nature of the international legal system. For example, the person who is against the legality of such intervention would argue that, under positive law, there is no exception to the prohibition of the use of force concerning the case of humanitarian intervention and thus the intervention in the present case was illegal. On the other hand, the person in support of this humanitarian intervention would use naturalistic arguments along the lines that the protection of fundamental human rights trumps positivistic and formalistic adherence to the prohibition of the use of force in such cases.

CHAPTER 2

Problem answer

This problem question concerns the application of multiple legal regimes in a dispute and the interrelationship among the sources of international law. The key question is whether the application of the reservation to the optional clause declaration covers all the legal claims put forward by State B or whether there are other sources of obligation available to the Court. This question resembles the *Nicaragua case* (1984), in view of the reservation of the USA concerning the application of multilateral agreements.

The reservation in question excludes the application of bilateral treaties; thus, you should first examine which aspects of the dispute are covered by the reservation. Apparently, the reservation would cover the claim regarding the expulsion of the nationals of State B from State A. Is there any corresponding customary law? Here, you will cite the aforementioned *Nicaragua case*, which explicitly stated that treaty and customary law can coexist alongside each other and that the application of one does not exclude the application of the other, and vice versa. Hence, if you can establish that the treaty has entered into customary law, then this claim would not be excluded from the reservation. This is dependent upon the existence of sufficient State practice based on the treaty provisions accompanied by *opinio juris* (see *North Sea Continental Shelf cases* (1969)). It seems difficult to support this contention, as we need practice from third States and not practice based solely upon a treaty. This notwithstanding, State B could argue that the systematic expulsion of its nationals by State A contravenes customary human rights law, for example, the prohibition of massive expulsion of aliens.

What about the general principles of good faith and *pacta sunt servanda*? The principle of good faith exists in all formal sources. However, it is not a self-standing legal obligation and if we consider that the treaty is excluded from the jurisdiction of the Court in light of the reservation, it is hard to argue that there is a breach solely on the basis of custom and 'general principles of law'. The same is true also for *pacta sunt servanda*.

Finally, with regard to the use of the territory of State A by State B, you can only argue that in light of the *Right of Passage case* (1960) there is a special or local custom established by the practice of both States and the respective *opinio juris*.

CHAPTER 3

Problem answer

1. Assess whether the interpretative declaration of State A is a disguised reservation. On the face of it, it seems like a reservation that sets a precondition for the application of the agreement. In view of its general character and the nature of the disarmament agreement, it would probably be incompatible with the object and purpose of the agreement (see Art 20 VCLT and *Reservations to Genocide Convention*, Advisory Opinion). This means that if you accept the permissibility school, it should have been declared null and void (cf the practice of the ECtHR in the *Belilos case* to sever such disguised reservations). On the contrary, if you accept the opposability school, the fact that no State objected means that it is permissible.

2. The application of Art 62 has been very restrictive. It has been invoked in few cases, most recently in the *Gabčíkovo-Nagymaros Project case* (1997), but it has never been successful. The problem here is the condition of 'unforeseen change of circumstances', which is not so obvious. Political tensions may arise and political relations never remain stable, and thus it is very hard to plead that this was 'unforeseen'. In light also of the sacrosanct principle *pacta sunt servanda*, it is difficult to consider the denunciation of the agreement by State A as lawful.

CHAPTER 4

Problem answer

1. The nuclear terrorism convention has only been ratified by the UK, but has not been transformed into its domestic legal order by means of an implementing statute. As a result, Antonio cannot be charged on the basis of the offence emanating from the convention as such. You may want to ponder, however, although no other facts are mentioned in the problem, whether the UK already possesses a statute whose provisions would give rise to a charge of nuclear terrorism. If so, Antonio could be tried under this specific statute. Otherwise, the terms of the convention are not enforceable in the UK's legal order.

2. If nuclear terrorism is a crime under customary international law, then there exists a significant body of case law that allows British courts to incorporate crimes under customary law without the need for implementing legislation. However, in order for such incorporation of a customary crime to take place, its existence must be affirmed by the courts and its application must not infringe fundamental rights, such as the prohibition of retroactive legislation.

3. UNSC resolutions have effect in the UK legal order on the basis of the United Nations Act 1946. Moreover, Orders in Council specify the precise terms and conditions for their implementation in the UK. However, the British government and the courts are obliged to construe relevant SC resolutions in conformity with the UK's human rights obligations, including its human rights statutes.

4. This means that if a SC resolution seemingly violates fundamental rights, such as the right of access to justice or the right to an adequate standard of living, it has to be implemented in such a way that the right in question is fully respected. This may require rescinding or amending the particular order or statute or simply providing a construction that is consonant with fundamental rights. The prevailing opinion in the CJEU and Europe is that SC resolutions can never be construed as authorizing the violation of fundamental rights.

CHAPTER 5

Problem answer

1. The Batas are a minority and minorities do not, as a rule, enjoy the right to secede from the central State. Minorities enjoy minority rights and any unilateral secession is not necessarily legitimate under international law, irrespective of whether they were abused by the government of the majority. At the very least, the Bata entity is not in a position to conduct its external affairs because, given the breach of the rule prohibiting minorities from seceding, other nations will not enter into relations with the Batas. The ICJ's opinion in the *Kosovo case* simply determined the legitimacy of Kosovo's unilateral declaration of independence, not the legality of the actual secession from Serbia.

2. Statehood through secession need not necessarily come about by the use of force, ie through an armed insurrection. The most legitimate way

of seceding is by a plebiscite that is consistent with the constitutional arrangements of the nation concerned. Equally, it may rest on an agreement among federated States within a single country, as was the case with the dissolution of the USSR in the early 1990s. However, the right to secession (as expressed through self-determination) against a racist, colonial, and oppressive regime can come about by the use of armed force. Force under such circumstances is exceptionally recognized as a legitimate tool for the secession of oppressed peoples. This seems to be the position of a big part of the international community in the case of Kosovo.

3. Minorities possess minority rights—that is, the right to use their own language and profess their particular culture and religion, among others. This right is enshrined in Art 27 UN Covenant on Civil and Political Rights (1966). They may also have, under the local constitution, rights to an autonomous or federal State, as is the case with Catalonia in Spain. This type of self-government or autonomy is a reflection of the internal dimension of self-determination that is applicable to minorities. Moreover, the central government has an obligation under international law to respect minority rights. Of course, a point can be made here that the Batas may claim some sort of de facto statehood by the mere fact of being in effective control of their territory.

4. There is a large body of precedent whereby the acts of an occupying power are given recognition by other nations, despite the fact that they do not recognize the legitimacy of the occupying power itself. This is the case with the TRNC described in this chapter.

CHAPTER 6

Problem answer

1. The particular offence has taken place in a number of jurisdictions, despite the fact that the offender initiated it in the UK. To start off with, the UK possesses territorial jurisdiction because part of the offence (the selling of the shares) occurred on its territory. At this point, it is also worth mentioning that, although the facts provided in the problem question do not provide anything else, it is possible that the UK enjoys further jurisdictional entitlements if its relevant statutes say so (eg nationality-based jurisdiction). This is irrespective of the fact that such broader jurisdictional competence may clash with that of Guatemala and Aruba. If the offender was ever arrested by Guatemalan authorities, then he could lawfully be extradited to the UK under the terms of their bilateral extradition agreement. Guatemala, equally, enjoys the type of territorial jurisdiction available to countries on whose territory a crime has been completed (the purchase of the shares). One could certainly advise the British government to make an official request to Aruba for the extradition of the offender, although there is no guarantee that this will take place, as there is no requirement on Aruba to accept such a request in the absence of a bilateral extradition treaty.

2. The particular conduct under consideration is not an offence in Aruba and hence normally a person should not be tried there under such a count because it would offend the principle that prohibits the application of retroactive legislation. However, the courts in Aruba may well assess that the particular conduct constitutes a crime under customary international law and decide that custom in Aruba may be incorporated in the legal system without parliamentary decree. In this case, they would have to assess whether this is in violation of the offender's rights. This is clearly not the case; he was well aware that this conduct was an offence in the UK, which is the place where he initiated the offence. Although you do not know anything about the law of Aruba, it is useful with such questions to import the legal principles of the system with which you are familiar.

CHAPTER 7

Problem answer

1. Serving presidents and heads of State enjoy personal immunity—that is, in respect of their person and not on the basis of the public nature of the functions they undertake. Therefore, they enjoy immunity at all times and all places, even when they are undertaking personal activities, as is the case here.

2. The answer remains the same as that above. Personal immunity persists at all times,

irrespective of the heinous nature of the crimes alleged to have been committed by the suspect. There is no solid precedent whereby national courts have violated a suspect's personal immunity. The only possibility to prosecute this person is through a UN Security Council referral to the International Criminal Court.

3. Once again, the operation of universal jurisdiction does not extinguish one's personal immunity. However, if country Y is a member of the International Criminal Court (ICC) Statute it may surrender the president of country X thereto.

4. This is certainly possible. One's immunity, whether personal or functional, may be waived by his or her executive authority (eg Parliament), upon which that person's immunity is lifted and the person may lawfully be tried before the courts of a foreign nation. This is a very rare phenomenon, however.

CHAPTER 8

Problem answer

1. Discuss the legality of the interdiction of the *MV So San* against the background of UNCLOS, other treaty law, and customary international law. Under UNCLOS, the UK does not hold such a right, as the right of visit is not granted for vessels suspected of being engaged in drug trafficking (Arts 108 and 110). The UK might have a legal basis for interdiction pursuant to the 1988 Vienna Convention on Trafficking in Narcotic Drugs, if both the UK and the flag State, Panama, are parties to said treaty. In this case, the boarding must be conducted in accordance with the terms of Art 17. The UK may also request the ad hoc consent of Panama and then board the vessel. Finally, as the law stands, the right of visit in respect of drug trafficking is not recognized under customary law.

2. The prerequisites for the assertion of enforcement jurisdiction on the high seas are as follows. The State concerned should have established prior legislative jurisdiction concerning the crime—in the present case, drug trafficking on the high seas. However, this presupposes that such jurisdiction is in accordance with international law; more specifically, in the present case, protective or universal jurisdiction ones. Moreover, as the crime is committed on board a foreign-flagged vessel, the UK must first be granted the right to exercise enforcement jurisdiction by the flag State, Panama. The latter State should waive its primary jurisdiction over the crimes pursuant to a treaty or on an ad hoc basis.

CHAPTER 9

Problem answer

1. The central issue is whether State A may invoke any circumstance precluding the ostensible wrongfulness of its conduct in relation to State B. Arguably, State A has breached its obligations from the bilateral agreement with B. This conduct is attributable to governmental authorities (ie the *de jure* organs of State A (Art 4 ARSIWA)); hence, State A incurs international responsibility for this wrongful act. Nevertheless, there are various circumstances precluding the wrongfulness of conduct. The more relevant one would be 'necessity' under Art 25 ARSIWA and customary law. To exculpate State A, you have to prove that the withholding of all profits from the joint venture was the only way State A could safeguard an essential interest threatened by a grave and imminent peril—that is, the survival of its population. It is true that in recent years the plea of necessity has been recognized by international jurisprudence as customary law, but it has been applied with extreme caution as a rather exceptional measure (eg *Gabčíkovo-Nagymaros Project case* (1997)). However, here it would not be so difficult to sustain this argument (cf *Société commerciale de Belgique* (1939)).

2. The measures that State B takes in response to the breach of the bilateral agreement would be assessed against the law of countermeasures. Reference should therefore be made to the conditions for the lawful adoption of countermeasures under Arts 49–54 ARSIWA and the respective customary law. In view of these provisions, it is readily apparent that the countermeasures were not in compliance with the relevant framework. Mainly, they were disproportionate to the alleged wrongful conduct of State A; in particular, the occupation of the island was in contravention of the prohibition of the use of force. This runs counter to Arts 26 and

50 ARSIWA. If it were only the freezing of assets, this would seem more proportionate and thus lawful as a countermeasure.

CHAPTER 10

Problem answer

1. The jurisdiction of the Court should be based on the consent of the parties to the dispute, expressed by various means. In the present case, the basis of jurisdiction invoked concerns the optional clause declarations under Art 36(2) ICJ Statute. The Court must first examine the application for provisional measures under Art 41 ICJ Statute; in this phase, the Court would examine only whether there is prima facie jurisdiction. The problem here lies in the reservation that State A has appended to the declaration excluding military measures for self-defence. While it is only the prima facie jurisdiction that it is required to satisfy in the proceedings for provisional measures, the Court would assess whether the measures, which State A has taken, are of a military nature. It is difficult to substantiate the argument that the expulsion of nationals falls under the scope of military measures for self-defence. Therefore, the Court has prima facie jurisdiction for the provisional measures phase and most probably also for the merits phase.

2. Consider Art 41 ICJ Statute and the significant case law of the Court. Having established the existence of prima facie jurisdiction, the Court would look at the irreparable harm or injury that State B may face and the seriousness of the danger, as well as the effectiveness of the requested measures. Additionally, as the jurisprudence dictates (*Provisional Measures on the Application of Revision of the Preah Vihear Judgment* (2011) and the *Costa Rica–Nicaragua case*), the Court would assess the plausibility of the claims in general. It is most probable that the Court would order provisional measures, especially if the planned expulsion of the nationals of State B satisfies the criteria of urgency and irreparable harm or injury. Moreover, the claims seem plausible, since the measures by State A are obviously disproportionate to the threat posed by State B. The Court would therefore order provisional measures, for example, regarding the expulsion of nationals, which would be binding on the respondent (see the *LaGrand case* (2001)).

CHAPTER 11

Problem answer

1. The primary consideration for the legality of the use of force is a prior 'armed attack' by the aggressor State against the victim State. This is a particularly high threshold to satisfy and, as noted by the ICJ in the *Nicaragua case*, the mere logistical support or the provision of weapons would not amount to an armed attack. As a result, despite the fact that country Y has incurred State responsibility for its actions against X, such actions do not give rise to self-defence by X against Y.

2. Civil conflicts constitute matters that fall within the exclusive jurisdiction of States. Hence, other States and international organizations are not entitled to intervene in such conflicts in favour of one or the other party. This rule against non-interference is stipulated in Art 2(7) UN Charter. The only exception to this rule concerns interventions by the UN Security Council, given that Arts 24(1) and 39 UN Charter confer upon it 'primary responsibility for the maintenance of international peace and security' and authority to determine any threat or breach to the peace or an act of aggression. Hence, the Council, acting under Chapter VII UN Charter, may lawfully intervene in civil wars and has, in fact, done so on numerous occasions. In the former Yugoslavia and Rwanda, for example, it went on to issue arms embargoes, deploy peacekeeping missions, limit use of force, establish of international criminal tribunals, among other things.

3. The *Caroline* incident is good enough precedent to justify the use of force against an imminent strike against the victim nation. Although this would not ordinarily satisfy the criteria under Art 51 for self-defence, under customary law there is significant agreement that imminent attacks (such as the amassing of forces and arsenal in full combat preparation, coupled with sufficient evidence that an attack is about to be launched) triggers the right to self-defence, at least under customary international law. Such anticipatory self-defence should be contrasted with

pre-emptive self-defence, whereby the attack is not necessarily imminent.

CHAPTER 12

Problem answer

1. In order to assess whether a reservation is valid, one must assess whether it is in conflict with the object and purpose of the particular convention. In the case of human rights treaties, there does not exist a hierarchy among the rights provided, other than the fact that some may be derogated from under very narrow circumstances in times of emergency, whereas others cannot. Given that this is not an emergency, the right to equality may not lawfully be subject to derogation. Equality is the cornerstone of an effective human rights regime and the perpetuation of inequality is a recipe for under-development and the perpetuation of disparities affecting other rights, such as ill health, lack of democratic governance, illiteracy, and many others. Moreover, equality does not even require the provision of resources by the State. It is clear, in any event, that this reservation is invalid because it is contrary to the object and purpose of the ECHR.

2. This second reservation has two strands. This suffers from the same defects as the previous reservation and is in conflict with the treaty's object and purpose. The second strand, however, suggests that the State in question is unable to provide a universal right to fair trial because of resource constraints. Hence, does this constraint justify the reservation in terms, at least, of the country's physical capacity to deliver the entitlement in question? No human rights treaty justifies a curtailment of civil and political rights on account of resource constraints, as the State could go on to argue that it will start to kill part of its prison population because it has insufficient resources to feed and house them. Clearly, this is unacceptable.

The basic issue here is whether there is in fact a state of emergency threatening the life of the nation and, if so, whether the measures adopted as a means of derogation are justified and are proportionate to the situation at hand. The first issue is subjective, but various thresholds have been discussed in the case law provided in the chapter. It is unlikely, however, that any human rights tribunal will accept that prolonged industrial strikes, no matter how disruptive they are, can ever threaten the life of a nation. This is usually reserved for situations of prolonged armed violence. As a result, the derogation is deemed unlawful.

CHAPTER 13

Problem answer

This case concerns the assumption of jurisdiction by the ICC. You should not allow yourself to be confused in situations where multiple States may be able to claim jurisdiction over an accused person. The relevant provision of the ICC Statute makes it clear that the surrender of a person to the Court may be made by a State party, regardless of whether said person is its national. Hence, the country where the offence occurred (territorial State) may just as well surrender the suspect (Art 12(2)(a)). In the case at hand, the UNSC intervenes and goes above the authority of both the territorial State and the State of which the accused is a national.

1. According to Art 13(b) ICC Statute, the UNSC may refer a situation to the Court, acting under Chapter VII of the UN Charter. When this is done, such referral (through a resolution) is not only binding on the States concerned, but also on the ICC. Complementarity only concerns the relationship between ICC member States and the Court; not the relationship between the UNSC and ICC/UN member States.

2. As has already been stated, Art 12(2)(a) allows the territorial State to surrender an accused person to the Court, irrespective of whether said person is a national of a State that is not a party to the ICC Statute.

Glossary

Act of State Foreign government conduct not susceptible to legal proceedings.

Anticipatory self-defence Self-defence in anticipation of another attack.

Armed attack High-intensity military force against a State.

Armed conflict Protracted inter-State armed violence or between States and non-States.

Baselines Points from which to measure the seaward breadth of maritime zones.

Collective security Authorization of armed force by the UN Security Council.

Constitutive recognition Recognition as necessary criterion for statehood.

Cultural relativism The idea that rights are validated by cultural criteria.

Custom The convergence of State practice and the conviction that it corresponds to an obligation (*opinio juris*).

Declaratory recognition Recognition simply serves to declare the fact of statehood.

Derogation Suspension of non-fundamental rights on account of public emergency.

Doctrine of transformation The two-step process of domesticating a treaty.

Dualism International and domestic law are distinct legal orders.

Effects doctrine Exercise of territorial jurisdiction because effects of conduct were felt there.

Exclusive economic zone (EEZ) Maritime zone up to 200 nautical miles seaward from baseline.

Expansive school Armed attack definition exists also in pre-UN Charter law.

Expropriation Nationalization of property of foreign nationals.

Extradition The surrender of a suspect by one country to another to stand trial.

Flag State The State wherein a ship is registered. This possesses jurisdiction for crimes committed by the ship.

Humanitarian intervention Military force by international community on humanitarian grounds.

Immunity Procedural bar to the ordinary jurisdiction of foreign courts.

Immunity from enforcement Judgments cannot be executed against property of States.

Immunity *ratione materiae* Afforded on the basis of the public nature of conduct (functional).

Immunity *ratione personae* Afforded on the basis of a person's status (personal).

Implied powers Powers conferred indirectly from an entity's constitutive instrument.

Incorporation doctrine International law becomes domestic law upon ratification.

Indivisibility The idea that human rights are inseparable.

Internal waters All water masses landward from baselines (ie rivers, lakes, deltas).

International organizations Entities set up by States and endowed with distinct legal personality.

Internationally wrongful act A violation of an international obligation by a State.

Jure gestionis Private conduct of governments.

Jure imperii Public government conduct.

Jurisdiction The power of States to enforce their laws over persons and property.

Jurisdiction, territorial Exercise of authority in one's own territory.

Jurisdiction, universal Exercise of authority irrespective of location in respect of certain crimes.

Jus cogens Peremptory (highest in hierarchy) rules of international law.

Justiciability That a particular entitlement is susceptible to enforcement proceedings.

Legality That which is lawful under international law.

Legitimacy That which receives universal approval, even if outside the ambit of law.

Locus standi The right (or standing) to bring a suit or claim.

Monism International and domestic law are part of the same legal order.

Non-interference Non-interference in the domestic affairs of other States.

Non-State entities Entities that are not States, such as terrorists, guerrillas, and multinational corporations.

Occupation Effective control over territory.

Persona non grata Non-welcome person.

Personality Possessing rights and duties and a capacity to enforce them under international law.

Ponsonby rule Treaties are ratified by the Queen following consideration by Parliament.

Pre-emptive self-defence Self-defence without being attacked first.

Progressive realization The idea that some rights are not immediately applicable.

Proportionality Response to conduct in proportion to that conduct.

Recognition Official acknowledgement of an entity's statehood.

Reprisal Unlawful response to prior unlawful conduct.

Reservation Unilateral statement that modifies or excludes treaty provisions for the signatory.

Restrictive school Armed attack definition is that found in the UN Charter.

Secession The break-up of a country into two or more new nations.

Self-defence Right of States to respond militarily to an armed attack.

Self-defence, anticipatory Use of force in anticipation of imminent armed attack.

Self-defence, pre-emptive Use of force to avert possible armed attack.

Self-determination Right of peoples to determine their collective status.

Soft law Non-binding but highly authoritative rules.

Sovereignty The authority of States to determine their affairs without intervention.

Sovereign States Independent States.

Standard-setting The idea of establishing non-binding but authoritative rules.

State immunity Right not to be sued before foreign courts.

Statehood Achieving the criteria for becoming a State.

Territorial jurisdiction The authority of the territorial State.

Territorial sea Maritime zone up to 12 nautical miles seaward from baseline.

Transformation doctrine International law becomes domestic law by a subsequent statute.

Treaties, self-executing Those treaties elaborate enough to be applied without implementing laws.

Ultra vires Exceeding one's vested powers.

Unilateral act Conduct undertaken by one State acting alone, which produces legal effects.

Universal jurisdiction The authority of all States over certain crimes.

Universalism The idea that rights apply equally to everyone, irrespective of culture.

Use of force Military force by one State against another.

Uti possidetis juris The drawing of borders based on colonial boundaries.

Index